CADOGAN
island guides

C000003374

THE DC

Cadogan Books Ltd
London House, Parkgate Road, London SW11 4NQ

The Globe Pequot Press
6 Business Park Road, PO Box 833, Old Saybrook, Connecticut 06475–0833

Copyright © Dana Facaros 1994
Contributors: Guy Dimond, Stephanie Ferguson and Sarah Hey

Illustrations © Pauline Pears 1986, Suzan Kentli 1993 and Horatio Monteverde 1994

Design by Animage
Cover illustration by Toby Morrison
Maps © Cadogan Guides, drawn by Thames Cartographic Ltd
Macintosh: Jacqueline Lewin and Typography 5

Editing: Guy Dimond
Managing: Vicki Ingle
Editorial Assistant: Emma Johnson
Proofreading: Stewart Wild

Series Editors: Rachel Fielding and Vicki Ingle

ISBN 0–947754–90–3

A catalogue record for this book is available from the British Library
Library of Congress Cataloging-in-Publication-Data available

Printed and bound by Scotprint Ltd,
Musselburgh, Scotland.

About the Author

Dana Facaros is a professional travel writer. Over the past ten years she has lived in several countries, concentrating on the Mediterranean area. In collaboration with her husband Michael Pauls she has written more than a dozen Cadogan Guides on, amongst others, Italy, Spain, France and Turkey. Her roots, however, are in the Greek Islands; her father comes from Ikaria. Dana's guide to all the Greek Islands, now in its fifth edition, was first published in 1979.

About the Contributors

Guy Dimond is a freelance travel writer and editor. He has visited most of the islands featured in this guide, and is editor of the series of Cadogan Guides to the Greek Islands. Freelance journalist and travel writer **Stephanie Ferguson** has travelled extensively throughout Greece and hopped round more than 40 islands. She fell under the spell of the country after a holiday in the Peloponnese in 1976, and since then has contributed to two guide books and has written features on Greece for a number of UK national publications. **Sarah Hey**, former editor of the English-language newspaper the *Corfu News*, has delivered yachts between the Ionian Islands and Mainland Greece. She is currently feature-writer on the *Yorkshire Evening Post*.

Author's Acknowledgements

I would like to thank the many members of the National Tourist Organization of Greece for their kind assistance in writing this guide, and the following people without whose moral, physical and financial assistance it would not have been possible: my parents and my grandmother, Mrs Despina Facaros, Joseph Coniaris, Sotiros S. Kouvaras of Ithaki, Filia and Kosta Pattakos, Carolyn Steiner and Julie Wegner .A special thanks goes to my better half, Michael, who added the bull; to my aunt and Ikariote informant Toula Cavaligos; and to Guy, Stephanie and Sarah for their invaluable amendments and additions.

Contents

Travel 2–20

Practical A–Z 23–46

Modern History, Art and Architecture 47–58

Maps

Choosing Your Island

An overall picture of the Dodecanese islands may help you pinpoint likely destinations. You may want to head for a lively cosmopolitan place, followed by a few days of absolute peace and quiet (say, Rhodes and then Halki). Below are thumbnail sketches, starting with the liveliest, trendiest and most touristy.

The queen of Greek tourism, **Rhodes** is large enough to absorb huge numbers of tourists, but suffers from pockets of mass package tourism of the least attractive type. Stay clear of those spots and there's plenty left. It has a stunning capital and charming mountain villages. The lovely island of **Kos** has lost much of its original character under the strain of mass package tourism, but there's plenty going on to keep you amused.

Arguably the best type of island holiday can be found on islands where there are enough tourists to ensure more than basic facilities—places with a choice of decent tavernas, a bar or two for an evening drink, and most of all, a place to sit out and watch life idle by. **Symi** falls happily into this category, with a mixture of rugged island scenery, typical villages, good restaurants and swimming. There are special gems like little **Patmos**, undeveloped but sophisticated, and known only for its monastery; or **Karpathos**, with dramatic scenery and strong folklore tradition.

There remain a few islands that come under the heading of 'almost away from it all'—not quite your desert island in that they have several places to stay, eat and explore, but beyond that not a lot to do after a couple of days, unless you are resourceful. This category includes **Astypalaia**, **Leros**, **Nissyros**, **Halki**, and **Kastellorizo**.

If, however, you genuinely want to get away from it all and don't mind eating in the same little taverna every night, then head for **Tilos** or **Lipsi**. On either of these islands you can treat yourself to some serious introspection and brush up on your modern Greek with the locals.

When to Go

When choosing your island(s), the time of the year is of paramount importance, and from mid-July to 20 August you can expect nothing but frustration on the more popular islands, or the smaller ones with a limited number of beds. Rhodes and Kos have succeeded, perhaps too well, in attracting tourists. Their climate, beaches, and natural beauty make them popular year round. Patmos is a major cruise ship port and can be suffocatingly packed with trippers in the summer. On the other hand, other islands remain on the fringes of mass tourism. Don't assume that the more isolated the island the cheaper the accommodation, as supply and demand dictate the prices. You could well pay more for a room in Kos, for example, than in the old town of Rhodes, where rooms are far more plentiful. Out of season you can pick and choose.

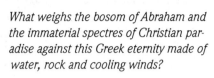

What weighs the bosom of Abraham and the immaterial spectres of Christian paradise against this Greek eternity made of water, rock and cooling winds?

Kazantzakis

Introduction

There's nothing like the Greek islands to make the rest of the world seem blurred, hesitant and grey. Their frontiers are clearly defined by a sea that varies from emerald and turquoise to indigo blue, with none of the sloppiness of a changing tide; the clear sky and dry air cut their mountainous contours into sharp outline; the whiteness and simplicity of their architecture is both abstract and organic. Even the smells, be they fragrant (lemon blossoms, incense, wild thyme, grilling fish) or whiffy (donkey flops, caique diesel engines, plastic melted cheese sandwiches) are pure and unforgettable. In such an environment, the islanders themselves have developed strong, open characters; they have bright eyes and are quick to laugh or cry or scream in fury, or inquire into the most intimate details of your personal life and offer unsolicited lectures on politics, how to brush your teeth properly or find a good husband.

Since the 1970s this clarity has been a magnet to tourists from the blurred, hesitant, grey world beyond. After shipping, tourism is Greece's most important source of income, to the extent that swallows from the north have become a regular fixture in the seasonal calendar: first comes Lent and Greek Easter, then the tourists, followed by the grape harvest, and in December, the olives. From June to September, ferries and flights are packed with holidaymakers, both Greek and foreign. Popular sites and beaches are crowded by day, and often by night as well, by visitors unable to find a room—they've been booked for months in advance.

Yet as each island has its own character, each has responded to the tourism cash cow in a slightly different way. On some, resort hotels have toadstooled up willy-nilly in search of the fast package-tour buck; some islands have sacrificed many charming old customs, environmental health, and even sanity itself in their desire to please all comers. And then there are other islands and villages, more self-reliant, clinging stubbornly to their traditions and doing all they can to keep outside interests from exploiting their coasts. Others, including some of the most visited islands, are enjoying a renaissance of traditional arts and customs, often led by the young who are pained to see their centuries-old heritage eroding into Euro-blandness.

If this book has any real purpose, it's to help you find the island of your dreams, whether you want all the mod-cons of home, sports facilities and disco dancing until dawn, or want to visit the ancient sites, study Byzantine frescoes and hone up on your Greek, or perhaps just escape to a secluded shore, where there's the luxury of doing nothing at all. Or perhaps you want a bit of each. For, in spite of all the rush to join the 20th century, the Greek islands have retained the enchantment that inspired Homer and Byron—the wine-dark sea, the scent of jasmine at twilight and nights alive with shooting stars.

The ancient Greeks dedicated the islands to the gods, and they have yet to surrender them entirely to us mortals. They have kept something pure and true and alive. Or as the poet Palamas wrote, 'Here reigns nakedness. Here shadow is a dream.'

The Dodecanese

Furthest from mainland Greece, the Dodecanese, or 'twelve islands' (although there are actually 16 inhabited ones in the *nomos*) only became Greek in 1948—officially, that is, for throughout centuries of occupations, the inhabitants of these islands have stubbornly clung to their Greek language, Orthodox religion and traditions. But their distance, and centuries of separation from the mainstream of Greek history, has dealt them a unique deck—medieval knights, Ottoman Turks and 20th-century Italians have all influenced the islands. Add to their distinct character and architecture a wealth of remarkable ancient and medieval monuments, a sunny climate and lush greenery, and you get an archipelago that never loses its fascination.

The 3000 islands of Greece (of which a mere 170 or so are inhabited) are divided into seven major groupings: the Cyclades in the Aegean, surrounding the once-sacred island of Delos; the Dodecanese, lying off the southwest coast of Turkey; the Northeastern Aegean islands, stretching from Thassos to Ikaria; the Ionian islands, sprinkled between Greece and Italy; the Saronic islands, in the Saronic Gulf; the Sporades, spread off the coast of Thessaly and Evia; and Crete, the largest island in Greece.

History

Lying just off the coast of precocious Asia Minor, the Dodecanese flourished in early antiquity. Various peoples lumped together as 'Aegeans' were their first inhabitants. They were subjugated by the seafaring Minoans, and when Crete fell in the 15th century BC, the Mycenaeans took over the Dodecanese; many islands sent ships to Troy. In the 12th–11th centuries BC the Dorians invaded the Dodecanese, heralding a dark age that lasted for three centuries.

Ionians eventually regained control of the islands, and by the Archaic period city-states, particularly on Rhodes and Kos, knew so much prosperity that they established colonies abroad. The Persians invaded the islands, and when they were defeated at Salamis, the Dodecanese joined the maritime league at Delos as a hedge against further attacks. Their greater distance from Athens, however, allowed them more autonomy than the Cyclades were permitted, and they produced many great artists and intellectuals, including Hippocrates, the father of medicine.

With the death of Alexander the Great, his general Ptolemy of Egypt controlled most of the Dodecanese. One of the greatest unsuccessful sieges in antiquity took place when one of Ptolemy's rival generals, Antigonos, sent his son Dimitrios to take Rhodes. Emboldened by its victory, in 164 BC Rhodes made an alliance with

Rome, enabling her to exert a powerful influence of her own over an empire of Greek islands.

St Paul visited some of the Dodecanese and began their early conversion to Christianity; St John the Theologian was exiled from Asia Minor to Patmos, where he converted the inhabitants and wrote the book of the *Apocalypse*, or *Revelations*. In 1095, the Dodecanese had their first taste of a more aggressive Christianity, when Crusaders en route to the Holy Land made them a port of call. The pillaging and piracy in which the Westerners occasionally indulged along the way climaxed in the capture of Constantinople in 1204.

In 1291, the tables turned when Jerusalem fell to the other side, the rising Ottoman Empire. This disrupted, among other things, the work of the Knights of St John, a wealthy order made up of the second and third sons of the cream of European nobility, who had devoted themselves to running a hospital for pilgrims in Jerusalem. The Knights abandoned Jerusalem for Cyprus, and eighteen years later set up headquarters on Rhodes, purchasing all the Dodecanese outright from Admiral Vinioli, a Genoese pirate. In 1309 they built a hospital and fortified Rhodes and the other islands against the Turks and pirates, the Knights themselves little better than pirates in their swift vessels made on Symi. Ottoman tolerance of their escapades soon wore thin, especially after the Knights took to letting Christian pirates pass through their territory unmolested, but stopped ships carrying Moslem pilgrims.

In 1522 Sultan Suleiman the Magnificent had had enough and attacked Rhodes (the third major Moslem offensive on the Knights) and all the men of the Dodecanese rallied to its defence. Only information from a traitor brought about the defeat of the Knights after a long siege. Always a gentleman, Suleiman permitted them and their followers to depart in safety with their possessions to their new fief, Malta, for which they paid the king of Spain their famous tribute of a golden falcon. Turkish occupation of the Dodecanese lasted until 1912, when the Italians took 'temporary possession' of the islands. This occupation was made 'permanent' after the Greek débâcle in 1920 by the second Treaty of Lausanne. Mussolini poured money into the islands, sponsoring massive public works programmes, reforestation, archaeological excavations and historical reconstructions. While Turkish rule had been depressing, negligent, and sometimes brutal, the fascists, in spite of their lavish expenditures, were even worse, outlawing the islanders' Orthodox religion and Greek language; even today you can find older people on the Dodecanese who are more comfortable speaking Italian. After the Second World War, the islands were reunited with Greece, the last territory gained by the government (in 1947); to encourage growth, especially through tourism, the islands were granted duty-free concessions.

Travel

By Air

If you're travelling from abroad to the Dodecanese, a direct flight is by far the simplest, fastest, and often the cheapest way to get there. Rhodes has a large international airport, and two other Dodecanese islands (Kos, Leros) also have regular international connections; nearby island airports, such as Samos and Crete, are also preferable to flying to Athens then taking a long ferry journey.

Charter Flights

Many charters go direct to the Dodecanese islands—Rhodes, Kos, Leros, or to nearby Samos—as well as to Athens and Thessaloniki. Charter flights have fixed outward and return dates, with the return date in less than one month. They are sold either with a package holiday or through 'consolidators' (travel agents) as a flight only. Charter flights to **Athens** and occasionally to the islands are frequent in the summer from European and North American capitals. Charters direct to Athens are available from Birmingham, Glasgow, Luton, Newcastle and Manchester. **In London** many travel agents offer cheap last-minute flights, and 'bucket shops' have made spare charter tickets their speciality (a return to Athens for £125 is possible). **Accommodation-included holidays** to the Dodecanese islands are often very cheap; from £160 for a week or 14 days isn't uncommon. Look through publications such as *Time Out*, the *Evening Standard* or the Sunday papers for cheap deals.

Americans and Canadians with more time than money may well find their cheapest way of getting to Greece is to take a trans-Atlantic economy flight to London and from there to buy a last-minute ticket to Greece. This may be difficult in July or August, however. Trans-Atlantic bargains can still be found, but bear in mind that the peak season runs from late May to mid-September.

There are several rules about charters to Greece. One is that a charter ticket is valid for a minimum of two nights and a maximum of four weeks. Visitors to Greece using a charter flight may visit Turkey or any other neighbouring country for the day, but must not stay overnight; the Turkish officials usually stamp your passport showing the dates of entry and exit. Even if you intend to stay longer than four weeks or travel to other countries, using just half a charter ticket may still work out less than a scheduled flight, so shop around.

When you buy a **flight-only charter ticket**, you will be issued with an accommodation voucher, which entitles you to stay at a (sometimes fictitious) hotel. This strange formality is a left-over from the days when charter tickets were only sold with accommodation included. It's unlikely the Greek customs officials will ask to see this voucher, but keep it handy until you're out of the airport just in case. **Student or youth charters** are exempt from the voucher system and are allowed to be sold as one-way tickets. Travelling this way you can stay for over a month as long as you are under 26 or a full-time, card-carrying student under 32.

Basic **travel insurance** is sometimes sold with charter tickets to Greece by travel agents. It is not compulsory to buy this, no matter what they might tell you. If they insist, look elsewhere.

Scheduled Flights

Scheduled flights rarely go from London directly to the islands, but there are plenty to Athens; they offer greater flexibility than charter flights, but generally cost more. Scheduled flights fly direct to Athens daily from London and New York. KLM flies via Amsterdam from Toronto, Montréal, Calgary and Halifax. While the basic carriers from the United States are Olympic Airways TWA, and Delta (via Frankfurt), from London it's Olympic Airways, British Airways or Virgin Atlantic. London offers the greatest variety of flights and the prices are often competitive close to the departure time if you book through a consolidator (travel agent) instead of directly with the airline. It's advisable to shop around and see which offers the best deal. **Superpex flights** offer substantially reduced fares, with flights from London to Athens ranging from £180 low season to £280 high season. They must, however, be paid for on the spot and are not refundable or flexible. American economy fares range from around $900 New York–Athens in low season to $1300 high season.

Olympic Airways	ℂ (071) 409 3400/493 3965 (London) ℂ (212) 838 3600 (New York) ℂ (01) 926 7251 (Athens)
British Airways	ℂ (081) 897 4000 (London)
Virgin Atlantic	ℂ (0293) 747747; rec. info. (0293) 511581 (London)
Delta	ℂ (800) 241 4141 (800) 221 1212 (New York)
Aer Lingus	ℂ (0232) 245151 (Dublin)
KLM	ℂ (514) 933 1314 (Montréal)
TWA	ℂ (800) 892 4141 (New York)

Bona-fide students under 26 are sometimes eligible for discounts, especially with Olympic Airways who currently offer 25% discount to **ISIC card holders** on all connecting flights from Athens to the islands, even when booked from London; Trailfinders, 42–50 Earls Court Road, W8 6EJ, © (071) 937 5400, STA Travel, 86 Old Brompton Road, London SW7 or 117 Euston Road, WC1, © (071) 937 9962; and Campus Travel, 52 Grosvenor Gardens, SW1 © (071) 730 8111 can get you some of the best current deals. Returning from Greece, it is advisable to confirm your return flight a few days prior to departure.

Don't forget that the Dodecanese are very close to airports in southern Turkey, though both Greek and Turkish authorities discourage this route of entry.

Flights from Athens to the Islands

Connecting flights from Athens to the islands are available on Olympic Airways, 11 Conduit Street, London W1R 0LP, © (071) 493 3965. Americans who do not have an Olympic Airways office in their town can call a toll-free no. (800) 223 1226 for information. At the time of writing, an additional flat fare of £50 will allow you to connect a flight landing at Athens to Kastellirozo, Leros, Kos, Rhodes, Karpathos and a handful of other adjacent Greek island airports, connections permitting. To be assured of a seat, especially in the summer, you should book your ticket as far in advance as possible. Infants up to 2 years old receive a 90% discount, and children of 2–12 years a 50% discount. Students only receive a 25% discount if the flight is a connecting one.

In recent years Olympic Airways has been offering island-to-island flights in season, a pleasant innovation that precludes the need to go via Athens. Although these have a habit of changing from year to year, routes between Herakleon (Crete) and Rhodes, Rhodes and Karpathos, Rhodes and Kassos, Rhodes and Kastellorizo, and between Rhodes and Kos are currently in operation. As the recently-privatized Olympic Airways no longer has a monopoly on inter-island flights, it's only a matter of time before other recently-formed Greek airlines set up in competition or try out new routes.

Olympic Airways (Athens)

6 Othonos, © 926 9111 (Int. andDom.)
Also 96 Leoforos Sygrou, © 926 7251–4

East Airport © 969 9703 (Int.)
West Airport © 936 9111 (Int. and Dom.)

Getting to and from Ellinikon Airport, Athens

Ellinikon Airport is divided into two: East (international airlines) and West (Olympic Airlines, both international and domestic flights). Double decker blue-and-yellow **express buses** leave for either terminal (but not both, so be sure you are getting on the right one) from Amalias Avenue, at the top of Syntagma Square, every 20 minutes between 6am and 9pm, every ½-hour between 9pm and 2am, and every hour from 2am to 6am. The fare is 160 dr. from 6am to midnight, 270 dr. otherwise. At the time of writing, this bus stop was being dug up for the new metro station, and the buses temporarily suspended.

The alternative, until these buses are reinstated, is the **public bus no. 133** from Othonos St, Syntagma Square (5.40am–midnight, every 15 minutes), or no. 122 from Vass. Olgas (5.30am–11.30pm, every 15 minutes); both go to the West terminal only. The fare is 75 dr. The East terminal may be reached by public bus no. 121 from Vass. Olgas Avenue (6.50am–10.50pm, every 40 minutes; 75 dr.). From Piraeus, express bus no. 19 goes to East and West terminals (160 dr.). The **metro** is an important means of getting across Athens, especially from Piraeus. It runs to Kifissia stopping at Thissio, Monastiraki, Omonia and Plateia Viktorias. Trolley buses run throughout the city centre from the Larissis station to Omonia and Syntagma and out to Koukaki, or linking Syntagma and Omonia with Patission and the National Archaeological Museum.

Taxis from Athens Airport

A taxi between Athens and the airport should cost you about 1100 dr. (more at night). Piraeus is particularly prone to cowboys preying on unsuspecting tourists heading from and to the ferries. Travellers should make sure they take proper yellow taxis with meters and official licence numbers. The tricksters hassle you (especially at Piraeus, less so at the airport) and charge 2–3,000 dr. for the journey; it should be around half that. If there's no meter, watch out. Prices are only double from 1–6am and on holidays such as Easter. You will have to pay surcharges on luggage, 50 dr. a piece, plus a 100 dr. supplement for an airport or Piraeus run.

In Athens cabs are difficult to find during the rush hour, when the drivers are knocking off for lunch, and when everyone is going back to work in the evenings. Hailing a cab is not for the faint-hearted. You almost have to hurl yourself in front of it and yell out your destination. Sharing is common and you all pay the full fare. Just check the meter reading when you get in so you don't get overcharged. Sharing (at full price) is also common on the islands.

There are no longer any direct trains from London to Athens, partly because of the civil war in former Yugoslavia. It is still possible to get to Athens by train, changing en route, if you really want to travel that way; it takes over three days. Call **British Rail International in London** ℂ (071) 834 2345. The route goes through Italy, either to Ancona or further south to Bari or Brindisi, and involves taking the ferry over to Corfu and Patras; these are now quite busy routes. British people under the age of 26 can travel by **InterRail** youth passes, which currently cost £249 for a month's rail travel in Europe—which gets you there and back via most places in Europe the train goes (excluding the UK, channel ferries and Spain). InterRail passes are also available to British residents over 26 for either 15 days or a month at a cost of £209 and £269 respectively. However they have the disadvantage that since France and Italy have pulled out of the over-26 scheme, and Serbia and Albania are off-limits, the only way you can get from London to Athens using this pass is by way of Hungary, Romania and Bulgaria, entering Greece north of Thessaloniki, which is rather a long way round. Americans and Canadians can buy 2-month **Eurail** and **Youth Eurail** passes before leaving home. However, the Eurail Pass is no bargain if you're only going to Greece, which has a limited rail service. For people over 60, the **Rail Europ** senior card saves up to 30% on rail fares in Greece and several other European countries, in Germany, and on most sea crossings. It costs £5 and can be purchased from British Rail by holders of a British Rail card.

The sad truth is that since the war in Yugoslavia, travelling by train is no longer an inexpensive, pleasant or easy method of getting to Greece; it's now cheaper, and a lot more comfortable, to fly, especially if you're heading for the Dodecanese. The train does have its uses though if you have plenty of time and want to stop off and see some of the rest of Europe en route.

There are domestic train routes on mainland Greece, but these are of little use if you're heading for the Dodecanese.

London to Athens

Taking a bus from London to Athens is always a possible alternative for those who are averse to air or train travel. It isn't usually much cheaper than a standby flight. But with 2½ days (or more) on the road and Adriatic ferry, adventures are practically included in the ticket price. **Eurolines,** 52 Grosvenor Gardens, Victoria, London, SW1W 0AU ℂ (071) 730 8235 offers 3-day journeys from London to Athens which cost around £218 return if you're over 26; there's a £12 saving if you're under 26. Departures from London are on Friday mornings in July, August and September only **Olympic Bus Ltd**, 70 Brunswick Centre, London WC1 1AE, © (071) 837 9141 offers 2½-day journeys from London to Athens via Brussels and Italy for a mere £50 one-way, or £100 return, departing London on Friday evenings. In Greece, you'll find agencies selling bus tickets on the most obscure islands, as well as in Athens; Filellinon St near Syntagma Square is Athens' budget travellers' boulevard, so check there for other possibilities.

Domestic Bus Services

The domestic bus service in Greece is efficient and regular, if not always a bargain. Each bus is decorated at the whim of its drivers, with pin-ups, saints, wallpaper, tinsel, tassels, and plastic hands which wave violently when the bus falls into a pothole. Local buses can be great fun; long-distance journeys are more testing.

There are never enough buses on the islands in the summer nor is it customary to queue. However, you will not be left behind if it is humanly possible for you to squeeze on. If you can wake up in time, you will find that buses are rarely crowded early in the morning.

Within the Athens area the bus fare is 75 dr. You must buy a ticket or book of ten tickets in advance from a kiosk or newsagent, then stamp one to validate it on boarding the bus—if you can fight your way to the machine, that is. If you don't and then get caught, you're liable for a fine 20 times the prevailing fare. The trolley buses operate in the same way as normal buses, but on fixed routes.

By Boat

The most common sea route to Greece is from Italy, with daily ferry services from Ancona, Bari, Brindisi, Otranto and Venice. The most popular of these is the daily service from Brindisi, which leaves at 10pm (connecting with the train from Rome) and arrives in Corfu the next morning. If you plan to sail in the summer, it's advisable to make reservations in advance, especially if you bring a car (most travel agents can do this for you). Students and young people can get a discount of up to 20%. Discounts of up to 20% are also offered when buying a return ticket. The quality of service among the different lines varies, of course; some ships are spanking clean and are plushly furnished, while others have been in service so long that they creak. However, the sullen demeanour of the crews seems to be uniform, unless you try a few words of Greek.

The main port of Greece, just outside Athens, is Piraeus. It's the main point of departure for the Dodecanese, and it's a long haul (11 hours or more).

Boats to the Islands

The daily newspaper *Naftemboriki* lists all the activities of the port at Piraeus and publishes weekly ship schedules. The National Tourist Office also publishes a monthly list of ship departures, both abroad and to the islands. These are more useful than it might at first seem; ferry schedules and routes change constantly.

A little travelling through the islands will soon show you that each boat is an individual. The many new ones are clean and comfortable and often air-conditioned. The older boats may lack some modern refinements but nevertheless they can be pleasant if you remain out on deck. The drinking water is never very good on the boats, but all sell beer, Coca Cola and lemon or orange soda. Biscuits and cigarettes complete the fare on the smaller boats, while the larger ones offer sandwiches, cheese pies or even full meals. Snacks tend to be pricier and of inferior quality to what you'll find on shore. If you're lucky, you'll have *souvlaki* sellers and pedlars offering nuts and *koulouria* (ringed biscuits) as the boat moves from island to island. The smallest boats which ferry you along the coast from beach to beach are called caiques, and usually have no facilities at all.

All the boats are privately owned and although the Greek government controls the prices some will be relatively more expensive, depending on the facilities offered, speed, etc. In most cases **children** under the age of 4 travel free, and between 4 and 10 for half-fare. Over 10 they are charged the full fare. In the

summer it is wise to buy tickets in advance, to guarantee a place, but you can always buy the ticket on board if you haven't had the time. Refunds are rarely given unless the boat itself never arrives, perhaps stuck in Piraeus for tax delinquencies. Boats will arrive late or divert their course for innumerable reasons, so if you have to catch a flight home allow for the eccentricities of the system and leave a day early to be safe.

When **purchasing a ticket**, either in Piraeus or on the islands, it's always best to do so from your ship's central agency. Other agencies may tell you that the boat is full, when in truth they've merely sold all the tickets allotted them by the central agency. On many islands, agents moonlight as bartenders or grocers and may only have a handwritten sign next to the door advertising their ship's departures.

Because Piraeus is so busy there's a new trend to use smaller mainland ports, especially Rafina and Lavrion. Neither of these is far from Athens, and bus connections are frequent; the bus stop is at Mavromateion. They are a bit of a bother for most tourists, though, which means that islands mainly served by these outlying ports are often quieter, if you take the trouble to go.

Most **inter-island ferries** have three or four classes: the first class, with an air-conditioned lounge and cabins (and often as expensive as flying); the second class, often with its own lounge as well, but smaller cabins; tourist class, with no cabins; and deck class, which is the norm, and usually gives you access to the typically large, stuffy rooms full of 'airline seats' and the snack bar area. As a rule the Greeks go inside and the tourists stay out—on summer nights in particular this is perhaps the most pleasant alternative if you have a sleeping bag.

You'd do well always to keep your ticket with you on a Greek ship, at least until the crew enacts its 'ticket control', a comedy routine necessitated by the fact that Greeks don't always check tickets when passengers board. Instead, after one or two pleas on the ship's loudspeaker system for passengers without tickets to purchase them forthwith, you suddenly find all the doors on the boat locked or guarded by a bored but obdurate sailor, while bands of officers rove about the boat checking tickets. Invariably mix-ups occur: children are separated from their parents, others have gone to the wc, someone has left a ticket with someone on the other side of the immovable sailor, crowds pile up at the doors, and stowaways are marched to the purser's office. In the worst cases, this goes on for an hour; on smaller ships it's usually over in 15 minutes.

Prices, though no longer cheap, are still fairly reasonable for passengers, rather dear for cars.

The following is a list of some of the more popular scheduled connections to the Dodecanese (and nearby islands) from Piraeus. Duration of each boat trip and the official guidelines for prices (supplied by the Greek tourist authorities in February 94) are given in drachmas but are subject to change without notice, and will vary between boats and ferry companies.

Piraeus to	2nd Class (dr.)	Tourist Class (dr.)	3rd Class (dr.)	Duration (hours)
Ag. Nik., Crete	9102	7012	5434	13
Astypalaia	n/a	5180	4109	13
Herakleon, Crete	253	5505	4031	12
Kalymnos	6950	n/a	4109	13
Karpathos	8434	6571	n/a	18
Kassos	n/a	n/a	4956	18
Kos	8500	n/a	5106	15
Leros	6950	n/a	4109	11
Rhodes	9206	n/a	5610	18
Samos (Karlovassi)	6255	n/a	3660	13
Sitia, Crete	10098	7029	5985	13
Symi	n/a	6586	4939	22
Tilos	7671	5857	4361	24

Not included in the above prices are port taxes (350 dr. approx) and VAT (currently 8%).

For the most recent information on inter-island sea connections, get a copy of the weighty *Greek Travel Pages* by International Publications in Athens, or *Key Travel Guide*, which is updated every week. Travel agents and the Greek National Tourist Offices sometimes have spare copies, and they're easy to find in Greece itself. Better still, the current edition of the *Thomas Cook Guide to Greek Island Hopping* (£9.95) is excellent for details of inter-island services.

Hydrofoils

There are currently three fleets of hydrofoils thumping between the islands of the Dodecanese. Hydrofoils as a rule travel twice as fast as ships and are twice as expensive (in some cases as much as a plane). In the peak season they are often fully booked, so buy tickets as early as you can. In a choppy sea a trip may leave you saddle-sore, and if the weather is very bad, they don't leave port. All the hydrofoils run throughout the year but are less frequent in winter. There are many new routes opening up in the Dodecanese, linking remoter islands with Rhodes and Kos. The routes and timetables are erratic, and change with little notice, so it's best to ask around at the tourist office or harbour; you may get a pleasant surprise and find a new route is being tried out. The ones which are most reliable are the Kos–Rhodes and Samos–Kos routes. ILIO hydrofoils began operations in 1993, and operate from the ports of Kalymnos and Samos; Dodecanese Hydrofoils run their airborne boats from Kos to Rhodes and up to Samos; while Zeus Lines runs shorter trips to Symi or to Marmaris from Rhodes.

Tourist Excursion Boats

These are generally slick and clean, and have become quite numerous in recent years. They are more expensive than the regular ferries or steamers, but often have schedules that allow visitors to make day excursions to nearby islands (though you can also take them one-way), and are convenient, having largely taken the place of the caique operators, many of whom now specialize in excursions to remote beaches instead of island-hopping on request. They may be the only transport available to the most remote islands, but do enquire about scheduled ferries. Friendly yachtsmen may give you a lift—it never hurts to ask.

Boats to Turkey

Whatever axes are currently being ground between Greece and Turkey, a kind of *pax tourista* has fallen over the mutually profitable exchange of visitors from the Dodecanese islands to the Turkish mainland. Connections run daily year-round between Rhodes and Marmaris (2½ hrs); between Kos and Bodrum daily in summer, less frequently in winter (45 mins); from Samos to Kuşadasi (near Ephesus) at least twice a day, April–October (1½ hrs); and from Lesbos (in the North East Aegean) to Ayvalik daily in summer (2 hrs). While there isn't much difference in crossing times, prices can vary enormously according to when you go and whose boat you take (both Greek and Turkish boats make the crossings). Generally speaking, the return fare is 8000 dr. There is a **uniform tax** from the Greek authorities for the crossing of 4000 dr., while the Turks tax you US$10 if you travel to Marmaris or Kuşadasi. On the whole, Turkish shops around the ports will take drachma, but the Greeks will not take Turkish lira—and the exchange rate between the two is pretty dreadful. Also, beware the **charter restriction**: things as they are, if you have spent a night in Turkey the Greek airport authorities might invoke the law and refuse you passage home on your flight.

Driving from **London to Athens** (and taking the ferry from Italy to Greece) at a normal pace takes around 3½ days, which is why one sees so few British cars in Greece. Unless you are planning to spend a few weeks covering large distances on land, a car is not really worth the expense and trouble of bringing it to Greece. There are many car hire companies on the mainland and the islands, if you feel a car is necessary; prices are, if anything, higher than the rest of Europe. An **International Driving Permit** is not required by EC citizens carrying an EC driving licence. Other nationals can obtain an International Driving Permit at home, or at one of the Greek Automobile Touring Club offices (ELPA, who charge around £10 for this), by presenting a national driving licence, passport, photograph—and fee of 5000 dr. In practice, tourists with bona-fide US, Australian or European driving licences can usually hire a car without fuss. The minimum age for driving is 18 years; 21 to 25 years for hire. If you're taking your own car, **The Motor Insurance Bureau** at 10 Xenofontos St, Athens, © (01) 323 6733, can tell you which Greek insurance company represents your own, or can provide you with additional cover for Greece.

Customs formalities for bringing in a car are very easy and usually take very little time. A Green Card (international third party insurance) is essential and you will get a carnet stamped in your passport. If your vehicle has EC number plates, you are allowed unlimited free use of your car in Greece. Non-EC vehicles have six months of free use in Greece, and after that you need to apply for a 9-month extension. If you leave Greece without your car, you must have it withdrawn from circulation by a customs authority. ELPA has a list of lawyers who can offer free legal advice on motorcars. They also have a 24-hour recording of information useful to foreign motorists, © 174.

Parking in the centre of Athens is forbidden outside designated parking areas. The traffic situation there is so bad that only cars with even number plates can park one day, cars with odd number plates the next. Local radio and newspapers tell drivers if they're on an odd or even day. Some families cheat by owning two cars. Police can unscrew the licence plates of illegally parked cars, and often do. While driving in the centre of Athens may be a hair-raising experience, most of the rest of Greece (busy towns and rough trails excepted) is easy and pleasant. There are few cars on most roads, even in summer, and all signs have their Latin equivalents. Traffic regulations and signalling comply with standard practice on the European Continent (i.e. driving on the right). Flocks of goats or sheep, old ladies on donkeys, and slow-moving lawnmower jitneys are some of the more interesting 'obstructions'. Crossroads and low visibility in the mountains are probably the greatest hazards. Where there are no right of way signs at a crossroads, give priority to traffic coming from the right, and always beep your horn on blind corners. Take special care when approaching an unguarded railway level crossing. It is also advisable to take a spare container of petrol along with you, as petrol stations are inconsistent in their frequency. There is a speed limit of 50kph (30mph) in inhabited areas: other speed limits are indicated by signposts in kilometres. Horn blowing is prohibited in Athens and other big cities, though you'd never guess it from the cacophony that starts when the red light changes to green. The **Greek Automobile Touring Club** (ELPA) operates a breakdown service (free if you've brought your AA/RAC membership card with you) within 60km (40 miles) of Athens or Patras: dial 104.

By Motorbike, Moped or Scooter

Safety considerations aside, mopeds, scooters and motorbikes are almost ideal for the islands in the summer. It almost never rains and what could be more pleasant than a gentle thyme-scented breeze freshening your journey over the mountains? Mopeds are both more economical and more practical than cars. They can fit into almost any boat and travel paths where cars fear to tread. Many islands have scooter rentals which are not expensive, and include third party coverage in most cases. To hire mopeds of under 125cc, you usually just have to leave your passport as security. For larger motorbikes of over 125cc, you must also show a valid car driving licence. For the largest motorbikes (over 250cc) you will need to show a full motorbike licence assuming that you can find a large motorbike for hire. Most of those smart-looking, 'born-to-be-wild' bikes on display outside hire shops belong to the staff and are left there as lures; they are not for hire. Check the mechanical condition of the bike you're hiring; they are often badly maintained and only given a cursory check between customers. It pays to hire early in the day, because the oldest and ropiest machines will be hired out last. Be warned that **moped accidents** are one of the most common ways that tourists get injuries in Greece—just look around the beach for evidence of grazed knees, scuffed elbows and legs in plaster, and they're the ones that were lucky. Greece has the second-worst road accident statistics in Europe (after Portugal), and Greek driving skills are not all they should be. So be very, very careful if you're not an experienced motorcyclist. Make sure your **travel insurance policy** covers moped accidents before you go on holiday—many policies exclude mopeds, or include them under additional cover—and try and avoid damaging the bike too, because the 'insurance' hire places offer is barely more than the legal minimum of third-party, and you'll be expected to pay for any damage more extensive than a puncture. Many British tour operators won't insure you for mopeds at all.

By Bicycle

Cycling has not caught on in Greece, either as a sport or as a means of transport, though you can usually hire a cheap (and badly maintained) mountain bike in most major resorts. If you can put up with an ill-fitting bike with gears that crash and brakes that squeal, they can be a pleasant enough way to get around on short journeys. If you're a keen cyclist, it's a much better idea to take your own bike with you. Check with your airline before flying; the usual stipulations apply, i.e. cover your bike with a cardboard 'bike box' (free from your local bike shop), turn the handlebars, take the pedals out (to prevent them from damaging other luggage), and let the tyres down to half the usual pressure (to prevent the inner tubes exploding at altitude). There is seldom any charge for carrying a bike on a plane, though you may be surcharged if the bike and your other luggage exceed the usual weight limit (most of the time bemused airline staff turn a blind eye). Trains in Greece carry bicycles for a small fee, and Greek boats generally take them along for nothing. Mountain bikes are a better choice for island roads than narrow-tyred racing and touring bikes. Gentle rides can be found on pancake-flat islands such as Kos. Pedal power rules in Kos town, almost like Amsterdam, with plenty of bikes for hire. On the islands you will find fresh water, places to camp, and a warm and surprised welcome in the villages. Make sure both you and your bike have comprehensive accident insurance before you go.

Hitch-hiking

With the rarest of exceptions, hitch-hiking, or 'autostop' as it is known in Greece, is perfectly safe and common practice on the islands and remote villages. However, the lack of cars makes it a not particularly speedy mode of transport. The Greek double standard produces the following percentages for hopeful hitch-hikers:

Single woman:	99% of cars will stop. You hardly have to stick out your hand. But be careful. Go for a car with a family or couple, and avoid single male drivers to be on the safe side.
Two women:	75% of cars will find room for you.
Woman and man:	50%; more if the woman is pretty.
Single man:	25% if you are well dressed with little luggage; less otherwise.
Two men:	start walking.

The best time for soliciting a ride is when you disembark from a ship. Ask your fellow passengers, or better still write your destination on a piece of paper (in Greek if possible) and pin it to your shirt with a naïve and friendly smile. What you lose in dignity you will generally gain in a lift. Strictly speaking hitching is illegal in Greece (though tolerated), so don't be offended if a truck driver sets you and your conspicuous backpack down just before a police checkpoint.

Specialist Holidays

A list of tour operators including specialist ones is available from the:

National Tourist Organization of Greece, ✆ (071) 734 5997 (London), ✆ (212) 421 5777 (New York), ✆ (312) 782 1084 (Chicago), ✆ (213) 6266696 (Los Angeles).   *agents*

American School of Classical Studies at Athens, 41E 72nd St, New York, NY 10021. Offers archaeological tours organized from the USA.
✆ (212) 861 0302 (New York)

Explore Worldwide, 1 Frederick Street, Aldershot, Hants. Walking holidays.
✆ (0252) 344161/319448

Laskarina Holidays, St Mary's Gate, Wirksworth, Derbyshire, DE4 4DQ. They organize painting holidays from studios and apartments (for hire) on Symi, and *caique* tours of the Dodecanese.   ✆ (0629) 824881

Manos Holidays, 168–172 Old Street, London EC1V 9BP. Nature weeks on Kos; Green beach spring-cleaning weeks on Lindos, Rhodes.
✆ (071) 216800

Peregrine Holidays, 40–41 South Parade, Summertown, Oxford, OX2 7JP. Nature and wildlife tours to the islands, plus Crete and the Peloponnese.
✆ (0865) 511642

Ramblers Holidays, Box 43, Welwyn Garden City, Hertfordshire, AL8 6PQ. Walking holidays with emphasis on archaeology and wildflowers.
✆ (0707) 331133

Specialist Vacations, 63 Cambridge Grove Road, Kingston-upon-Thames, Surrey, KT1 3HB. Painting holidays on Symi, Kastellorizo, Halki and Nissyros. ✆ (081) 974 8373

Swan Hellenic Ltd, 77 New Oxford Street, London, WC1A 1PP. The cruise ship 'Orpheus' is the best choice for culture seekers; it sails to the ancient sites of the Mediterranean, including the Greek Islands. 14-day cruises cost around £1500 to £2000, but that includes meals, excursions, port taxes and even tip.
✆ (071) 831 1515 (London); ✆ (617) 266 7465 (Boston, MA)

Waymark Holidays, 44 Windsor Road, Slough, SL1 2EJ. Walking holidays.
✆ (0753) 516477

Customs and Immigration

The formalities for foreign tourists entering Greece are very simple. **American**, **Australian** and **Canadian** citizens can stay for up to three months in Greece simply on presentation of a valid passport. However, unless you are entering with a car, immigration officials no longer stamp EC passports. **South Africans** are permitted two months.

If you want to extend your stay in Greece, you must report to the police 10 days before your visa runs out. (If you are staying in Athens, register at the Athens Alien Dept, 173 Alexandras Ave, 115 22 Athens, ✆ (01)646 8103). Take your passport, four photographs, and bank exchange receipts. The rules vary from province to province, but you will most likely receive a slip of paper authorizing you to stay for a period of up to six months; this will cost you 11,000 dr. This has to be renewed at the end of every six successive months that you remain in Greece.

If you are about to visit Turkish-occupied North Cyprus, make sure the Turkish authorities stamp a removeable piece of paper in your passport; visitors to North Cyprus since the Turkish occupation are not allowed re-entry to Greece.

Yachting

One of the great thrills of sailing the Greek waters is the variety of places to visit in a relatively short time, with the bonus that nowhere in Greece is far from safe shelter or harbours with good facilities for yachtsmen. There is little shallow water, except close to the shoreline, few currents and no tides or fog. The 100,000 miles of coastline, and a collection of islands and islets numbering three thousand, provide a virtually inexhaustible supply of secluded coves and empty beaches, even at the height of the tourist season. Equally, there are berthing facilities in the most popular of international hotspots—it's all there beneath the blue skies and bright sunshine. **The Greek National Tourist Organization** has initiated a programme of rapid expansion in the face of mounting competition from Turkey and Spain; facilities are being improved and new marinas are being constructed throughout the country.

Greek weather guarantees near-perfect sailing conditions, the only real problem being the strong winds in parts of the country at certain times of the year, notably April to October, when most yachtsmen are at sea.

The Ionian Sea and the west coast of the Peloponnese are affected by the *maistros*, a light-to-moderate northwest wind which presents itself in the afternoon only. Less frequently there are westerly winds, from moderate to strong, to the west and south of the Peloponnese. To the south of Attica, and east of the Peloponnese, the sea is to a great extent sheltered by land masses and it is not until summer that the menacing *meltemi* blows. The Aegean Sea is affected by a northwest wind in the south, and a northeasterly in the north, and when the *meltemi* blows in August and September, it can reach force eight, testing all your skills at the helm. The Turkish coast has light, variable breezes which are rudely interrupted by the forceful *meltemi*.

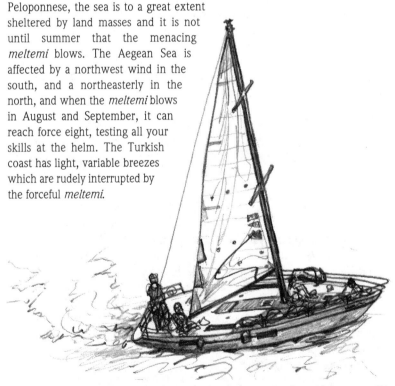

This chart shows average wind speeds (in knots) during the months April to October.

Area	Apr	May	Jun	Jul	Aug	Sep	Oct
N.E. Aegean (Limnos)	NE 10.2	NE 8.2	NE 8.2	NE 10.2	NE 10.2	NE 10.2	NE 11.4
Thrakiko (Thassos)	NE 1.4	NE 1.4	NE 1.4	NE 1.4	NE 1.4	NE 1.6	NE 2.3
Kos–Rhodes (Kos)	W/NW 13.6	W/NW 13.0	NW 13.0	NW 13.6	NW 13.6	NW 13.0	W/NW 11.4
S.W. Aegean (Milos)	N 9.0	SW 6.6	N 6.6	N 8.6	N 8.6	N 8.6	N 9.8
W. Cretan (Chania)	SW 5.0	N/NW 4.4	N/WN 4.4	N/NW 4.4	N 4.1	N 4.1	N 3.8
E. Cretan (Herakleon)	NW 6.6	NW 4.4	NW 6.2	NW 8.2	NW 7.4	NW 6.6	NW 5.8
E. Cretan (Sitia)	NW 6.6	NW 5.0	NW 7.0	NW 8.6	NW 8.2	NW 6.6	NW 5.0
Kythera (Kythera)	NE 9.8	W 8.2	W 7.8	NE 7.4	NE 8.2	NE 9.0	NE 10.6
Samos Sea (Samos)	NW 9.4	NW 7.8	NW 9.4	NW 11.0	NW 10.2	NW 8.6	NW 7.0

If you wish to **skipper a yacht** anywhere within the Greek seas, you must consult the *Compile Index Chart of Greek Seas*, otherwise known as *XEE*, published by the Hellenic Navy Hydrographic Service. Basically it is a map of Greece divided into red squares, each with an index number, from which you can select the appropriate charts and order them accordingly (cost approx. 1500 dr.). For non-Greeks, 2500 dr. will buy you what is known as *XEE 64*, a booklet of abbreviations explaining the signs on the charts, with texts in English and Greek. You also need one of the *Pilot* series books, which cost 2500 dr. each and cover the following areas in great detail:

Pilot A: South Albania to Kythera; Ionian Sea, Corinthian Gulf and North Peloponnese shores.

Pilot B: Southeastern Greek shores; Crete, Eastern Peloponnese, Saronic Gulf and Cyclades.

Pilot C: Northeastern Greek shores; Evoikos, Pagassitikos, Sporades, Thermaikos, Chalkidiki.

Pilot D: North and Eastern Aegean shores; Eastern Macedonia, Thrace, Limnos, Lesbos, Chios, Samos, the Dodecanese and Asia Minor.

These describe geographical data, possible dangers, and the present state of transportation and communication. All ports and marinas are mentioned, including where to obtain fresh water and fuel, and there are descriptions of visible inland features. The Hydrographic Service constantly updates the books and sends additional booklets to authorized sellers and to all port authorities, where you may consult them. The nautical charts are updated using the latest most sophisticated methods, and follow standardized dimensions. They are on a 1:100,000 scale for bigger areas and 1:750,000 for ports. Heights and depths are given in metres with functional conversion tables for feet and fathoms.

Further information is provided in booklets called *Notes to Mariners*, published monthly and available for consultation at port authorities. These give information on any alterations to naval charts you have purchased for your voyage. Besides all this there is the Navtex service. A special department of the Hydrographic Service keeps you informed about the weather or any special warnings for the day, through telex, or Navtex. The text is in Greek and English, and there are four retransmission coastal stations covering the Greek seas. Weather forecasts for yachtsmen are broadcast at intervals throughout the day on VHF Channel 16 (in Greek and English); security warnings are also broadcast on this channel, e.g. dangerous wrecks, lights not in operation, etc.

Bunkering Ports and Supply Stations

These are the main ports where fuelling facilities and provisions may be obtained:

Adamas (Milos)*, Aegina, Ag. Nikolaos (Kea), Ag. Nikolaos (Crete)*, Alimos Marina, Argostoli (Kefalonia)*, Chios*, Ermoupolis (Syros)*, Flisvos Marina, Gouvia Marina*, Gythion*, Chalkida*, Chania (Crete)*, Hydra, Itea*, Kalymnos, Kamares (Sifnos), Kapsali (Kythera), Kastellorizo, Kastro (Andros), Katakolo*, Katapola (Amorgos), Kavala*, Kimi (Evia), Korinthos*, Kos*, Lakki (Leros), Lavrion*, Lefkas, Limeni (Mani), Limaria (Skyros), Mirina (Limnos)*, Mytilini*,

Monemvasia, Mykonos*, Nafpaktos, Naxos, Nea Roda, Palea Epidavros, Paleokas-tritsa, Parga, Parikia (Paros), Pigadia (Karpathos), Pilos*, Poros, Porto Koufo, Porto Rafti, Preveza*, Rhodes (Mandraki)*, Skala (Patmos)*, Skiathos*, Skopelos, Spetses, Thessaloniki Marina*, Thessaloniki Port*, Tinos, Vathi (Ithaca)*, Volos*, Vouliagmeni Marina, Zea Marina.

indicates official ports of entry and exit, where there are port, customs and health authorities, as well as immigration and currency control services. Others are: Herakleon, Kimissi (Evia), Pithagorion and Vathi (Samos), Fira (Santorini), and Kali Limenes (Crete).

Main Port Authorities

Piraeus	✆ (01) 451 1311
Elefsina	✆ (01) 554 3504
Thessaloniki	✆ (031) 531504
Corfu	✆ (0661) 39918
Herakleon	✆ (081) 244912
Chios	✆ (0271) 23097
Kavala	✆ (051) 224472
Patras	✆ (061) 341024
Rhodes	✆ (0241) 22220
Volos	✆ (0421) 38888

Yachts entering Greek waters must fly the code flag 'Q' until cleared by entry port authorities. Upon arrival the **port authority** (*Limenarkion*) issues all yachts with a transit log, which entitles the yacht and crew to unlimited travel in Greek waters. It also allows crew members to buy fuel, alcohol and cigarettes duty free. It must be kept on board and produced when required, and returned to the customs authorities on leaving Greece at one of the exit ports. Permission is normally given for a stay of 6 months, but this can be extended. Small motor, sail or rowing boats do not require a 'carnet de passage', and are allowed into Greece duty free for 4 months. They are entered in your passport and deleted on exit. For more information, apply to the **Greek National Tourist Organization**, 4 Conduit Street, London, W1R 0DJ, ✆ (071) 734 5997, who produce a useful leaflet *Sailing the Greek Seas*.

Anyone taking a yacht by road is strongly advised to obtain boat registration documentation from the **DVLA**, Swansea, SA99 1BX, ✆ (0792) 783355. The **Royal Yachting Association**, R.Y.A. House, Romsey Road, Eastleigh, Hampshire, SO5 4YA, ✆ (0703) 629962, is a useful source of information.

Monthly Mooring Rates (dr.)

In Alimos Marina (Athens)	**summer**	**winter**
Up to 7m	3300	2800
8–17m	3600	2900
18m and above	3700	3000

Yacht Charter

Chartering yachts is very popular these days, and as the promotional literature says, can be cheaper than staying in a hotel (if you have enough friends or family to share expenses). Between the various firms (the National Tourist Organisation has a list) there are over a thousand vessels currently available in all sizes, with or without a crew (though without a crew—bareboat charter—both the charterer and another member of the party must show **proof of seamanship**: a sailing certificate or letter of recommendation from a recognized yacht or sailing club). There are various options: motor yachts (without sails), motor sailors (primarily powered by motor, auxiliary sail power) and sailing yachts (with auxiliary motor power). Charters can be arranged through licensed firms of yacht brokers, or by contacting yacht owners directly. The **Yacht Charter Association**, 60 Silverdale, New Milton, Hampshire, BH25 7DE, ℂ (0425) 619004, supplies a list of its recognized yacht charter operators and offers advice on chartering overseas. For more information on chartering in Greece, write to:

The Hellenic Professional Yacht Owners Association, 43 Freatidos St, Zea Marina, 18536 Piraeus. ℂ (01)452 6335

Greek Yacht Brokers and Consultants Association, 7 Filellinon St, 105 57 Athens. ℂ (01)323 0330

Greek Yacht Owners Association, 10 Lekka St, 185 37 Piraeus.
ℂ (01)452 6335

One of the largest and most reputable firms is **Valef**, located at 22 Akti Themistokleous, Piraeus, ℂ (01)428 1920, fax 428 1926 (in the USA: 7254 Fir Rd, PO Box 391, Ambler, PA 19002). They have more than 300 craft, accommodating 4–50 people in comfort.

Yacht Charter Operators Based in England

Bareboat yacht charter prices start from around £350–£400 per week for a 31-ft boat in low season and £2,500 for a 48-ft boat in high season. Prices peak during July and August and are lower during the spring and autumn months.

BUOYS Cruising Club, 8 Chase Side, Enfield, Middlesex, EN2 6NF. Offers charters from Athens. ✆ (081) 367 8462

Carefree Sailing Ltd, 122 Pavilion Gardens, Laleham, Middlesex, TW18 1HW. Offers charters from Corfu, Lesbos and Rhodes. ✆ (0784) 462796

Creative Holidays & Cruises, 36 Chalton Street, London, NW1 1JB. Offers charters from Piraeus. ✆ (071) 383 4243

Marinair, 188 Northdown Road, Cliftonville, Kent, CT9 2QN. Offers charters from Corfu, Rhodes, Kos and Athens. ✆ (0843) 227140

McCulloch Marine, 60 Fordwych Road, London, NW2 3TH. Offers charters from Athens. ✆ (081) 452 7509

Tenrag Yacht Charters, Bramling House, Bramling, Canterbury, Kent, CT3 1NB. Offers charters from Poros and Skiathos. ✆ (0227) 721874

World Expeditions Ltd, 8 College Rise, Maidenhead, Berkshire, SL6 6BP. From Athens and a number of Greek islands. ✆ (0628) 74174

A number of English-based **flotilla companies** offer one- or two-week sailing holidays, the airfare being included in the total cost. High season prices for a fortnight's holiday range from £550 per person to £1000 per person, depending on the number of people per yacht; expensive enough, but much cheaper than a yacht charter. The yachts have 4–6 berths, are supervised by a lead boat, with experienced skipper, engineer and hostess. Flotilla companies based in England include:

Odysseus Yachting Holidays, 33 Grand Parade, Brighton, BN2 2QA. ✆ (0273) 695094

Sovereign Sailing, Groundstar House, 390 London Road, Crawley, West Sussex, RH10 2TB. ✆ (0293) 599944

Practical A–Z

Average Daily Temperatures

	ATHENS	CRETE (HERAKL'N)	CYCLADES (MYKONOS)	DODECS (RHODES)	IONIAN (CORFU)	N.E. AEGEAN (MYTILINI)	SARONIC (HYDRA)	SPORADES (SKYROS)
	F° C°	F° C°	F° C°	F° C°	F° C°	F° C°	F° C°	F° C°
JAN	**48 11**	54 12	54 12	**54 12**	50 10	50 10	53 12	51 10
FEB	**49 11**	54 12	54 12	**54 13**	51 10	48 10	53 12	51 10
MAR	**54 12**	58 14	56 13	**58 14**	52 12	52 12	56 13	52 11
APR	**60 16**	62 17	60 17	**60 17**	60 15	60 16	61 16	58 15
MAY	**68 20**	68 20	68 20	**66 20**	66 19	68 20	68 20	66 19
JUN	**76 25**	74 24	74 23	**73 21**	71 21	74 24	76 25	74 23
JUL	**82 28**	78 26	76 25	**78 27**	78 27	80 27	82 28	77 25
AUG	**82 28**	78 26	76 25	**79 27**	78 26	80 27	81 28	78 25
SEP	**76 25**	76 24	74 23	**78 25**	74 23	74 23	76 25	71 22
OCT	**66 19**	70 21	68 20	**72 21**	66 19	66 19	71 21	65 19
NOV	**58 15**	64 18	62 17	**66 17**	58 15	58 15	62 17	58 15
DEC	**52 12**	58 14	58 14	**58 14**	54 12	52 12	58 15	51 12

Two Greek measurements you may come across are the *stremma*, a Greek land measurement (1 stremma = ¼ acre), and the *oka*, an old-fashioned weight standard, divided into 400 *drams* (1 *oka* = 3lb; 35 *drams* = ¼lb, 140 *drams* = 1lb).

The **electric current** in Greece is mainly 220 volts, 50Hz; plugs are continental two-pin.

Greek time is Eastern European, or two hours ahead of Greenwich Mean Time.

Embassies and Consulates

Australia	37 D. Soutsou St, 115 21 Athens, ℭ 644 7303
Austria	26 Leof. Alexandras, 106 83 Athens, ℭ 821 1036
Canada	4 I. Gennadiou St, 115 21 Athens, ℭ 723 9511
France	7 Vass. Sofias, 106 71 Athens, ℭ 361 1665
Germany	10 Vass. Sofias, 151 24 Athens, ℭ 369 4111
Ireland	7 Vass. Konstantinou, 106 74 Athens, ℭ 723 2771
Japan	Athens Twr., 2–4 Messogion St, 115 27 Athens, ℭ 775 8101

New Zealand	15–17 Tsoha Street, Athens, ✆ 641 0311–5
South Africa	124 Kifissias & Iatridou, 115 10 Athens, ✆ 692 2125
United Kingdom	1 Ploutarchou St, 106 75 Athens, ✆ 723 6211
US	91 Vass. Sofias, 115 21 Athens, ✆ 721 2951
United Nations	36 Amalias Ave, Athens, ✆ 322 9624

Food and Drink

Eating Out

Eating establishments in Greece are categorized into Luxury, A, B, and C classes. Prices are controlled by the Tourist Police, who also enforce sanitary and health regulations.

The menu in Luxury restaurants is often 'international', with little to reveal that you're in Greece; in others you will find the more basic and authentic Greek cuisine. This is steeped in rich golden olive oil and the ingredients are fresh and often produced locally. It is quite usual in all but the snootiest eating places to examine the dishes (on display behind glass, or in the kitchen) before making a choice. There is usually a menu posted on the door with an English translation, listing the prices, but it's better still to see what the dish of the day is.

The availability and variety of fish depends on the catch. Sadly, seafood has become one of the most expensive meals you can order. A combination of increased demand, marketing to Athens, and greedy, unsound fishing practices (such as illegal dynamiting) has decreased the fish population in the Mediterranean, so that what was once common and cheap is now costly and in some places quite rare. Each type of fish has its own price, then your portion is costed by its weight. Restaurants which specialize in fish are called *psarotavernas*.

Pork has taken the place of lamb as the most common meat in Greek tavernas since the country joined the European Community. Almost all *souvlaki* (the ubiquitous chunks of meat grilled on a stick) you get these days is pork, though lamb, roasted or stewed, is still widely available. Beef and chicken are often stewed in a sauce of tomatoes and olive oil, or roasted, accompanied by potatoes, spaghetti or rice. Village feasts, or *paniyiri*, often feature wild goat meat with rice or potatoes. A Greek salad can be just tomatoes or just cucumbers, or village-style *horiatiki* with tomatoes, cucumbers, black olives, peppers, onions and *feta* cheese—a small one for one person and a big one for two or three. You eat this during the meal, dipping your bread in the olive oil. Desserts are not generally eaten in Greece, but in the summer dinner is generally followed by melon or watermelon.

Restaurants (*estiatórion*) serve baked dishes and often grills as well. Restaurants serving just a grill and roasts are called *psistariá. Tavernas* may serve baked dishes or a grill or both, and is less formal than a restaurant. Don't be alarmed if food arrives tepid; Greeks believe this is better for the digestion. A sweet shop, or *zacharoplasteíon,* offers honey pastries, cakes, puddings and drinks and sometimes home-made ice cream. Many also serve breakfast, along with the less common dairy shops, or *galaktopoleíon* which sell milk, coffee, bread, yoghurt, rice pudding and custard pies. Cheese pastries (*tyropitta*) and 'tost' can appear almost anywhere. Lager beer is now common in most restaurants, Amstel and Heineken being the most popular, and wine is popular with most meals.

Prices on Greek menus are written first without, then with, service and tax charges. If you are served by a young boy (*mikró*), give him something or leave it on the table—tips are generally all he earns. If you've been given special service, you may leave a tip for your waiter on the plate. The amount varies; up to 10 per cent is quite sufficient in most places.

Wine

The best-known wine of Greece, *retsina*, has a very distinctive taste of pine resin, dating from the time when Greeks stored their wine in untreated pine casks. It is an acquired taste, and many people can be put off by the pungent odour and sharp taste of some bottled varieties. Modern retsinas show increasingly restrained use of resin; all retsinas are best appreciated well-chilled. Draught retsina (*retsina varelisio*) can be found only on some islands, but in Athens it is the accepted, delicious accompaniment to the meal. Any taverna worth its salt will serve it, and if it's not available you're in the wrong place, unless you've chosen a foreign or fairly exclusive Greek restaurant. In cases of desperation, where no barrelled retsina is on offer, the wine house Kourtakis produces

a very acceptable bottled version at a low price. Retsina is admirably suited to Greek food, and after a while a visitor may find non-resinated wines a rather bland alternative. Traditionally it is served in small tumblers, and etiquette requires that they are never filled to the brim or drained empty; you keep topping up your colleagues' glasses, as best you can. There is a great deal of toasting throughout the meal (*stin yamas*—to our health, *stin yassas*—to your health), and by all means clink glasses with someone else, but on no account bring your glass down on another person's (unless your intentions for the evening are entirely dishonourable).

Ordinary red and white house wines are often locally-produced bargains—*krasi varelisio* or *krasi heema*, *krasi* meaning wine, *varelisio* from the barrel; *heema*, means 'loose'. The customary way of serving these is in small, copper-anodized jugs, in various metric measures (500ml and 250ml being the most common; a standard wine bottle holds 750cl). These are generally fine, though you may be unlucky and get one that's a stinker.

Greece has an ample selection of medium-priced red and white wines, often highly regionalized with each island and village offering their own unique wines. There are many indigenous Greek grape varieties which avoid the tyranny of Cabernet Sauvignon and Chardonnay. All the principal wine companies— Boutari, Achaia-Clauss, Carras, Tsantali, Kourtaki—produce acceptable table wines at very affordable prices. These large Greek wine producers have been investing heavily in new equipment and foreign expertise over the last decade, and it shows; even that humblest of bottles (and Greece's best-seller) *Demestika* has become very acceptable of late, and bears little resemblance to the rough stuff that earned it some unflattering, sound-alike nicknames. Look out for the nobler labels; Boutari *Naoussa* is an old-style, slightly astringent red, while Boutari's *Grande Réserve* is their best red; *Lac des Roches* is their most popular white on the islands. *Peloponnesiakos* from Achaia-Clauss is an easy-drinking, light white wine which is faddishly popular at the moment anywhere within exportable distance of the Peloponnese. From Carras, *Château Carras* is a Bordeaux-style red wine made from the Cabernet Sauvignon and Merlot grapes; if you're lucky you might find *Carras Limnio*, a good dinner wine. Boutari's *Santorini* is their finest island white, while in Rhodes CAIR supplies Greece with its sparkling *methode traditionelle* white, *Caïr*. Emery produces some good whites including Villare.

In recent years small wine producers have become very fashionable with the wine-drinking elite of Greece. Some of these island wine-makers are superb; others deserve obscurity. But for the most part, you are unlikely to come across them in the average taverna. If you're a wine buff, it's worth seeking them out from local recommendations in off-licences and high-class restaurants; or better still, consult Maggie McNie of the **Greek Wine Bureau** in London © (071) 823 3799, who is a Master of Wine and probably the best-qualified expert on Greek wines; she can tell you what to try, or what to bring back with you.

Samos produces an excellent dessert *Muscat*, There are various local spirits too; on Nissyros *soumada* liqueur is made from almonds.

Cafés

Cafés or *kafeneíons* (in small towns these are frequented almost exclusively by men, who discuss the latest news, and play cards or backgammon) serve Greek coffee (*café hellinikó*), which is the same stuff as Turkish coffee. There are 40 different ways to make this, although *glykó* (sweet), *métrio* (medium) and *skéto* (no sugar) are the basic orders. It is always served with a glass of water. Nescafé with milk has by popular tourist demand become available everywhere, though Greeks prefer it iced, with or without sugar and milk, which they call *frappé*. Soft drinks and *ouzo* round out the average café fare.

Ouzo—like its Cretan cousin *raki*—is a clear anise-flavoured aperitif which many dilute (and cloud) with water. It can be served with a little plate of snacks called *mezédes* which can range from

grilled octopus through nuts to cheese and tomatoes, though these days you must request *mezédes* especially in tourist areas. Brandy, or Metaxa (the Greeks know it by the most popular brand name), is usually a late-night treat. The more stars on the label (from three to seven) the higher the price, and in theory at least, the better the quality. In tourist haunts, milkshakes, fruit juices, cocktails and even capuccino are readily available; in the backwaters you can usually get ice cream and good Greek yoghurt.

Bars

In the last few years the influx of tourists has resulted in the growth of trendy bars, usually playing the latest hit records and serving fancy cocktails as well as standard drinks. These establishments come to life later in the evening, when everyone has spent the day on the beach and the earlier part of the evening in a taverna. They close at 3 or 4am, although amid protest, the Greek Government plans to make this 2am (the Goverment claims the nation is nodding off at work after a night on the tiles). In general they're not cheap, sometimes outrageously dear by Greek standards, and it can be disconcerting to realize that you have paid the same for your Harvey Wallbanger as you paid for the entire meal of chicken and chips, salad and a bottle of wine, half an hour before in the taverna next door. Cocktails have now risen to beyond the 1000 dr. mark in many bars, but before you complain remember that the measures are triples by British standards. If in doubt stick to beer, ouzo, wine and Metaxa (Metaxa and coke, if you can stomach it, is generally about half the price of the better-known Bacardi and coke). You may have difficulty in finding beer, as the profit margin is so small that many bars stop serving it in the peak season, thus obliging you to plump for the higher-priced drinks. One unfortunate practice on the islands is the doctoring of bottles, whereby some bar owners buy cheaper versions of spirits and use them to refill brand name bottles. The only way to be sure is to see the new bottle being opened in front of you.

A list of items which appear frequently on Greek menus is included in the language section at the end of the guide.

Health

In theory there is at least one doctor (*iatrós*) on every island, whose office is open from 9 to 1 and from 5 to 7. On many islands too there are hospitals which are open all day, and usually have an outpatient clinic, open in the mornings. British travellers are often urged to carry a **Form E111**, available from DSS offices (apply well in advance on a form CM1 from post offices), which admit them to the most basic IKA (Greek NHS) hospitals for treatment; but this doesn't cover medicines or nursing care, which still have to be paid for. In any case, the E111 seems to be looked on with total disregard outside of Athens. Private doctors and hospital stays can be very expensive, so you should take out a travel **insurance** policy, then claim your money back on return to the UK. Greek General Practitioners' fees are, however, usually reasonable.

If you have a serious injury or illness, consider leaving Greece for treatment back home if you are well enough to travel, because even the best hospitals (in Athens) lag many years behind northern Europe or the USA in the modernity of their methods of care and treatment. It's quite common for families to bring food in for the patient. So make sure your **holiday insurance** also has adequate repatriation cover.

Most doctors pride themselves on their English, as do their friends the pharmacists (found in the *farmakeio*), whose advice on minor ailments is good, although their medicine is not particularly cheap. If you forgot to bring your own condoms and are caught short, they are widely available from *farmakeio* and even kiosks, with lusty brand names such as 'Squirrel' or 'Rabbit'. If you can't see them on display, the word *kapotes* (condom) gets results. You can also get the Pill, *xapi antisiliptiko*, morning-after Pill and HRT over the pharmacy counter without a prescription. Be sure to take your old packet to show them the brand you use.

A few hints: Coca Cola or retsina reduces the impact of the oil in Greek foods. Fresh parsley can also help stomach upsets.

Money

The word for **bank** in Greek is *trápeza*, derived from the word *trapezi*, or table, used back in the days of money changers. On all the islands with more than goats and a few shepherds there is some sort of banking establishment. If you plan to spend time on one of the more remote islands, however, such as Kastellorizo, it is safest to bring enough drachma with you. On the other hand, the small but popular islands often have only one bank, where exchanging money can take a long time. Waiting can be avoided if you go at 8am, when the banks open (normal banking hours are 8–2, 8–1 on Fri). Most island banks are closed on Saturdays and Sundays. Better still, **post offices** will exchange cash, travellers's cheques and Eurocheques; they also charge less commission than banks, and the queues are usually shorter. The numbers of 24-hour **automatic cash-tellers** are growing in Athens and large resorts.

Credit cards can be used to withdraw cash at banks; put your account into credit before going abroad, and this will often be the cheapest way to transfer money. The Commercial Bank of Greece will allow you to withdraw money by Visa, and the National Bank of Greece will exchange on Access (MasterCard). Money can also be withdrawn from some automatic tellers (24 hours daily).

Bank cards There are increasing numbers of cash dispensers for Eurocheque cards, Cirrus and Plus cards in Athens and the big tourist resorts.

Eurocheques are accepted in banks and post offices.

Traveller's cheques are always useful even though commission rates are less for cash. The major brands of traveller's cheques (Thomas Cook and American Express) are accepted in all banks and post offices; take your passport as ID, and shop around for commission rates.

Running out? Athens and Piraeus, with offices of many British and American banks, are the easiest places to have money sent by cash transfer from someone at home if you run out—though it may take a few days. If there's no bank on the island you're on, the shipping agent will change money, and the post office will change Eurocheques.

The **Greek drachma** is circulated in coins of 100, 50, 20, 10, 5, 2 and 1 drachma and in notes of 100, 500, 1000 and 5000 drachma.

Museums

All significant archaeological sites and museums have regular admission hours. Nearly all are **closed on Mondays**, and open other weekdays from 8 or 9 to around 2, though outdoor sites tend to stay open later, until 4 or 5pm. As a rule, plan to visit cultural sites in the mornings to avoid disappointment, or unless the local tourist office can provide you with current opening times. Hours tend to be shorter in the winter. **Students** with a valid identification card get a discount on admission fees; on Sundays admission is generally free for EC nationals.

If you're currently studying archaeology, the history of art or the Classics and intend to visit many museums and sites in Greece, it may be worth your while to obtain a free pass by writing several weeks in advance of your trip to the Museum Section, Ministry of Science and Culture, Aristidou 14, Athens, enclosing verification of your studies from your college or university. Entrance fees for sites or museums are not listed in this book. Count on 400–600 dr. in most cases; exceptions are the Acropolis and National Archaeology Museum in Athens at 1500 dr.

Greek music is either city music or village music. The music of the city includes the popular tunes, *rembetika* (derived from the hashish dens of Asia Minor) and most bouzouki music, whereas village music means traditional tunes played on the Greek bagpipes (*tsamboúna*), the clarinet (*klaríno*), the violin and sometimes the dulcimer (*sandoúri*). Cretan music specializes in the lyre (*lyra*) and is in a category of its own.

On the islands you can hear both city and village music, the former at the *bouzoukia*, or **Greek nightclubs**, which usually feature certain singers. Many play records or washed-out muzak until midnight as the customers slowly arrive. Smaller, rougher night clubs are called *boites* or *skilakia* —'dog' shops. You generally buy a bottle of white wine and fruit and dance until four in the morning, though expect to pay a pretty drachma for the privilege. To hear **traditional music**, you must go into the villages, to the festivals or weddings. In many places Sunday evening is an occasion for song and dance. Village music is generally modest and unpretentious, while city music is the domain of the professional singers, although any bold member of the audience with a good voice can get up to sing a few songs. After a few hours of drinking, a particular favourite or a good dancer is liable to make the enthusiasts forget the law against *spásimo*, or **plate breaking**, and supporters may end up paying for missing place settings. If the mood really heats up, men will dance with wine glasses or bottles on their heads, or even sink their teeth into a fully-set table and dance without spilling a drop. When the matrons begin to belly-dance on the table, you know it's time to leave.

In the tavernas you're liable to hear either **city or village music**. Some put on permanent shows, and others have music only occasionally. Athens is awash with tourist shows and discotheques during the summer but starts pulsating to all kinds of Greek music in November, when Plaka is returned to the Athenians. Most musicians on the islands go to Athens in the winter.

The lyrics to most Greek songs deal with the ups and downs of love; *s'agapoh* which you hear in nearly every song means 'I love you'. Serious composers (Mikis Theodorakis is the best known) often put poetry to music, providing splendid renderings of the lyrics of George Seferis and Yannis Ritsos. The guerrillas (*partizanis*) and the Communists have a monopoly on the best political songs, many by Theodorakis. Cretan songs are often very patriotic (for Crete) and many are drawn from the 17th-century epic poem, the *Erotókritos*, written in the Cretan dialect by Vitzentzios Kornáros.

Every island in Greece has its special dance, although today it is often only the young people's folkdance societies that keep them alive, along with the island's traditional costumes. The best time to find them dancing is on each island's Day of Liberation from the Turks or any other anniversary of local significance. One of the best-known professional folkdance companies, based in Athens, is **Dora Stratou Greek Folk Dances**, Dora Stratou Theatre, Philopappou Hill, © 324 4395 or © 921 4650. From beginning of May to end of September. Shows begin at 10pm every day, with an additional show at 8pm on Wednesdays and Sundays. Tickets average 1200 dr.; 700 dr. for students.

Although these shows are beautiful and interesting, there's nothing like getting up to dance yourself—a splendid way to work off the big dinner just consumed at a *paniyiri.* For a brief overview of the most popular dances, *see* p.64.

National Holidays

Note that most businesses and shops close down for the afternoon before and the morning after a religious holiday. If a national holiday falls on a Sunday, the following Monday is observed. The Orthodox Easter is generally a week or so after the Roman Easter.

1 January	New Year's Day	*Protochroniza;* also *Aghios Vassilis* (Greek Father Xmas)
6 January	Epiphany	*Ta Fórce/Epifania*
circa 14 March	'Clean Monday' (precedes Shrove Tuesday, and follows a three-week carnival)	*Kathari Deftéra*
25 March	Greek Independence Day	*Evangelismós*
circa 29 April	Good Friday	*Megáli Paraskevi*
circa 1 May	Easter Sunday	*Páscha*
circa 2 May	Easter Monday	*Theftéra tou Páscha*
circa May	Labour Day	*Protomaya*
15 August	Assumption of the Virgin	*Koímisis tis Theotókou*
28 October	'Ochi' Day (in celebration of Metaxas' 'no' to Mussolini)	

| **25 December** | Christmas | *Christoúyena* |
| **26 December** | Gathering of the Virgin | *Sinaxi Theotóku* |

In Greece, Easter is the big national holiday, the equivalent of Christmas and New Year in northern climes and the time of year when far-flung relatives return to Greece to see their families back home; it's a good time of year to visit for atmosphere, with fireworks and feasting. On Kalymnos and Symi they even throw dynamite. After the priest has intoned: *'O Christos Aneste!'*—Christ has risen!—families return home with lighted candles, mark the sign of the cross on the doorpost, and tuck into a special meal of *mayaritsa* soup. On Easter Sunday the Paschal lamb is spit-roasted and music and dancing goes on day and night. After Easter and May 1, spring (*anixi*—the opening) has offically come, and the tourist season begins.

Festival dates for saints' days vary over a period of several given days, or even weeks, due to the Greek liturgical calendar; we have given the 1994 dates when known, but check these locally, if you can, for following years.

Packing

Even in the height of summer, evenings can be chilly in Greece, especially when the *meltemi* wind is blowing. Always bring at least **one warm sweater** and a pair of long trousers. Those who venture off the beaten track into the thorns and rocks should bring sturdy and comfortable shoes—trainers (sneakers) are good. Cover the ankles if you really like wilderness, where scorpions and harmful snakes can be a problem. Plastic beach shoes are recommended for rocky beaches, where there are often sea urchins; you can easily buy them near any beach if you don't want to carry them around with you.

Summer travellers following whim rather than a pre-determined programme should bring a **sleeping bag**, as lodgings of any sort are often full to capacity. Serious sleeping-baggers should also bring a Karrimat or similar insulating layer to cushion them from the gravelly Greek ground. Torches are very handy for moonless nights, caves and rural villages.

On the pharmaceutical side, **seasickness pills**, insect bite remedies, tablets for stomach upsets and aspirin will deal with most difficulties encountered. Women's sanitary towels and sometimes Tampax are sold from general stores, but on remote islands you'll need to seek out the *farmakeio;* if there's no pharmacy, you've had it. Soap, washing powder, a clothes line and especially a towel are necessary for those staying in class C hotels or less. Most important of all, buy a

universal-fitting sink plug if you like sinks full of water; Greek sinks rarely have working ones. A knife is a good idea for *paniyiria*, where you are often given a slab of goat meat with only a spoon or fork to eat it with. A photo of the family and home is always appreciated by new Greek friends.

On all the Greek islands except for the most remote of the remote you can buy whatever you forgot to bring. **Toilet paper and mosquito coils** are the two most popular purchases on arrival. However, special needs such as artificial sweeteners, contact lens products and so on can generally be found in Athens and the more popular islands.

Let common sense and the maxim 'bring as little as possible and never more than you can carry' dictate your packing; work on the theory that however much money and clothing you think you need, halve the clothing and double the money.

Photography

Greece lends herself freely to beautiful photography, but a fee is charged at archaeological sites and museums. For a movie camera of any kind, including camcorders, you are encouraged to buy a ticket for the camera; with a tripod you pay per photograph at sites, but cameras (especially tripod-mounted ones) are **not allowed in museums**, for no particular reason other than the museum maintaining a monopoly on its own (usually very dull) picture stock. 35mm film, both print and slide, can be found in many island shops, though it tends to be expensive and the range of film speeds limited (100 ASA and 64 ASA are easily available though if you take slides). Disposable and underwater cameras are on sale in larger holiday resorts. Large islands even have 24-hour developing services, though again this costs more than at home.

The light in the summer is often stronger than it seems and is the most common cause of ruined photographs; opting for slow film (100ASA or less) will help. Greeks usually love to have their pictures taken, and although it's more polite to ask first, you should just go ahead and take the photo if you don't want them to rush off to beautify themselves and strike a pose. You should avoid taking pictures of the aircraft, military installations and barracks, communications systems on mountain tops, and Army look-out posts. The Photography Forbidden sign shows a camera with a cross through it and speaks for itself.

If you bring an expensive camera to Greece, it never hurts to **insure** it. Above all, never leave it alone 'for just a few minutes'. Although Greeks themselves very rarely steal anything, other tourists are not so honest.

Signs for post offices *(tachidromío)* as well as postboxes *(kourti)* are bright yellow and easy to find. Many post office employees speak English. Stamps can also be bought at kiosks and in some tourist shops, although they charge a small commission. Stamps are *grammatósima*. Postcards can take up to three weeks to arrive at their destinations, or only a week if you're lucky; letters sent abroad are faster, taking just over a week, depending on the route. If you're really in a hurry you can send letters *Express* for extra cost.

If you do not have an address, mail can be sent to you *Poste Restante* to any post office in Greece, and can be picked up with proof of identity. After one month all unretrieved letters are returned to sender. If someone has sent you a parcel, you will receive a notice of its arrival, and you must go to the post office to collect it. You will have to pay a handling fee of 650dr, and customs charges and duties should the parcel contain dutiable articles. 'Fragile' stickers attract scant attention. In small villages, particularly on the islands, mail is not delivered to the house but to the village centre, either a café or bakery. Its arrival coincides with that of a ship from Athens.

If you want to mail a package, any shop selling paper items will wrap it for a small fee.

Watersports

Naturally these predominate in the islands. All popular beaches these days hire out pedal boats and windsurf boards; some have paragliding and jet skis. Waterskiing prevails on most islands and large hotel complexes. Several islands offer sailing and windsurfing instruction. For more details contact:

Hellenic Yachting Federation, 7 Akti Navarchou Kountourioti, Piraeus, © 413 7351

Greek Windsurfing Association, 7 Filellinon St, Piraeus, © 323 3696

Nudism is forbidden by law in Greece, except in designated areas, such as the more remote beaches of Mykonos. In practice, however, many people shed all in isolated coves, at the far ends of beaches, or ideally on beaches accessible only by private boat; Rhodes has a particularly high nudity quotient. On the other hand, topless sunbathing is now legal on the majority of popular beaches *away* from settlements. Do exercise discretion. It isn't worth wounding local sensibilities, no matter how prudish other people's attitudes may seem. You could be arrested on the spot and end up with three days in jail or a stiff fine. Canoodling on public beaches in broad daylight can also offend.

Underwater activities with any kind of breathing apparatus are strictly forbidden to keep divers from snatching any antiquities and to protect marine life. However, snorkelling is fine, and Rhodes has a diving school. Even if you already know how to dive, you have to go out with their boats.

Average Sea Temperatures

Jan	Feb	Mar	Apr	May	Jun	Jul	Aug	Sep	Oct	Nov	Dec
59°F	59°F	59°F	61°F	64°F	72°F	75°F	77°F	75°F	72°F	64°F	63°F
15°C	15°C	15°C	16°C	18°C	22°C	24°C	25°C	24°C	22°C	18°C	17°C

Land Sports

Tennis is very popular in Athens with numerous clubs from Glyfada to Kiffissia. Rhodes also has a club; Sports Club of Rhodes, ✆ (0241) 25905.

Otherwise there are courts at all major resort hotels, where, if you are not a resident, you may be allowed to play in the off season.

There is a golf course on Rhodes, and it admits non-members.

The **Afandou Golf Club**, 19km (12 miles) from Rhodes town, ✆ 51255, has 18 holes, par 70. The club has equipment hire and shop, lounges, changing rooms, and a restaurant. Fees are from 3000 dr. per round, or 16,000 dr. for seven rounds in one week, lessons 4000 dr. per half hour.

Many small riding stables offer horse riding on the islands. In Athens, call the **Riding Club of Greece**, Paradissos, ✆ 682 6128 and Riding Club of Athens, Gerakos, ✆ 661 1088.

Telephones

The *Organismos Telepikoinonia Ellathos*, better known as OTE, has offices in the larger towns and at least one on every island that has a telephone service; these are the best place to make international calls. You can call both direct and collect (reverse charges), although the latter usually takes at least half an hour to put through. On the larger islands you may dial abroad direct (for Great Britain dial 0044 and for the USA 001 before the area code). A 3-minute call to the UK will cost about 750 dr., to the US 1600 dr. You should also use OTE for calling other places in Greece. Telegrams can be sent from OTE or the post office.

Payphones don't exist as such; the few that there were have been replaced with cardphones during the summer of 1993. Calls can be made from kiosks (more expensive), *kafeneíons*, and shops (always ask first). **Phonecards** have now come to Athens and the busier resorts but some islands only have the blue booths without the phones *in situ* yet. Buy a card when you arrive at the airport, or at *periptera* for 1000 dr for 100 units or *monades*.

It is often impossible to call Athens from the islands in mid-morning; chances improve in the evening. To defeat the beeps, whirrs, and buzzes you often get instead of a connection, wait for the series of six clicks after the area code is dialled before proceeding.

Toilets

It's customary in Greece to put the used toilet paper in a special wastebasket beside the toilet (which is emptied regularly); this is a habit left over from the days when toilet paper blocked the inadequate Greek plumbing. However, Greek plumbing has improved remarkably in the past few years, especially in the newer hotels. However, public toilets and those in cheaper hotels and pensions often have their quirks. **Tavernas, *kafeneíons*, and sweet shops** almost always have facilities (it's good manners to buy something before you excuse yourself); there are public pay toilets in strategic area of the towns.

In older pensions and tavernas, the plumbing often makes up in inventiveness for what it lacks in efficiency. Do not tempt fate by disobeying the little notices 'the papers they please to throw in the basket'—or it's bound to lead to trouble. Also, a second flush in immediate succession will gurgle and burp instead of swallow. Many places in Greece have only a ceramic hole. Women who confront this for the first time should take care not to wet their feet: squat about halfway and lean back as far as you can. Always have paper of some sort handy.

If you stay in a private room or pension you may have to have the electric water heater turned on for about 20 minutes before you take a shower, so if you were promised **hot water** but it fails to appear, ask the proprietor about it. In most smaller *pensions*, water is heated by a solar panel on the roof, so the best time to take a shower is in the late afternoon, or the early evening (before other residents use up the finite supply of hot water). In larger hotels there is often hot water in the mornings and evenings, but not in the afternoons. Actually 'cold' showers in the summer aren't all that bad, because the tap water itself is generally lukewarm, especially after noon. A good many showers are of the hand-held variety; sinks in Greece rarely have plugs.

Greek tap water is perfectly safe to drink, but on some islands like Halki and Kalymnos it's very salty and undrinkable. Big plastic bottles of spring water are widely available, even on ships, and taste better than tap water. On dry islands, remember to ask what time the water is turned off.

Tourist Information

If the **Greek National Tourist Organization** (in Greek the initials are: EOT) can't answer your questions about Greece, at least they can refer you to someone who can.

In Athens

EOT Information Desk: National Bank of Greece, Syntagma Square, 2 Karageorgi Servias St, ✆ (01) 322 2545, 323 4130.
EOT, East Airport: ✆ (01) 969 9500.
Head Office: 2 Amerikis St, Athens 10564, ✆ (01) 322 3111; fax 322 2841.

In Australia

51–57 Pitt St, Sydney, NSW 2000, ✆ 241 1663/4; fax 235 2174.

In Canada

1300 Bay St, Toronto, Ontario, ✆ (416) 968 2220, fax 968 6533.
1233 De La Montagne, Montreal, Quebec, ✆ (514) 871 1535, fax 871 1535.

In Great Britain

4 Conduit St, London W1R 0DJ, ✆ (071) 734 5997, fax 287 1369.

In the US

Head Office: Olympic Tower, 645 Fifth Ave, 5th Floor, New York, NY 10022, ✆ (212) 421 5777; fax 826 6940.
168 N. Michigan Ave, Chicago, Ill. 60601, ✆ (312) 782 1084; fax 782 1091.
611 West Sixth St, Suite 2198, Los Angeles, Calif. 90017, ✆ (213) 626 6696; fax 489 9744.

Islands without a branch of the EOT often have some form of local tourist office; if not, most have **Tourist Police** (often located in an office in the town's police station). You can always tell a Tourist Policeman from other cops by the little flags he wears on his pocket, showing which languages he speaks. They have information about the island, and can often help you find a room. In Athens there are four Tourist Police stations, and a magic telephone number—171. The voice on 171 not only speaks good English, but can tell you everything from ship departures to where to spend the night.

Tourist Police in Athens

Dimitrakopoloulou 77, Veikou (the new home of 171)
Larissa Train Station, © 821 3574
West Airport, Olympic Airways, © 981 4093
East Airport, © 969 9523

At Piraeus the Tourist Police are on Akti Miaouli, © 452 3670/418 4815.

Travelling with Children

Greece is one of the best Mediterranean countries to bring a child, as children are not barely tolerated as they are in more 'sophisticated' holiday resorts, but are generally enjoyed and encouraged. Depending on their age, they go **free** or receive **discounts** on ships and buses. You can also save on hotel bills by bringing sleeping bags for the children. However, if they're babies, don't count on island pharmacies stocking your baby's brand of milk powder or baby foods—they may have some, but it's safest to bring your own supply. Disposable nappies, especially Pampers, are widely available, even on the smaller islands. Travelling with a baby is like having a special passport. Greeks adore them, so don't be too surprised if your infant is passed round like a parcel. Greek children usually have an afternoon nap, so do their parents, so it's quite normal for Greeks to eat *en famille* until the small hours. The attitude to children is very different to the British one of being seen but not heard—Greek children are spoiled rotten. Finding a **babysitter** is never a problem.

Superstitions are still given more credit than you might expect; even in the most cosmopolitan of households, you'll see babies with amulets pinned to their clothes or wearing blue beads to ward off the evil eye before their baptism. Beware of commenting on a Greek child's intelligence, beauty or whatever, as this may call down the jealous interest of the old gods. The response in the old days was to spit in the admired child's face, but these days, superstitious grannies will say the ritual 'phtew—phtew—phtew', as if spitting, to protect the child from harm.

Hotels

All hotels in Greece are divided into six categories: Luxury, A, B, C, D and E. This grading system bears little relationship to the quality of service or luxury; it's more to do with how the building is constructed, size of bedrooms, etc. If the hotel has a marble-clad bathroom it gets a higher rating. For this reason, some D and C class hotels can be better than Bs. You may come across government-run hotels, *Xenias*, many of which look like barracks. Some of these are better than others.

prices

Prices are set and strictly controlled by the Tourist Police. Off season you can generally get a discount, sometimes as much as 40%. In the summer season prices can be increased by up to 20%. Other charges include an 8% government tax, a 4.5% community bed tax, a 12% stamp tax, an optional 10% surcharge for stays of only one or two days, an air conditioning surcharge, as well as a 20% surcharge for an extra bed. All of these prices are listed on the door of every room and authorized and checked at regular intervals. If your hotelier fails to abide by the posted prices, or if you have any other reason to believe all is not on the level, take your complaint to the Tourist Police.

1994 hotel rates (drachma) for mid–high season (1/5/94–30/9/94)*

Single room with bath	9–30000	6.7–15000	6.7–10000	4.5–8000	2.7–5000
Double room with bath	13.1–35000	9.9–17000	5.7–14000	4.6–10000	4–6000

*1994 maximum prices were still not confirmed at the time of writing, as the change of Government in late 1993 disabled the civil service and EOT for months; the above prices are based on the most up-to-date information available in Spring 1994.

Prices for E hotels are about 20% less than D rates.

During the summer, hotels with restaurants may require guests to take their meals in the hotel, either full pension or half pension, and there is no refund for an uneaten dinner. Twelve noon is the official check-out time, although on the islands it is usually geared to the arrival of the next boat. Most Luxury and class A, if not B, hotels situated far from the town or port supply buses or cars to pick up guests.

Hotels down to class B all have private bathrooms. In C most do. In D you will be lucky to find a hot shower, and in E forget it. In these hotels neither towel nor soap is supplied, although the bedding is clean.

The importance of reserving a room in advance, especially during July and August, cannot be over-emphasized. **Reservations** can be made through the individual hotel or:

The Hellenic Chamber of Hotels, 24 Stadiou St, 105 61 Athens, © (01) 323 6962 (from Athens: between 8 and 2); fax (01) 322 5449.

In the 'Where to Stay' sections of this book, accommodation is listed according to the following price categories:

luxury	15,000 dr. and above
expensive	8–15,000 dr.
moderate	4–8000 dr.
cheap	4000 dr. and below

Please note that prices quoted are for **double rooms**.

Rooms (Domatia) in Private Homes

These are for the most part cheaper than hotels and are sometimes more pleasant. On the whole, Greek houses aren't much in comparison to other European homes mainly because the Greeks spend so little time inside them; but they are clean, and the owner will often go out of his or her way to assure maximum comfort for the guest. Staying in someone's house can also offer rare insights into Greek domestic taste, which ranges from a near-Japanese simplicity to a clutter of bulging plastic cat pictures that squeak when you touch them; lamps shaped like ships, made entirely of macaroni; tapestries of dogs shooting pool; and flocked sofas covered in heavy plastic that only the Patriarch of the Orthodox Church is allowed to sit in. Increasingly, however, rooms to rent to tourists are built in a separate annexe and tend to be rather characterless.

While room prices are generally fixed in the summer (the going rate in high season is now 4000 dr.) out of season they are always negotiable with a little finesse, even in June.

Prices depend a lot on the island; fashionable ones like Mykonos or Santorini are very expensive. Speaking some Greek is the biggest asset in bargaining, although not strictly necessary. Claiming to be a poor student is generally effective. Always remember, however, that you are staying in someone's home, and do not waste more water or electricity than you need. The owner will generally give you a bowl to wash your clothes in, and there is always a clothes line.

The Tourist Police on each island have all the information on rooms and will be able to find you one, if you do not meet a chorus of Greeks chanting 'Rooms? Rooms?' as you leave the boat. Many houses also have signs.

Youth Hostels

Some of these are official and require a **membership card** from the **Association of Youth Hostels**, or alternatively an International Membership Card (about 2500 dr.) from the Greek Association of Youth Hostels, 4 Dragatsaniou St, Athens, © 323 4107; other hostels are informal, have no irksome regulations, and admit anyone. There are official youth hostels on the islands of Corfu and Santorini. Most charge extra for a shower, sometimes for sheets. Expect to pay 600–1200 dr. a night, depending on the quality of facilities and services offered. The official ones have a curfew around midnight.

Camping Out

The climate of summertime Greece is perfect for sleeping out of doors. Unauthorized camping is illegal in Greece, although each village on each island enforces the ban as it sees fit. Some couldn't care less if you put up a tent at the edge of their beach; in others the police may pull up your tent pegs and fine you. All you can do is ask around to see what other tourists or friendly locals advise. In July and August you only need a sleeping bag to spend a pleasant night on a remote beach, cooled by the sea breezes that also keep hopeful mosquitoes at bay. Naturally, the more remote the beach, the less likely you are to be disturbed. If a policeman does come by and asks you to move, though, you had best do so; be diplomatic. Many islands have privately-operated camping grounds—each seems to have at least one. These are reasonably priced, though some have only minimal facilities. The National Tourist Office controls other, 'official', campsites which are rather plush and costly.

There are three main reasons behind the camping law: one is that the beaches have no sanitation facilities for crowds of campers; secondly, forest fires are a real hazard in summer; and thirdly, the law was enacted to displace gipsy camps, and is still used for this purpose. If the police are in some places lackadaisical about enforcing the camping regulations, they come down hard on anyone lighting any kind of fire in a forest, and may very well put you in jail for two months; every year forest fires damage huge swathes of land.

National Tourist Office of Greece **camping rates** per day during high season:

	dr.	
Adult	600 –	800
Child (4–12)	300 –	500
Caravan	1000 –	1300
Small tent	500 –	650
Large tent	900 –	1200
Car	150 –	200

Renting a House or Villa

On most islands it is possible to rent houses or villas, generally for a month or more at a time. Villas can often be reserved from abroad: contact a travel agent or the National Tourist Organisation (NTOG) for names and addresses of rental agents. In the off season houses may be found on the spot with a little enquiry; with luck you can find a house sleeping 2–3 people, and depending on the facilities it can work out quite reasonably per person. Islands with sophisticated villa rentals (i.e. with a large number of purpose-built properties with all the amenities, handled by agents in Athens, Great Britain and North America) are Rhodes and Symi. The NTOG has a list of agents offering villas and apartments. Facilities normally include a refrigerator, hot water, plates and utensils, etc. Generally, the longer you stay the more economical it becomes. Things to check for are leaking roofs, creeping damp, water supply (the house may have a well) and a supply of lamps if there is no electricity.

Art Centres of the School of Fine Arts

Four of the five annexes of the Athenian School of Fine Arts are located on the islands, with one on Rhodes. These provide inexpensive accommodation for foreign artists (for up to 20 days in the summer and 30 in the winter) as well as studios, etc. One requirement is a recommendation from the Greek embassy in the artist's home country. Contact its Press and Information Office for further information.

Self-catering Holidays

Airtours, Wavell House, Helmshore, Rossendale, Lancashire, BB4 4NB. Self-catering on Rhodes, Kos, and Kalymnos. © (0706) 260000

Filoxenia Tours, Sourdock Hill, Barkisland, Halifax, West Yorks HX4 0AG. Exclusive tailor-made holidays in many places, including Leros and Astypalaia. © (0422) 375999

Greek Sun Holidays, 1 Bank Street, Sevenoaks, Kent, TN13 1UW. Apartments and studios on Amorgos, Ikaria, Karpathos, Kassos, Kos, Lipsi, Nissyros, Samos and Telendos, to name a few.   ✆ (0732) 740317

Laskarina Holidays, St Mary's Gate, Wirksworth, Derbyshire, DE4 4DQ. Villas, village houses and apartments on Alonissos, Symi, Halki, Tilos, Telendos, Kalymnos, Leros, Lipsi, Astypalia and Nissyros.   ✆ (0629) 824881

Manos Holidays, 168–172 Old Street, London EC1V 9BP. Accommodation in major resorts, plus less-known islands.   ✆ (071)216 8000

Women Travellers

Greece is fine for women travellers but foreign women travelling alone can be viewed as an oddity in some places. Be prepared for a fusillade of questions. Greeks tend to do everything in groups or *pareas* and can't understand people who want to go solo. That said, Greece is a choice destination for women travelling on their own. Out of respect Greeks on the whole refrain from annoying women as other Mediterranean men are known to do, while remaining friendly and easy to meet; all the Greek men from sixteen to sixty like to chat up foreign women, but extreme coercion and violence such as rape is rare. Men who try to take advantage of women or chase tourists are generally looked down on and have bad reputations. While some Greek men can't fathom what sexual equality might mean—they are usually the same who hold the fantasy that for a woman a night without company is unbearable mortification of the flesh—they are ever courteous and will rarely allow even the most liberated female (or male) guest to pay for anything.

In the major resorts like Rhodes, tourist women are considered fair game, fish to be harpooned in more ways than one by the local lads throughout the season. A *kamaki* is a harpoon in Greek, and also the name given to the Romeos who usually roar about on motorbikes, hang out in the bars and cafés, and hunt in pairs or packs. Their aim is to collect as many women as possible, notching up points for different nationalities. There are highly professional *kamakis* in the big resorts, gigolos who live off women tourists, gathering as many foreign hearts plus gold chains and parting gifts as they can; they overwinter all over the world with members of their harem. Other Greeks look down on them, and consider them dishonourable and no good.

Many young Greek women are beginning to travel alone—that leggy blonde with the rucksack could just as well be Greek as Swedish nowadays—but this is no indication that traditional values are disappearing. Although many women in the larger towns now have jobs, old marriage customs still exert a strong influence, even in Athens. Weddings are sometimes less a union of love than the closing of a lengthily negotiated business deal. In the evenings, especially at weekends, you'll see many girls of marriageable age join the family for a seaside promenade, or *volta*, sometimes called 'the bride market'. A young man, generally in his late twenties or early thirties, will spot a likely girl on the promenade or will hear about her through the grapevine. He will then approach the father to discover the girl's dowry—low wages and high housing costs demand that it contains some sort of living quarters from the woman's father, often added on top of the family house. The suitor must have a steady job. If both parties are satisfied, the young man is officially introduced to the daughter, who can be as young as 16 in the villages. If they get along well together, the marriage date is set. The woman who never marries and has no children is sincerely pitied in Greece. The inordinate number of Greek widows (and not all wear the traditional black) is due to the traditional 10- to 20-year age difference between husband and wife.

Because foreign men don't observe the Greek customs, their interest in a Greek woman will often be regarded with suspicion by her family. Although the brother probably won't brandish a knife at a man for glancing at his sister, he is likely to tell him to look elsewhere.

Working

If you run out of money in Greece, it usually isn't too difficult to find a temporary job on the islands, ranging from polishing cucumbers to laying cement. The local *kafeneíon* is a good place to enquire. Work on yachts can sometimes be found by asking around at the Athenian marinas. The theatre agents, for work as extras in films, are off Academias Ave, by Kanigos Square. Teachers may apply to one of the seven English/American schools in Athens, or apply as an English teacher to a *frontistirion*, a poorly-paid, private school. The *Athens News*, the country's English daily, and *The Athenian*, a monthly publication, often have classified advertisements for domestic, tutorial, and secretarial jobs.

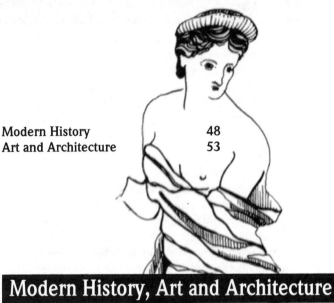

Modern History, Art and Architecture

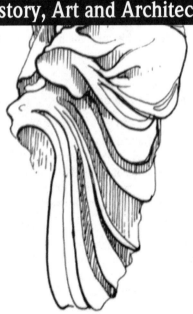

Unless you're one of those dullards who unplug themselves from their earphones and novels only to take photographs of donkeys, then you'll want to meet the Greeks. Although the massive influx of foreign visitors in recent years has had an inevitable numbing effect on the traditional hospitality offered to strangers, you will find that almost everyone you meet is friendly and gracious, and the older islanders—especially in the small villages—full of wonderful stories.

And rare indeed is the Greek who avoids talking about politics. It was Aristotle, after all, who declared man to be a political animal and if Greeks today have any link with their Classical past it is in their enthusiasm for all things political. An enthusiasm especially evident during an election, when all means of transport to the Greek islands are swamped with Athenians returning to their native villages to vote. Some knowledge of modern history is essential in understanding current Greek views and attitudes, and for that reason the following outline is included. Ancient and Byzantine history, which touches Greece less closely today, is dealt with under Athens and the individual islands.

The Spirit of Independence

From ancient times to the end of the Byzantine Empire, Greek people lived not only within the boundaries of modern-day Greece but throughout Asia Minor, in particular that part of Asia Minor now governed by Turkey. Constantinople was their capital, and although founded as a new Rome by Constantine, it was Greek. Not even during the 400-year Turkish occupation did these people and their brethren in Europe stop considering themselves Greeks—and the Turks, for the most part, were content to let them be Greek as long as they paid their taxes.

The revolutionary spirit that swept through Europe at the end of the 18th and beginning of the 19th centuries did not fail to catch hold in Greece, by now more than weary of the lethargic inactivity and sporadic cruelties of the Ottomans. The Greek War of Independence was begun in the Peloponnese in 1821, and it continued for more than six years in a series of bloody atrocities and political intrigues and divisions. In the end the Great Powers, namely Britain, Russia and France, came to assist the Greek cause, especially in the decisive battle of Navarino (20 October 1827) which in effect gave the newly formed Greek government the Peloponnese and the peninsula up to a line between the cities of Arta and Volos. Count John Capodistria of Corfu, ex-secretary to the Tsar of Russia, became the first President of Greece. While a king was sought for the new state, Capodistria followed an independent policy which succeeded in offending the pro-British and pro-French factions in Greece—and also the powerful Mavromikhalis family who assassinated him in 1831. Before the subsequent anarchy spread too far, the Great Powers appointed Otho, son of King Ludwig I of Bavaria, as King of the Greeks.

The Great Idea

Under Otho began what was called The Great Idea of uniting all the lands of the Greek peoples with the motherland, although Athens lacked the muscle to do anything about it at the time. Otho was peaceably ousted in 1862 and the Greeks elected William George, son of the King of Denmark, as 'King of the Hellenes'. By this they meant all the Greek people, and not merely those within the borders of Greece. The National Assembly drew up a constitution in 1864 which made the nation officially a democracy under a king, a system that began to work practically under Prime Minister Kharilaos Trikoupis in 1875. With the long reign of George I, Greece began to develop with an economy based on sea trade. The Great Idea had to wait for an opportune moment to ripen into reality.

In 1910 the great statesman from Crete, Eleftherios Venizelos, became Prime Minister of Greece for the first time. Under his direction the opportune moment came in the form of the two Balkan Wars of 1912–13, as a result of which Crete, Samos, Macedonia and southern Epirus were annexed to Greece. In the meantime King George was assassinated by a madman, and Constantine I ascended to the throne of Greece. Constantine had married the sister of Kaiser Wilhelm and had a close relationship with Germany, and when the First World War broke out, so did a dispute as to whose side Greece was on. Venizelos supported the Allies and Constantine the Central Powers, although he officially remained neutral until the Allies forced him to mobilize the Greek army. Meanwhile, in the north of Greece, Venizelos had set up his own government with volunteers in support of the Allied cause.

After the war to end all wars The Great Idea still smouldered, and Venizelos made the blunder of his career by sending Greek forces to occupy Smyrna (present-day Izmir) and advance on Ankara, the new Turkish capital. It was a disaster. The Turks, under Mustapha Kemal (later Ataturk) had grown far more formidable after their defeat in the Balkan War than the Greeks had imagined. In August 1922 the Greek army was completely routed at Smyrna, and many Greek residents who could not escape were slaughtered. Constantine immediately abdicated in favour of his son George II, and died soon afterwards. The government fell and Colonel Plastiras with his officers took over, ignobly executing the ministers of the previous government. Massive population exchanges were made between Greece and Turkey to destroy the rationale behind Greek expansionist claims, and the Greeks were confronted with the difficulties of a million Anatolian refugees.

In 1929 a republic was proclaimed which lasted for ten shaky years, during which the Greek communist party, or KKE, was formed and gained strength. After the brief Panglos dictatorship, the Greeks elected Venizelos back as President. He set the present borders of Greece (except for the Dodecanese Islands, which belonged to Italy until 1945). During his term of office there was also an unsuccessful uprising by the Greek Cypriots, four-fifths of the population of what was then a British Crown Colony, who desired union with Greece.

World War–Civil War

The republic, beset with economic difficulties, collapsed in 1935, and King George II returned to Greece, with General Metaxas as his Prime Minister. Metaxas took dictatorial control under the regime of 4 August, which crushed the trade unions and all leftist activities, exiling the leaders. Having prepared the Greek army long in advance for the coming war, Metaxas died in 1941 after his historic 'No!' to Mussolini. In 1940, with Italian troops on the Albanian border, Greece was the first Allied country voluntarily to join Britain against the Axis. The Greek army stopped the Italians and then pushed them back into Albania.

But by May 1941 all of Greece was in the hands of the Nazis, and George II was in exile in Egypt. The miseries of Occupation were compounded by political strife, fired by the uncertain constitutionality of a monarch who had been acting for so many years without parliamentary support. The Communist-organized EAM, the National Liberation Front, attacked all the competing resistance groups so rigorously that they came to support the monarchy as a lesser evil than the Communists. These Monarchists were supported in turn by the British. Nothing could be done, however, to prevent Civil War from breaking out three months after the liberation of Greece. The army of the EAM almost took Athens before the King finally agreed not to return to Greece without a plebiscite.

After the World War and the Civil War the country was in a shambles, economically and politically. Americans began to supersede the British in Greek affairs, and acted as observers in the elections of March 1946. A few months later the King was officially welcomed back to Greece, although he died a year later to be succeeded by his brother Paul.

Recovery and the Issue of Cyprus

Recovery was very slow, despite American assistance. Stalin also became very interested in the strategic location of Greece. In a roundabout way this caused the second Civil War in 1947 between the Communists and the government. The Americans became deeply involved defending the recent Truman Doctrine (on containing Communism, especially in Greece) and government forces finally won in October 1949, allowing the country to return to the problems of reconstruction.

With the Korean War in 1951 Greece and Turkey became full members of NATO, although the Cyprus issue again divided the two countries. In 1954, the Greek Cypriots, led by Archbishop Makarios, clamoured and rioted for union with Greece. Either for military reasons (so believe the Greeks) or to prevent a new conflict between Greece and Turkey, the Americans and British were hardly sympathetic to Cyprus' claims. Meanwhile Prime Minister Papagos died, and Konstantinos Karamanlis replaced him, staying in office for eight years. The stability and prosperity begun under Papagos increased, and agriculture and tourism began to replace Greece's traditional reliance on the sea. The opposition to Karamanlis criticized him for his pro-Western policy, basically because of the Cyprus bugbear, which grew worse all the time. Because of the island's one-fifth Turkish population and its strategic location, the Turks would not agree on union for Cyprus—the independence or partitioning of the island was as far as they would go. Finally in 1960, after much discussion on all sides, Cyprus became an independent republic and elected Makarios its first President. The British and Americans were considered to be good friends again.

Then once more the economy began to plague the government. The royal family became unpopular, there were strikes, and in 1963 came the assassination of Deputy Lambrakis in Thessaloniki (see the film *Z*) for which police officers were tried and convicted. Anti-Greek government feelings rose in London, just when the King and Queen were about to visit. Karamanlis advised them not to go, and their insistence sparked off his resignation. George Papandreou of the opposition was eventually elected Prime Minister. King Paul died and Constantine II became King of Greece.

In 1964 violence broke out in Cyprus again, owing to the disproportional representation in government of the Turkish minority. A quarrel with the King led to Papandreou's resignation resulting in much bitterness. The party system deteriorated and on 21 April 1967 a group of colonels established a military dictatorship. George Papandreou and his son Andreas were imprisoned, the latter charged with treason. Col. George Papadopoulos became dictator, imprisoning thousands without trial. In 1967 another grave incident occurred in Cyprus, almost leading to war. King Constantine II fled to Rome.

Moral Cleansing

The proclaimed aim of the colonels' junta was a moral cleansing of 'Christian Greece'. Human rights were suppressed, and the secret police tortured dissidents—or their children. Yet the British and American governments tolerated the regime, the latter very actively because of NATO. The internal situation went from bad to worse, and in 1973 students of the Polytechnic school in Athens struck. Tanks were brought in and many were killed. After this incident popular feeling rose to such a pitch that Papadopoulos was arrested, only to be replaced by his arrester, the head of the military police and an even worse dictator, Ioannides. The nation was in turmoil. Attempting to save his position by resorting to The Great Idea, Ioannides tried to launch a coup in Cyprus by assassinating Makarios, intending to replace him with a president who would declare the long-desired union of Cyprus with Greece. It was a fiasco. Makarios fled, and the Turkish army invaded Cyprus. The dictatorship resigned and Karamanlis returned to Athens from Paris where he had been living in exile. He immediately formed a new government, released the political prisoners and legalized the Communist party. He then turned his attention to Cyprus, where Turkish forces had occupied 40% of the island. But the Greek army was not strong enough to take on the Turks, nor did the position taken by the British and the American governments help.

Today's Republic

On 17 November 1974 an election was held, which Karamanlis easily won. The monarchy did less well and Greece became the republic it is today. In 1977 Archbishop Makarios died leaving the Cyprus issue unresolved in the minds of the Greeks, although the Turks seem to consider it well nigh settled. This remains one of the major debating points in Greek politics. The desire for social reform and an independent foreign policy were to be the ticket to Andreas Papandreou's Socialist victories in the 1980s. His party, PASOK, promised withdrawal from NATO and the removal of US air bases, along with many other far-reaching reforms. In practice, the new government found these impossible to implement, and the arrogant Papandreou succeeded in alienating nearly all of Greece's allies while overseeing a remarkable economic boom, thanks to the growth of tourism and EC loan money. In the end, scandals and corruption brought PASOK down; Papandreou's open affair with a much younger woman—Dimitri Liani, now his wife—and the Bank of Crete corruption scandal didn't go down well in an essentially conservative country. This led to PASOK losing power in 1990.

Mitsotakis and the New Democracy (ND) conservatives took a slim majority in the elections to grapple with Greece's economic problems. ND immediately launched a wave of austerity measures which proved even more unpopular than Papandreou—a crackdown on tax evasion, which is rife in Greece; a wage freeze for civil servants; privatisation of most state-run companies, including Olympic Airways; and steep increases in charges for public services. This sparked off a wave of strikes in 1991 and 1992. By late 1992 Mitsotakis was also involved in political scandals, and in 1993 a splinter party formed, Political Spring, led by Antonis Samaras. The principal effect of this was to split the votes and thereby topple ND when a general election was held in October 1993.

PASOK, led again by the ageing Andreas Papandreou, won the election, and proceeded to build a political dynasty that would make Bill Clinton jealous; he appointed his young wife as chief of staff, made his son the deputy foreign minister, and even made his own doctor the minister of health. 75-year-old Papandreou's own health is poor, and most Greeks doubt his ability to administer the medicine Greece needs. The big issues on the agenda for the next year or so are the continuing economic problems, the rising foreign debt, the influx of Albanian refugees, and the Macedonian question, on which Greece seems prepared to defy all of her allies, even at the risk of igniting an all-out Balkan war.

A Brief Outline of Greek Art and Architecture

Neolithic to 3000 BC

The oldest known settlements on the Greek islands date back to approximately 6000 BC—Knossos, Phaistos and the cave settlements of **Crete**, obsidian-exporting Phylokope on **Milos**, sophisticated Paleochoe on **Limnos** and Ag. Irene on **Kea**. Artistic finds are typical of the era elsewhere—dark burnished pottery, decorated with spirals and wavy lines and statuettes of the fertility goddess in stone or terra cotta.

Bronze Age: Cycladic and Minoan styles (3000–1100 BC)

Contacts with Anatolia and the Near East brought Crete and the Cyclades to the cutting edge of not only Greek, but European civilization. Around 2600 BC Cycladic dead were buried with extraordinary white marble figurines, or idols that border on the modern abstract (in the museums in **Naxos** and **Athens**). In the same period the first Minoans in Crete were demonstrating an uncanny artistic talent in their polychrome pottery—Kamares ware—and their stone vases (carved to resemble ceramic) and gold jewellery. They buried their dead in round *tholos* tombs up to 18 m in diameter. Hieroglyphs, learned from the Egyptians, were used to keep track of the magazines of oil, wine and grain stored in huge *pithoi* which characterize Minoan palaces and villas.

By the Middle Minoan period (2000–1700 BC) Crete ruled the Aegean with its mighty fleet. The Minoan priest-kings were secure enough from external and internal threats to build themselves unfortified palaces and cities, inevitably centred around a large rectangular courtyard. They installed a system of canals and drains which suggests that the Romans were hardly the first to take regular baths. Hieroglyphic writing was replaced by the still undeciphered script Linear A. Cretan civilization reached its apogee in the Late Minoan period (1700–1450 BC), when the Minoans had colonies across the Aegean and their elegant ambassadors figured in the tomb paintings of the Pharaohs; their own palaces at **Knossos, Phaistos, Zakros, Mallia** and at their outpost of Akrotiri on the island of **Santorini** were adorned with elegant frescoes of flowers, animals, human figures and bull dancers and other treasures now in the archaeology museums of **Herakleon** and **Athens**.

Built mostly of wood and unbaked brick, the Minoan palaces collapsed like card castles in a great natural disaster when the volcanic island of Santorini exploded *c.* 1450 BC. The Achaeans of Mycenae rushed in to fill the vacuum of power and trade in the Aegean, taking over the Minoan colonies; their influence extended to the language of Linear B, which has been deciphered as a form of early Greek. The Achaeans adopted the Minoans' artistic techniques, especially in goldwork and ceramics. Little of this ever reached the islands, although many have vestiges of the Achaeans' stone walls, known as *cyclopean* after their gigantic blocks. As impressive as they are, they failed to keep out the northern invaders known as the Dorians, who destroyed Aegean unity and ushered in one of history's perennial Dark Ages.

Geometric (1000–700 BC) and Archaic (700–500 BC)

The break-up of the Minoan and Mycenaean world saw a return to agriculture and the development of the *polis* or city-state. In art the Geometric period refers to the simple, abstract decoration of the pottery; traces of Geometric temples of brick and wood are much rarer. The temple of Apollo at **Dreros** on Crete and the first Temple of Hera on **Samos** were built around the 8th century, although both pale before the discovery in 1981 of the huge sanctuary at **Lefkandi** on Evia, believed to date from *c*. 900 BC. The most complete Geometric town discovered so far is Zagora on **Andros**.

The Archaic Period is marked by the change to stone, especially limestone, for the building of temples and a return to representational art in decoration. The first known stone temple—and a prototype of the Classical temple with its columns, pediments and metopes—was **Corfu**'s stout-columned Doric Temple of Artemis (580 BC), its pediment decorated with a formidable 10-ft Medusa (now in Corfu's museum). The beautiful Doric Temple of Aphaia on **Aegina** was begun in the same period and decorated with a magnificent 6th-century pediment sculpted with scenes from the Trojan war (now in Munich). The excavations at Emborio, on **Chios**, are among the best extant records we have of an Archaic town; the 6th-century Efplinion tunnel at Pythagorio, **Samos** was the engineering feat of the age.

This era also saw the beginning of life size—and larger—figure sculpture, inspired by the Egyptians: poses are stiff, formal, and rigid, one foot carefully placed before the other. The favourite masculine figure was the *kouros*, or young man, originally one of the dancers at fertility ritual (see the marble quarries of **Naxos** and the *Kriophoros* of **Thassos**); the favourite feminine figure was the *kore*, or maiden, dressed in graceful drapery, representing Persephone and the return of spring. The Archaeology Museum in **Athens** has the best examples of both. The 7th century also saw the development of regional schools of pottery, influenced by the black-figured techniques of Corinth: **Rhodes** and the Cycladic islands produced some of the best.

Classic (500–380 BC)

As Athens became the dominant power in the Aegean, it attracted much of the artistic talent of the Greek world and concentrated its most refined skills on its showpiece Acropolis, culminating with the extraordinary mathématical precision and perfect proportions of the Parthenon, the greatest of all Doric temples, yet built without a single straight line in the entire building. Nothing on the islands approaches it, although there are a few classical-era sites to visit: **Limen** on Thassos and **Eretria** on Evia, **Lindos, Kamiros** and **Ialysos** on Rhodes.

Hellenistic (380–30 BC)

This era brought new stylistic influences from the eastern lands, conquered and hellenized by Alexander the Great and his lieutenants. Compared to the cool, aloof perfection of the Classical era, Hellenistic sculpture is characterized by a more emotional, Mannerist approach, of windswept drapery, violence, and passion. Much of what remains of **Samothrace**'s Sanctuary of the Great Gods, and the Louvre's dramatic *Victory of Samothrace* are from the Hellenistic period. Ancient Rhodes was at the height of its powers, and produced its long-gone Colossus, as well as the writhing *Laocoon* (now in the Vatican museum) and Aphrodite statues in the **Rhodes** museum. Houses became decidedly more plush, many decorated with mosaics and frescoes as in the commercial town of **Delos** and in the suburbs of **Kos**.

Roman (30 BC–AD 529)

The Pax Romana ended the rivalries between the Greek city-states and pretty much ended the source of their artistic inspiration, although sculptors, architects, and other talents found a ready market for their skills in Rome, cranking out copies of Classic and Hellenistic masterpieces. The Romans themselves built little in Greece: the stoa and theatre of Heroditus Atticus (160 AD) were the last large monuments erected in ancient Athens. On the islands, the largest site is **Gortyna**, the Roman capital of Crete.

Byzantine (527–1460)

The art and architecture of the Byzantine Empire began to show its stylistic distinction under the reign of Justinian (527–565), and the immediate post-Justinian period saw a first golden age in the splendour of Ag. Sofia in Istanbul and the churches of Ravenna, Italy. On the islands you'll find only the remains of simple three-naved basilicas—with two important exceptions: the 6th-century Ekatontapyliani of **Paros** and 7th-century Ag. Titos at **Gortyna**, Crete.

After the austere anti-art puritanism of the Iconoclasm (726–843) the Macedonian style (named after the Macedonian emperors) slowly infiltrated the Greek provinces. The old Roman basilica plan was jettisoned in favour of what became the classic Byzantine style: a central Greek-cross plan crowned by a dome, elongated in front by a vestibule (narthex) and outer porch (exonarthex) and in the back by a choir and three apses. **Dafni** just outside Athens and Nea Moni on **Chios** with its massive cupola, are superb examples; both are decorated with extraordinary mosaics from the second golden age of Byzantine art, under the dynasty of the Comnenes (12th–14th centuries). As in Italy, this period marked a renewed interest in antique models: the stiff, elongated hieratic figures with staring eyes have more naturalistic proportions in graceful, rhythmic compositions; good examples are at **Dafni**. The age of the Comnenes also produced some fine painting: the 12th-century frescoes and manuscripts at the Monastery of St John on **Patmos**; the beautifully-frescoed early 13th-century Kera Panayia at **Kritsa**, near Ag. Nikolaos on Crete. Crete's occupation by Venice after 1204 marked the beginning of an artistic cross-fertilization that developed into the highly-esteemed Cretan school of icon painting, most conveniently seen in the Byzantine museums in Ag. Katerina in **Herakleon** and in **Athens**.

What never changed was the intent of Byzantine art, which is worth a small digression because in the 14th century Western sacred art went off in an entirely different direction—so much so that everything before is disparagingly labelled 'primitive' in most art books. One of the most obvious differences is the strict iconography in Byzantine painting: if you know the code you can instantly identify each saint by the cut of beard or his or her attribute. Their appeal to the viewer, even in the 11th century when the figures were given more naturalistic proportions, is equally purely symbolic; a Byzantine Christ on the Cross, the Virgin *Panayia*, the 'all-holy', angels, saints and martyrs never make a play for the heartstrings, but reside on a purely spiritual and intellectual plane. As Patrick Leigh Fermor wrote: 'Post-primitive religious painting in the West is based on horror, physical charm, infant-worship and easy weeping.' Icons and Byzantine frescoes never ask the viewer to relive vicariously the passion of Christ or coo over Baby Jesus; Byzantine angels never lift their draperies to reveal a little leg; the remote, wide-eyed Panayia has none of the luscious charms of the Madonna. They never stray from their remote otherworldliness.

And yet, in the last gasp of Byzantine art under the Paleologos emperors (14th–early 15th centuries), humanist and naturalistic influences combined to produce the Byzantine equivalent of the Late Gothic/early Renaissance painting in Italy, in Mistras in the Peloponnese. It is the great might-have-been of Byzantine art: after the Turkish conquest the best painters took refuge on Mount Athos, or on the islands ruled by Venice, but none of their work radiates the same charm or confidence in the temporal world.

Turkish Occupation to the Present

The Turks left few important monuments in Greece, and much of what they did build was wrecked by the Greeks after independence. **Rhodes** town has the best surviving mosques, hammams, houses and public buildings, not only because the Turks loved it well, but because it only became Greek in 1945. **Crete** and **Corfu** have a number of fine Venetian relics: impressive fortifications and gates, fountains, public buildings and town houses. Elsewhere, islands with their own fleets, especially **Hydra**, **Spetses** and **Symi** have impressive captain's mansions, while other islands continued traditional architectural styles: the whitewashed asymmetry of the Cyclades, the patterned sgraffito in the mastic villages of Chios, the Macedonian wooden upper floors and balconies of the northernmost islands.

In the 19th century, public buildings in both Athens and **Syros** (briefly Greece's chief port) are fairly bland neo-Classical works; a host of neo-Byzantine churches went up, while many older ones were unfortunately tarted up with tired bastard painting, Byzantine in iconography but most of it no better than the contents of a third rate provincial museum in Italy.

On the whole, the less said about 20th century architecture on the islands the better: the Fascist architecture left by the Italians on the Dodecanese islands has a sense of style, which is more than can be said of the cheap concrete slabs that have gone up elsewhere. Prosperity in the 1980s has brought an increased interest in local architecture and historic preservation: following the lead of the National Tourist Organization's traditional settlement programme, private individuals have begun to restore old monasteries, abandoned villages, and captains' mansions, while many of the newest resort developments are less brash and more in harmony with local styles. One individual who won't be restoring any of his Palaces is ex-King Constantine of Greece, whose properties were expropriated by the Papandraeus Government in 1994.

Topics

For years Greek environmentalists have pushed for legislation to protect rare species of wildlife in the Aegean and Ionian Seas. National parks, wildlife sanctuaries and hunting laws are well regulated on the mainland, but it is the fragile ecosystems of the dying seas that cry out most desperately for protection. In the early 1980s, efforts to save the Mediterranean green loggerhead turtle centred on Zakynthos; information kiosks sprouted on the island, representing not only a conscious effort to protect marine life, but also the first public information outlets directly in conflict with the mighty gods of tourism. Because the turtles lay their eggs on the sandy beaches, sometimes immediately in front of resort hotels, the noise, lights, and innocent trampling of buried turtle eggs was destroying a turtle population already struggling against a hundred natural predators. Controls and schedules were imposed on the use of beaches by tourists, infuriating local proprietors who saw their incomes threatened, while to environmentalists, who considered tourists little better than 'terrorists', the regulations hardly went far enough. Gradually both sides have moderated their stance to reach a compromise: tourists must respect the turtles, an attitude that has proved profitable in drawing eco-tourists.

The crystalline seas around the Northern Sporades have been chosen as the country's first, and only, marine wildlife reserve, largely as an attempt to preserve the most endangered mammal in Europe, the monk seal. There are only 300 monk seals remaining in Greek waters, and some estimates put the world population at a mere 500. Over-fishing has reduced the population's food supply, and mass tourism has forced the seals away from beaches to more secluded spots (mostly sea caves). Although legislation controls tourist and fishing activities in the marine park, the logistics problem of patrolling the sea remains staggering. Laws limiting large-scale fishing are constantly flouted—demand for fish has drained the Aegean's key resource by nearly 60 per cent.

Since international attention has been focused on the monk seals and their dwindling numbers, a research station and rehabilitation centre have been established on the island central to the park, Alonissos. The Hellenic Society for the Study and Protection of Monk Seals (HSSPMS) has managed to rehabilitate five orphaned seals in recent years—a 20 per cent increase in the park's population of 30, and the best population stabilizer ever, as seals will not breed in captivity. Combined with the orphan programme and their public awareness drive, the HSSPMS is beginning to bring the species back from the brink of extinction. Tourists have helped by observing the park laws, such as not entering caves where seals are born and suckled, and not disturbing islands known to be inhabited by seals. Some islanders have responded enthusiastically, acting as voluntary, part-time rangers, and reporting orphaned or injured seals to the HSSPMS.

Another endangered species in this marine park is Eleanora's Falcon, a small migratory falcon which nests almost exclusively in the Sporades in spring and summer. Many other birds use the Northern Sporades as a stepping stone on their migratory paths—swallows, storks, herons and egrets all pass at one time of the year or another, and take advantage of sanctuary. If you see a dolphin, consider yourself lucky. Not for superstitious reasons (although local fishermen paint dolphins on their boats), but because there are so few. As for turtles in the Aegean, well, if you see one, put it down to the effects of *ouzo*.

The biggest hurdle faced by Greek environmentalists is the lack of local support. Businesss people fear that even the slightest restrictions on tourist activity will make tourists and their money stay away. The facts prove the contrary. Island councils, restaurants, hotels and tour boat operators are gradually becoming aware that people long to go to places where the environment is healthy and clean. They are happy to see wildlife in its natural habitat, even if only a glimpse. Tourists tend to return to places with natural beauty, enticed by harmony with nature, and locals are slowly beginning to realize that Greece fits the bill.

As for creatures unfortunately *not* on the endangered list, the wily mosquito tops the list for pure incivility. Most shops stock the usual defences: lotions, sprays and insect coils; or pick up one of those inexpensive electric mosquito repellents that fit right in the wall plug and don't stink as badly as the smouldering coils. The most effective repellents contain high proportions of Deet; Autan and Jungle Formula (on sale in the UK, sometimes from airport chemists) do the job. Jungle Formula contains more Deet and tends to be more effective.

Public insect enemy Number Two is the wasp, either taking bites out of that honey *baklava* you've just ordered, or spoiling your picnic on the beach (a special hazard on the lush Ionian islands). Dangers lurk in the sea as well: harmless pale brown jellyfish (*médusas*) may drift in anywhere depending on winds and currents, but the oval transparent model (*tsouitres*) are stinging devils that can leave scars on tender parts of your anatomy if you brush against them. Pincushiony black sea urchins live on the rocks of rocky beaches, and must be avoided. The spines may break and embed themselves, deeper still if you try to force them out; the Greeks recommend olive oil and a lot of patience to get the spine to slip out. As first aid, they suggest peeing on them to take away the sting (if you're a woman, summon a friend). They hurt like hell, so on rocky beaches it makes sense to wear sandals or plastic shoes in the water if you're likely to be putting your feet down on the rocks.

Much less common are Greece's shy scorpions, who hide out in between the rocks in rural areas; unless you're especially sensitive, their sting is no more or less painful than a bee's. Always avoid the back legs of mules, unless you've been properly introduced. The really lethal creatures are rare: the small, grey-brown viper that lives in the nooks and crannies of stone walls, where it is well camouflaged, only comes out occasionally to sun itself. Although seldom seen (it prefers abandoned villages and quiet archaeological sites), the Greeks are terrified of it; the mere word *fithi* (snake) will turn the most stout-hearted villager to jelly. Mountain sheepdogs are a more immediate danger in outer rural areas; by stooping as if to pick up a stone to throw, you might keep a dog at bay.

Sharks seldom prowl near the coastal regions of Greece. Blood attracts them, so if you are wounded, swim for shore without delay. Divers should ask their Greek confrères about other dangerous fish in the area, such as the weaver, an unlikely delicacy whose razor-sharp fins can kill.

Macedonia

The signs at Athens Airport proclaim: Macedonia is Greek. If that doesn't sink in, then the slogans on the new phonecards drive the message home: Macedonia is One and Only and it is Greek. And don't think you can escape hearing about the issue by flying off to the distant islands; the Greeks are obsessed with the subject, and it's worth knowing some historical background in case you become embroiled in a discussion about it.

The Greek government, and the nation, emphatically denies recognition of the independent Republic of Macedonia in the former Yogoslavia. Ever since the province bordering Greek Macedonia declared itself independent and adopted the M-word in April 1993, nationalistic fervour has broken out and the Greeks are outraged, wearing lapel pins featuring the symbol of Alexander the Great, Macedonia's most famous son.

Ironically Greece, host nation of the EU in 1994, is pitting itself against EC moves to recognize the former Yugoslav state. Campaigners argue that Macedonia has been Greek for 3,000 years (some claim 4,000 years), and thus has a copyright on the name. They fear borders will be re-drawn, there is even threat of invasion, and say Ancient Macedonia was a Hellenistic civilisation, not a Slavic one, as the Slavs didn't settle on the Balkan peninsula until the 6th century AD.

Macedon was a backwoods kingdom on the fringes of Greek civilization until the advent of Philip II (reigned 359–336 BC), who, aided by the discovery of gold and his own unconventional military tactics, created the most effective army in Greece. As the Greek states squabbled among themselves, he annexed Thessaly (352 BC), and in 338 BC gobbled up the rest of Greece by crushing the last-minute anti-Macedonian coalition of Athens and Thebes. Philip forced the city-states into a pan-Hellenic league that took orders from him. The first was to raise a massive army against the Persians. Philip was assassinated, leaving the vast army to his son Alexander, who had been carefully groomed to think like a true Greek by the greatest teacher of the day–Aristotle.

Alexander had inherited all of his father's military genes, and then some. After a quick razing of Thebes to keep the quarrelsome Greeks in their place, he took his pan-Hellenic army to Persia and began his inexorable conquest that stretched to India before his army staged a sit-down strike and refused to march another step. Although much of his great empire died with him or was divided up into chunks by his generals (his Ptolemies in Egypt, the Seleucids of Syria), his greatest achievment in the eyes of the Greeks was the hellenisation (read civilisation) of his conquests. Greek became the lingua franca and the gods of Olympus usurped the temples of their barbaric brethren. Yet during his lifetime, Alexander was looked down on by the Greeks as little more than a barbarian himself.

From 215–146 BC Rome meddled increasingly in Greek affairs, at first partici-pating in the Macedonian Wars between Phillip V of Macedon and the rival Aetolian and Achaian federations. Philip was forced into an alliance with Rome in 200 BC and the Macedon kingdom was destroyed in 168 BC to become the Roman province of Macedonia; under the later Ottoman empire the population of Mace-donia, a region with hazily-defined borders, was such a mixture of Greeks, Albanians, Serbs, Bulgarians and Romanians that it gave rise to the French word for salad *(macédoine)*.

As the Ottoman Empire died its slow death in the early 1900s, Macedonia became a hotbed of rival nationalistic groups. When the two Balkan wars erupted in 1912 Greece gained southern Macedonia, Salonika and Kavala, just beating the Bulgarians in the rush for territory. Disagreements over the borders have rankled ever since; in the murky Balkan fruit salad, names count for a lot.

Fiercely proud and defensive after centuries of domination, the Greeks believe it is an outrage for the name of Macedonia to be adopted by the former Yugoslav state. To them the golden age of their cultural history has been usurped and acceptance of any EC recognition is unlikely.

In the homogenized European Community of the 1990s, only the Spaniards and Greeks still dance to their own music with any kind of spontaneity, and it's no coincidence that both have untranslatable words to describe the 'spirit' or 'mood' that separates going through the steps and true dancing. In Spain, the word is *duende*, which, with the hard driving rhythms of flamenco, has an ecstatic quality; in Greek, the word is *kefi*, which comes closer to 'soul'. For a Greek to give his all, he must have *kefi*; to dance without it could be considered dishonest. The smart young men in black trousers and red sashes who dance for you at dinner probably don't have it; two craggy old fishermen, in a smoky café in Crete, who crank up an old gramophone and dance for their own pleasure, do. You can feel the *kefi* at Easter when the village elders join hands and dance an elegant *kalamatiano*, or when a group of children celebrate the local saint's day in North Karpathos. Any sensitive person can't help but be moved by the atmosphere, especially in contrast with the stark, technically perfect stage performances of the dance troupes under the Acropolis or in the old fort of Corfu. If the *kefi* moves you to leap up and dance, your Greek friends will see you in a new light, your bond with Greece established, and you may find it just that bit harder to book your ticket home.

Nearly every island has its own dance, some of which are extremely difficult. Then there are the dances everyone knows, from the elementary 'one two three kick kick', or *Sta Tria*, footed in a circle with hands on shoulders. The circle is never complete, however: even in this simple dance a man or woman will lead, handkerchief in hand, setting the pace and supplying the special effects with leaps, foot slaps, kicks, little skips or whatever he or she likes. Cretans are among the most energetic leaders—some are almost contortionists.

Sta Tria often begins slowly and picks up to a furious pace towards the end. The *sýrto*, on the other hand, retains its slow graceful pace throughout. It has only six easy steps which are repeated until the end, but watch the leader for variations. This is considered the oldest Greek dance of all, dating back to Hellenistic, if not Homeric times. The *kalamatíanos*, a 12-step dance, takes some practice. If a Greek invites you to dance the *bállos*, the most common couple's dance, follow your partner's lead and hope for the best. While there are certain set steps to the *tsíftetéli*, or belly dance, it has become a free-spirited dance for the loose limbed and requires plenty of nerve (or wine) to pull off successfully.

The *zembekiko* is normally but not exclusively performed by men, a serious, deliberate solo dance with outstretched arms, evoking the swooping flight of the eagle; a companion will go down on one knee to encourage the dancer and clap out the rhythm. The *hasápiko*, better known as the Zorba dance, and traditionally performed by two men, will require some practice but is well worth learning—like Alan Bates who finally began to fathom *kefi* from Anthony Quinn at the end of the film *Zorba the Greek*. Plenty of practice and energy are the rules for joining in most Cretan dances, where the music demands furious, machine-gun fire steps and hops that go on until your adrenalin has pumped its last. But toss back another *raki*, and before you know it you'll be up dancing another *pentozal* or *podokto*.

You can get off on the right foot with *Greek Dances* by Ted Petrides (published by Lycabettus Press in Athens), supplemented by some private coaching from the Greeks—or their children, who usually have more patience.

Orthodoxy

With the exception of a handful of Catholics in the Cyclades, nearly all Greeks belong to the Orthodox, or Eastern church; indeed, being Orthodox and speaking Greek are the two most important criteria in defining a Greek, whether born in Athens, Alexandria or Australia. Orthodoxy is so fundamental that even the greatest sceptics can hardly conceive of marrying outside the church, or neglecting to have their children baptized.

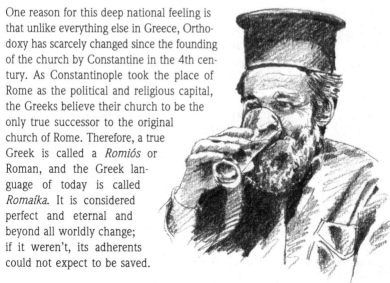

One reason for this deep national feeling is that unlike everything else in Greece, Orthodoxy has scarcely changed since the founding of the church by Constantine in the 4th century. As Constantinople took the place of Rome as the political and religious capital, the Greeks believe their church to be the only true successor to the original church of Rome. Therefore, a true Greek is called a *Romiós* or Roman, and the Greek language of today is called *Romaíka*. It is considered perfect and eternal and beyond all worldly change; if it weren't, its adherents could not expect to be saved.

Hence, the Greeks have been spared the changes that have rocked the West, from Vatican II to discussions over women in the clergy to political questions of abortion, birth control and so on—matters on which Orthodoxy has always remained aloof. Much emphasis is put on ceremony and ritual, the spiritual and aesthetic, with very little appeal to the emotions.

This explains the violence of Iconoclasm, the one movement to change the rules. Back in the early 8th century Byzantine Emperor Leo III the Isaurian, shamed by what his Moslem neighbours labelled idolatry, deemed the images of divine beings to be sacrilegious. Iconoclasm began the rift with Rome, that worsened in 800 when the Pope crowned Charlemagne as emperor, usurping the position of the Emperor of Constantinople. Further divisions arose over the celibacy of the clergy (Orthodox may marry before they are ordained) and the use of the phrase 'and the son' in the Holy Creed, the issue which caused the final, fatal schism in 1054 when the Pope's representative Cardinal Humbert excommunicated the Patriarch of Constantinople.

After the fall of the Byzantine Empire (that 'thousand-year-long mass for the dead' as one recent Greek writer put it), the Turks not only tolerated the Orthodox church, but they had the political astuteness to impart considerable powers to the patriarch. The church was thus able to preserve many Greek traditions and Greek education through the dark age of Ottoman rule; on the other hand it often abused this power against its own flock, especially locally. According to an old saying, priests, headmen and Turks were the three curses of Greece and the poor priests (who in truth are usually quite amiable fellows) have not yet exonerated themselves from the list they now share with the king and the cuckold.

The extraordinary quantity of churches and chapels on some islands has little to do with the priests, however. Nearly all were built by families or individuals, especially by sailors, seeking the protection of a patron saint. Some were built to keep a promise, others in simple thanksgiving. Architecturally they come in an endless variety of styles depending on the region, period and terrain, as well as the wealth and whim of the builder. All but the tiniest have an *iconostasis*, or altar screen, made of wood or stone to separate the *heiron* or sanctuary, where only the ordained are allowed, from the rest of the church. Most of the chapels are now locked up, ever since light-fingered tourists decided that icons make lovely souvenirs; if you track down the caretaker, do dress discreetly (no shorts!) and leave a few drachmas for upkeep.

Almost all these chapels have only one service a year, on the name day of the patron saint (name days are celebrated in Greece more widely than birthdays,

'Many years!' *(Chrónia pollá!)* is the proper way to greet someone on their name day). This annual celebration is called a *yiortí* or more frequently *paniyiri*, and is the cause for feasts and dancing before or after the church service. If feasible, *paniyiria* take place directly in the churchyard, if not, in neighbouring wooded areas or in tavernas. The food can be superb but is more often basic and plentiful; for a set price you receive more than your share and a doggy bag full, generally of goat. *Paniyiria* (festivals) are also the best places to hear traditional island music and learn the dances, and it's sad that they're only a fond memory in most major tourist centres. The Assumption of the Virgin, 15 August, is the largest *paniyiri* in Greece apart from Easter, the biggest holiday. The faithful sail to Tinos, the Lourdes of Greece, and to a dozen centres connected with Mary, making mid-August a very uncomfortable time to travel among the islands, especially the Cyclades. Not only are the ships packed to the brim, but the *meltemi* wind also blows with vigour, and Greek matrons, the most ardent pilgrims of all, are the worst of all sailors.

Orthodox weddings are another lovely if long-winded ritual. The bride and groom stand solemnly before the chanting priest, while family and friends in attendance seem to do everything but follow the proceedings. White crowns, bound together by a white ribbon, are placed on the heads of bride and groom, and the *koumbáros*, or best man, exchanges them back and forth. The newlyweds are then led around the altar three times, which spurs the guests into action as they bombard the happy couple with fertility-bringing rice and flower petals. After congratulating the bride and groom guests are given a small *boboniéra* of sugared almonds. This is followed by the marriage feast and dancing, which in the past could last up to five days. If you are in the vicinity of a village wedding you may be offered a sweet cake; you may even be invited to come along to the feasting as a special guest.

Baptisms are cause for similar celebration. The priest completely immerses the baby in the Holy Water three times (unlike Achilles, there are no vulnerable spots on modern Greeks) and almost always gives the little one the name of a grandparent. For extra protection from the forces of evil, babies often wear a *filaktó*, or amulet, the omnipresent blue glass eye bead. If you visit a baby at home you may well be sprinkled first with Holy Water, and chances are there's a bit of beneficial garlic squeezed somewhere under the cradle. Compliments to the little one's parents should be kept to a minimum; the gods do get jealous.

Funerals in Greece, for reasons of climate, are carried out as soon as possible, and are announced by the tolling of the village church bells. The dead are buried for three to five years (longer if the family can pay) after which time the bones are exhumed and placed in the family box to make room for the next resident. *Aforismós*, or Orthodox excommunication, is believed to prevent the body decaying after death—the main source of Greek vampire stories. Memorials for the dead take place three, nine and forty days after death, and on the first anniversary. They are sometimes repeated annually. Sweet buns and sugared wheat and raisin *koúliva* are given out after the ceremony; children wouldn't miss them for the world.

The *Periptero* and the Plane Tree

In Greece you'll see it everywhere, the greatest of modern Greek inventions, the indispensable *periptero*. It is the best-equipped kiosk in the world, where people gather to chat, make local or international calls, or grab a few minutes' shade under the little projecting roof. The *periptero* is a substitute bar, selling everything from water to cigarettes to ice cold beer; an emergency pharmacy stocked with aspirin, mosquito killers, condoms and sticking plaster; a convenient newsagent for Greek and international publications, from *Ta Nea* to *Die Zeit*; a tourist shop offering travel guides, postcards and stamps; a toy shop for balloons, plastic swords and My Little Pony; a general store for shoelaces, batteries and rolls of film. In Athens they're at most traffic lights. On the islands they are a more common sight than a donkey. You'll wonder how you ever survived before *peripteros* and the treasures they contain.

The other great meeting centre of Greek life is the mighty plane tree, or *platanos*, for centuries the focal point of village life, where politics and philosophy have been argued since time immemorial. Since Hippocrates the Greeks have believed that plane shade is wholesome and beneficial (unlike the ennervating shadow cast by the fig) and one of the most extraordinary sights in the islands is 'Hippocrates' plane tree' on Kos, propped up on scaffolding and as protected as any national monument would be. In Greek the expression *herete mou ton platano* loosely translates as 'go tell it to the marines', presumably because the tree has heard all that nonsense before. For a Greek village the *platanos* represents that village's identity; the tree is a source of life, for it only grows near abundant fresh water; its deep roots a symbol of stability, continuity and protection—a huge majestic umbrella, even the rain cannot penetrate its sturdy leaves. Sit under its spreading branches and sip a coffee as the morning unfolds before you; the temptation to linger there for the day is irresistible.

Shirley Valentines

Know thyself

—inscription over the gate of the oracle at Delphi

There isn't an island without at least one Shirley Valentine, drawn years ago by something special, a holiday romance perhaps that turned into a love affair with a place rather than a person, an enjoyment of living in a country where eccentrics are welcomed rather than scorned. Shirley Valentines come in all shapes and sizes, male or female, young or old, cynical or innocent, birdwatchers or bartenders, pensioners from New York, English gym teachers and marine insurance agents, lost souls from Hamburg, Dutch advertising execs, an occasional black sheep or social misfit; all characters who have found their Atlantis, and can now only live as strange birds in foreign nests.

These people have become part of island daily life and, as far as many locals are concerned, add a missing ingredient. They know their island well, and are usually a good source of information, whether it be tracking down the friendliest watering hole, or blackmailing the builder who promised to turn up weeks ago. Björn from Stockholm has been there for years, married a local girl and can outswear the locals. Penny from Bath can drink the village boys under the table. She has her reasons for doing so; her heart is broken with regularity, and every day brings tears and laughter, but turning Ipanemian brown under the Greek sun, far from the monochrome office blocks, and watching the sun set at the most beautiful time of the day brings a serenity and happiness previously unknown.

'Greece' once remarked President Karamanlis, 'reminds me of an enormous madhouse'. True or not, whether the Shirley Valentines have a streak of madness in them, Greece has allowed them to invent for themselves a way of living their fantasies, of building a new personality that was just under the surface anyway.

When You've Gone

As the days shorten and the cafés close, the last forlorn tourists sit on the deserted waterfront, and the empty echoes of summer fade away. There's now a chill to the wind as the waiters collect up the tables and chairs, no longer needed for the rest of the year, and the island returns to normality. The discotheques, not long ago throbbing to Right Said Fred, close down; the bouzouki replaces the electric guitar, boogie gives way to the *zembekiko* and the overall tempo of life changes. The real Greece re-emerges, the islanders claim back their island. Plastic cafés are re-transformed into lively little *ouzeri*, and it is time to sit and reflect on the summer, count the precious drachmas and lick wounds. The evening stroll, or *volta* returns with full intensity, and the greeting is *Kalo chimona*, or 'Have a good winter'. Wild seas reclaim the beaches; the last Coca Cola can is washed away as the pebbles are rinsed of suntan lotion. Even the swallows decamp, and head south to warmer climes. As the wind kicks up, bare-bones ferry schedules go haywire; fresh vegetables, meat and milk become scarce on many islands, and many a meal consists of beans or lentils, sardines and pasta.

Cold, wet and windy, the Greek winter takes hold of the summer paradise, and men huddle in the *cafenia* dicussing politics and tourist conquests, playing cards and *tavli* (backgammon), watching blue movies. Gambling becomes a craze in the winter and fortunes made in the summer can be lost at the turn of a card. Women stay at home and do their needlework or watch soaps on TV. The sun's warmth is replaced by the warmth of the family, and grandma can now take repossession of her little room rented out on the black to backpackers. The only voices in the main street are those of the children wandering in a ragged line to the village school, clutching their schoolbags and midday snacks of bread and spam. The few hardy perennial foreign residents make a reappearance in the cafés, and the lingua franca once again returns to demotic Greek.

The summer spirit flickers briefly in winter's depths, and the gentle sun some-times provides enough warmth to sit out by the still, sparkling blue sea, watching the caiques come in with their haul. Spring, the loveliest of all seasons in Greece, sees the trees blossom and the islands transformed into carpets of flowers, as Easter approaches. Even the most boisterous Greeks are subdued in the week preceding the Easter weekend, which erupts into a frenzy of dancing, rejoicing, eating and drinking, as fireworks light up the midnight sky. *Christos anesti!* is the greeting, 'Christ has risen!' and millions of candles are lit around the country.

Like magic any harsh memories of the previous summer are forgotten, vendettas are forgiven, and a rejuvenated population prepares itself for a new season, painting café chairs, mending shopfronts, whitewashing walls. There's a feeling of expectancy in the air as, first the swallows, then the tourists arrive, and the whole show winds up again.

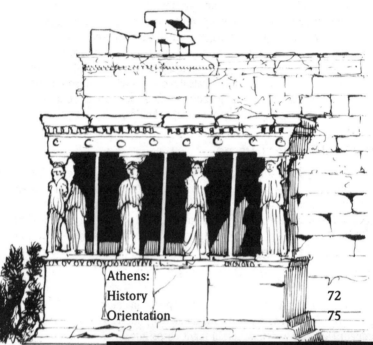

Athens and Piraeus

Many travellers to the Greek islands eventually find themselves in Athens and Piraeus, but it's rarely love at first sight; Athens, with its ramshackle architecture and grubby, dusty exterior, wins no beauty prizes. Look closely, however, and you may be won over by this urban crazy quilt of villages—small oases of green parks hidden amidst the hustle and bustle; tiny family-run tavernas tucked away in the most unexpected places; the feverish pace of its nightlife and summer festivals devoted to wine and song; and best all, the Athenians themselves, whose friendliness belies the reputation of most inhabitants of capital cities.

An Historical Outline of Athens

Inhabited by pre-Hellenic tribes in the Neolithic Age (c. 3500 BC) Athens made its proper debut on the stage of history in the second millennium, when Ionians from Asia Minor invaded Attica and established several small city-states. Their main centre was Kekropia, named for the serpent god Kekrops (he later became connected with King Erechtheus, who was himself a snake from the waist down and is considered to be the original founder of Athens). The owl was sacred to Kekropia—as it was to the goddess Athena, and her worship and name gradually came to preside in the city.

In the 14th century BC Athens, as part of the Mycenaean empire of the Achaeans, invaded Crete, fought Thebes, and conquered Troy, but managed to escape the subsequent Dorian invasion which brought chaos into the Mycenaean world. Two hundred years later, however, it was Attica's turn to meet the uncouth Dorians, who brought with them Greece's first Dark Age. This endured until the 8th century BC, far too long for the sophisticated Ionians and Aeolians, who went back to their homelands in Asia Minor and settled many of the Aegean islands.

Sometime during the 8th century all the towns of Attica were peaceably united, an accomplishment attributed to the mythical King Theseus (1300 BC). Athens was then ruled by a king (the chief priest), a *polemarch* (or general), and an *archon* (or civil authority), positions that became annually elective by the 6th century. The conflict between the landed aristocracy and rising commercial classes gradually brought about the solution of democratic government, beginning under the reforms of Solon. Yet under every stone there lurked a would-be tyrant; Solon was still warm in the grave when Pisistratos, leader of the popular party, made himself boss (545 BC) and began the naval build-up that first made Athens a threat to the other independent city-states of Greece.

Pisistratos' son was followed by another reformer, Kleisthenes, who discarded Athens' ancient but unsatisfactory political classifications by dividing the population into ten tribes. Each selected by lot 50 members of the people's assembly, from which a further lot was drawn to select an archon, creating ten archons in all, one from each tribe. The head archon gave his name to the Athenian year.

Meanwhile, as Persian strength grew in the east, Ionian intellectuals and artists settled in Athens, bringing with them the roots of Attic tragedy. They encouraged Athens to aid the Ionians against the Persians, an unsuccessful adventure that landed the city in the soup when Darius, the King of Kings, turned to subdue Greece, and in particular Athens, which posed the only threat to the Persian fleet. In 490 BC Darius' vast army landed at Marathon only to be defeated by a much smaller Athenian force under Miltiades. Powerful Sparta and the other Greek states then recognized the eastern threat, but continued to leave 'national' defence primarily in the hands of the Athenians and their fleet, which grew ever mightier under Themistocles. However, it failed to keep the Persians from having another go at Greece, and in 480 BC the new king Xerxes showed up with the greatest fleet and army the ancient world had ever seen. Athens was destroyed, but the Persian navy was neatly outmanouevred by the Athenian ships at Salamis and the invasion was finally repelled by the Athenians and Spartans at the battle of Plataea.

Having proved her naval might, Athens set about creating a maritime empire, not only to increase her power but also to stabilize her combustible internal politics. She ruled the confederacy at Delos, demanding contributions from the islands in return for protection from the Persians. Sea trade became necessary to support the city's growing population, while the founding of new colonies around the Mediterranean ensured a continual food supply to Athens. The democracy became truly imperialistic under Pericles, who brought the treasure of Delos to Athens to skim off funds to rebuild and beautify the city and build the Parthenon. It was the golden age of Athens, the age of the sculptures of Phidias, the histories of Herodotos, the plays of Sophocles and Aristophanes, the philosophy of Socrates.

The main cause of the Peloponnesian War (431–404 BC) was concern over Athenian expansion in the west. Back and forth the struggle went, Sparta with superiority on land, Athens on the seas, until both city-states were near exhaustion. Finally Lysander captured Athens, razed the walls, and set up the brief rule of the Thirty Tyrants.

Although democracy and imperialism made quick recoveries (by 378 the city had set up its second Maritime League), the Peloponnesian War had struck a blow from which Athens could not totally recover. The population grew dissatisfied with public life, and refused to tolerate innovators and critics to the extent that Socrates was put to death. Economically, Athens had trouble maintaining the trade she so desperately needed. Yet her intellectual tradition held true in the 4th century, bringing forth the likes of Demosthenes, Praxiteles, Menander, Plato and Aristotle.

Philip II of Macedon took advantage of the general discontent and turmoil to bully the city-states into joining Macedon for an expedition against Persia. Athenian patriotism and independence were kept alive by the orator Demosthenes until Philip subdued the city (338). He was assassinated shortly before beginning the Persian campaign, leaving his son Alexander to conquer the East. When Alexander died, Athens had to defend herself against his striving generals, beginning with Dimitrios Poliorketes (the Besieger) who captured the city in 294. Alexandria and Pergamon became Athens' intellectual rivals, although Athens continued to be honoured by them.

In 168 BC Rome captured Athens, but gave her many privileges including the island of Delos. Eighty years later Athens betrayed Roman favour by siding with Mithridates of Pontos, for which Sulla destroyed Piraeus and the walls of the city. But Rome always remembered her cultural debt; leading Romans attended Athens' schools and gave the city great gifts. Conversely many Greek treasures ended up in Rome. St Paul came to preach to the Athenians in AD 44. In the 3rd century Goths and barbarians sacked Athens, and when they were driven away the city joined the growing Byzantine Empire.

Justinian closed the philosophy schools in AD 529 and changed the temples to churches and the Parthenon into a cathedral. By now Athens had lost almost all of her former importance. She became the plaything of the Franks after they pillaged Constantinople in 1204. St Louis appointed Guy de la Roche as Duke of Athens, a dukedom which passed through many outstretched hands: the Catalans, Neapolitans and Venetians all controlled it at various times. In 1456 the Turks took Athens, turning the Parthenon into a mosque and the Erechtheion into a harem. While attacking the Turks in 1687 Morosini and the Venetians blew up part of the Parthenon, where the Turks had stored their gunpowder. A year later the Venetians left, unsuccessful, and the citizens who had fled returned to Athens. In 1800 Lord Elgin began the large-scale removal of monuments from Athens to the British and other museums.

In 1834, after the War of Independence, Athens—then a few hundred war-scarred houses deteriorating under the Acropolis—was declared the capital of the new Greek state. Otho of Bavaria, the first King of the Greeks, brought his own architects with him and laid out a new city on the lines of Stadiou and El. Venezelou streets, which still boast most of Otho's neo-Classical public buildings. The rest of the city's architecture was abandoned to unimaginative concrete blocks, spared monotony only by the hilly Attic terrain. More and more of these hills are being pounded into villas and flats by the ubiquitous cement mixer; greater Athens squeezes in over three million lively, opiniated inhabitants (a third of the entire Greek population) who thanks to native ingenuity and EC membership are now more prosperous than they have been since the age of Pericles. Unfortunately this means a million cars now crawl the ancient streets, creating the worst smog problem east of Los Angeles, and one that threatens to choke this unique city.

Modern Athens currently has a new problem with ethnic tensions. The Gipsies have traditionally been looked on as the underclass in Greece, blamed for wrongdoings and thefts. But since thousands of impoverished refugees poured into northern Greece from Albania in 1990 they have become the new whipping boys, especially those who are not ethnically Greek. Albanians are blamed for an increase in street crime and burglaries in the cities.

Many Albanians have moved into Athens, adding to the unemployment problem in the eyes of Athenians. There has been an increase in housebreaking, theft from cars, and other crimes previously unknown in the suburbs of Athens; inevitably, the immigrants, with their visible poverty, have become the new scapegoats.

Orientation

Syntagma (or **Constitution**) **Square** is to all intents and purposes the centre of the the city, and it's here that the **Parliament Building** is to be found, backing on to the **National Gardens** and **Zappeion Park**, a haven of green and shade to escape the summer heat, with ducks to feed and a hundred benches useful for grabbing a few winks. The square itself is a busy roundabout with traffic whizzing past, but this doesn't seem to deter the people sitting feet away at the outdoor tables of the numerous overpriced cafés.

From Syntagma it's a short walk down to the far more interesting **Plaka**, the medieval centre of Athens at the foot of the Acropolis, where many of the older houses have been converted into intimate tavernas or bars, each tinkling away with its own electric bazouki. This is also a good place to look for mid-priced accommodation, and a fun part of the city to wander around in the evening.

During the day meander through Athens' nearby flea market district, to the west of **Monastiraki Square** (and metro), where bulging shops sell everything from good quality woollen goods and fake Caterpillar boots to furniture and second hand fridges. To reach the flea market, you'll find several streets en route that all claim to be the flea market, but are nothing more than tourist traps selling tat such as engraved souvenirs of Athens, fur coats, fake icons, and lots of t-shirts with 'Hellas' printed on them.

A 10-minute walk from Syntagma will take you to **Kolonaki Square**, Athens' Knightsbridge in miniature, complete with fancypants shops and restaurants (all of course expensive) and plenty of well-heeled Athenians to patronize them. Up from the square (it's a long haul on foot, but there's a funicular) is the hill of **Lycavitos**, illuminated like a fairytale tower at night. On the top sits the chapel of **St George**, a restaurant/bar and a cannon fired on national holidays. It offers the best panoramic views of Athens, including a sweeping vista down to the sea at Piraeus, *nefos* (Athens' special brand of smog) permitting.

A 20-minute walk from Syntagma, along Vass. Sofias, brings you to the Hilton Hotel, a useful landmark. Behind it are the essential Athenian neighbourhoods of **Ilissia** and **Pangrati**, the best place to get a feel for everyday life in the city. Lose yourself in their backstreets and you may find your own little taverna, of which there are plenty, rather than restrict yourself to the tourist haunts in the centre.

From Zappeion Park buses run frequently down to the coast and suburbs of **Glyfada**, **Voula** and **Vouliagmenis**. Glyfada, close to the airport, is a green and pleasant suburb, and the town itself has grown into a busy resort and a rival Kolonaki. Many smart city dwellers shop at the ritzy boutiques, and there are even a couple of well-designed (but small, fortunately) indoor shopping centres.

Here and further down the coast at Voula are pay beaches run by EOT, the National Tourist Organisation. The water is generally clean, but nothing like the more remote islands. There's also good swimming beyond Voula in the rocky coves at Vouliagmenis. Beyond Vouliagmenis, the road continues along the coast to **Sounion** and its **Temple of Poseidon** (440 BC), famous for its magnificent position and sunsets and where there's always at least one tourist searching for the column where Byron carved his name.

Agora Museum (the Theseum and Ancient Agora)

Open 8.30–3, closed Mon, adm.

The Agora was not only the market but the centre of Athenian civic and social life where citizens spent much of their day; here Socrates questioned their basic conceptions of life and law. In 480 BC the Persians destroyed all the buildings of the Agora, which were rebuilt in a much grander style; many suffered the wrath of the Romans and fires set by the barbarians. Only the foundations remain of the **Bouleuterion** or council house, and the neighbouring Temple of the Mother of the Gods, the **Metroon**, built by the Athenians in reparation for their slaying of a priest from the cult. The round **Tholos** or administration centre is where the administrators or *prytanes* worked, and as some had to be on call day and night, kitchens and sleeping quarters were included. Its final reconstruction took place after Sulla's rampage in 88 BC. Only a wall remains of the **Sanctuary of the Eponymous Heroes of Athens**, the ten who gave their names to Kleisthenes' ten tribes. The **altar of Zeus Agoraios** received the oaths of the new archons, a practice initiated by Solon.

The 4th-century **Temple of Apollo** was dedicated to the mythical father of the Ionians, who believed themselves descended from Ion, son of Apollo. The huge statue of Apollo in the Agora museum once stood inside the temple. Almost nothing remains of the **Stoa Basileios**, or of Zeus Eleutherios, which played a major role in Athenian history as the court of the annual archon, where trials concerning the security of the state took place. By the Stoa of Zeus stood the **Altar of the Twelve Gods**, from which all distances in Attica were measured. Alongside it ran the **Panathenaic Way**; some signs of its Roman rebuilding may be seen by the Church of the Holy Apostles. After crossing the Agora, this ceremonial path ascended to the Acropolis, where devotees celebrated the union of Attica. South of the Altar of Twelve Gods is the site of the Doric **Temple to Ares** (5th century BC). The **Three Giants** nearby were originally part the **Odeon of Agrippa** (15 BC); parts of the orchestra remain intact after the roof collapsed in AD 190. Confusingly, the site and the giants were reused in the façade of a 5th-century AD gymnasium, that served for a century as the site of the University of Athens until Justinian closed it down. Near the **Middle Stoa** (2nd century BC) are ruins of a **Roman temple** and the ancient shops and booths. On the other side of the Middle Stoa is the people's court, or **Heliaia**, organized by Solon in the 6th century BC to hear political questions; it remained active well into Roman times.

Between the **South and East Stoas** (2nd century BC) is the 11th-century **Church of the Holy Apostles** (Ag. Apostoli), built on the site where St Paul addressed the Athenians and restored, along with its fine paintings, in 1952. Across the Panathenaic Way run the remains of **Valerian's Wall** thrown up in AD 257 against the barbarian, its stone cannibalized from Agora buildings wrecked by the Romans. Between Valerian's Wall and the Stoa of Attalos are higgledy-piggledy ruins of the **Library of Pantainos**, built by Flavius Pantainos in AD 100 and destroyed 167 years later. Finds from the entire Agora are in the museum in the **Stoa of Attalos**, the 2nd-century BC portico built by King Attalos II of Pergamon, reconstructed by John D. Rockefeller.

The same ticket gets you into the mid-5th-century BC **Theseum**, nothing less than the best-preserved Greek temple in existence. Doric in order and dedicated to Hephaistos, the god of metals and smiths, it may well have been designed by the architect of the temple at Sounion. It is constructed almost entirely of Pentelic marble and decorated with metopes depicting the lives of Heracles and Theseus (for whom the temple was named). Converted into a church in the 5th century, it was the burial place for English Protestants until 1834, when the government declared it a national monument.

The Acropolis

Mon–Fri 8–5, Sat and Sun 8.30–3, adm.

The naturally-fortified **Acropolis** was inhabited from the end of the Neolithic Age. The Mycenaeans added a Cyclopean wall and the palace of their king. This was later replaced by a temple to the god of the spring, Poseidon, and to Athena. In mythology, these two divinities took part in a contest to decide who would be the patron of the new city. With his trident Poseidon struck the spring Klepsydra out of the rock of the Acropolis, while Athena invented the olive tree, which the Athenians judged the better trick.

The tyrant Pisistratos ordered a great gate constructed in the wall, but Delphi cursed it and the Athenians dismantled it. In 480 BC the temple's cult statue of Athena was hurried to the protection of Salamis, just before the Persians burnt the Acropolis. Themistocles built a new rampart out of the old Parthenon, and under Perikles the present plan of the Acropolis buildings was laid out.

The path to the Acropolis follows the Panathenaic Way, laid out at the consecration of the Panathenaic Festival in 566 BC. The Acropolis entrance is defended by the **Beulé Gate** (named after Ernest Beulé, the archaeologist who found it); the monumental stairways were built by the Romans and the two lions are from Venice. The reconstructed Panathenaic ramp leads to the equally reconstructed

Propylaia, the massive gateway replacing Pisistratos' cursed gate, built by Pericles' architect Mnesikles. The ancient Greeks considered the Proplyaia the architectural equal of the Parthenon itself, although it was never completed because of the Peloponnesian War. On either side of the Propylaia's entrance are two wings; the north held a picture gallery (Pinakotheke) while the smaller one to the south consisted of only one room of an unusual shape, because the priests of the neighbouring Nike temple didn't want the wing in their precinct. The original entrance had five doors, the central one pierced by the Panathenaic Way.

Temple of Athena Nike

The Ionic Temple of Athena Nike, or *Wingless Victory*, was built by the architect Kallikrates in 478 BC of Pentelic marble. Inside was kept the cult statue of Athena, a copy of a much older wooden statue. Its lack of wings, unlike later victory statues, gave it its second name. In 1687 the Turks destroyed the temple to build a tower. It was rebuilt in 1835 and again in 1936, when the bastion beneath it threatened to crumble away. The north and western friezes were taken to England by Lord Elgin and have been replaced by cement casts. From the temple of Athena Nike the whole Saronic Gulf could be seen in the pre-smog days, and it was here that Aegeus watched for the return of his son Theseus from his Cretan adventure with the Minotaur. Theseus was to have signalled his victory with a white sail but forgot; at the sight of the black sail of death, Aegeus threw himself off the precipice in despair.

The Parthenon

The Parthenon, the glory of the Acropolis and probably the most famous building in the world, if not the most imitated, is a Doric temple constructed between 447 and 432 BC under the direction of Phidias, the greatest artist and sculptor of the Periclean age. Originally called the Great Temple, it took the name Parthenon (Chamber of Virgins) a hundred years after its completion. Constructed entirely of Pentelic marble, it originally held Phidias' famous statue of Athena Parthenos, more than 36ft high and made of ivory and gold. Look closely, and you'll see that the Parthenon's foundation is curved slightly to prevent an illusion of drooping caused by straight horizontals. To make the columns appear straight the architect bent them a few centimetres inward. Corner columns were made wider to complete the illusion of perfect form.

The outer colonnade consists of 46 columns and above them are the remnants of the Doric frieze left behind by the beaverish Lord Elgin: the east side portrayed the battle of giants and gods, the south the Lapiths and Centaurs (mostly in the

British Museum today), on the west the Greeks and the Amazons, and on the north the battle of Troy. Little remains of the pediment sculptures of the gods. Above the interior colonnade, the masterful Ionic frieze designed by Phidias himself shows the quadrennial Panathenaic Procession in which Athena was brought a golden crown and a new sacred garment, or *peplos*.

The Parthenon's roof was blown sky high in 1687 when a Venetian bomb hit the Turks' powder stores inside; the destruction was continued in 1894 by an earthquake and today the nefarious *nefos* smog threatens to give the kiss of death to this graceful prototype of a thousand bank buildings. Entrance within the Parthenon itself is forbidden, to save on wear and tear. What is intriguing—and sometimes you can see the work in progress—is that after all these years the Greek government has decided to pick up all the pieces lying scattered since Morosini's day, and reconstruct as much of the temple as possible.

The Erechtheion

The last great monument on the Acropolis is the Erechtheion, a peculiar Ionic temple that owes its idiosyncrasies to the various cult items and the much older sanctuary it was built to encompass. Beneath the temple stood the Mycenaean House of Erechtheus, mentioned by Homer, and the primitive cult sanctuary of Athena; on one side of this grew the Sacred Olive Tree created by Athena, while under the north porch was the mark left by Poseidon's trident when he brought forth the divine spring. The tomb of Kekrops, the legendary founder of Athens, is in the Porch of the Maidens or Caryatids, where Erechtheus died at the hand of either Zeus or Poseidon. Within the temple stood the ancient cult statue of Athena Polias, endowed with the biggest juju of them all, solemnly dressed in the sacred *peplos* and crown.

After the Persian fires, the sanctuary was quickly restored, but the marble temple planned by Pericles was not begun until 421 BC. Used as a church in the 7th century, it became a harem under the Turks, who used the sacred place of the trident marks as a toilet. Lord Elgin nicked parts of this temple as well, including one of the caryatids which you can now see in the British Museum; acidic air pollution has forced the Greek government to replace the other girls with casts.

Basically the Erechtheion is a rectangular building with three porches. Inside were two cellas, or chambers: the East Cella dedicated to Athena Polias, the smaller to Poseidon–Erechtheus. Six tall Ionic columns mark the north porch where the floor and roof were cut away to reveal Poseidon's trident marks, for it was sacrilegious to hide something so sacred from the view of the gods. The six famous maidens gracefully supporting the roof on their heads are another Ionian motif.

The Acropolis Museum

(open Tues–Fri 8–4.30, Mon 10–4.30, Sat and Sun 8.30–2.30)

The museum houses sculptures and reliefs from the temples, in particular the Erechtheion's maidens, or Kores. But frankly, the museum's contents are far less impressive than the site outside, unless you're a scholar of classics or have a big interest in archaeology.

Below the Acropolis is the **Areopagos**, or hill of Ares, the god of war. There sat the High Council, who figured so predominantly in Aeschylos' play *The Eumenides* where mercy defeated vengeance for the first time in history during the trial of the matricide Orestes. Although Pericles removed much of the original power of the High Council, under the control of the ex-archons it continued to advise on the Athenian constitution for hundreds of years.

The Theatres

*Prices vary: 800 dr. is the current rate of admission to the site of The **Acropolis**, for an adult without a concession.*

On the south side of the Acropolis are two theatres. The older, the **Theatre of Dionysos**, was used from the 6th century BC when Thespis created the first true drama, and was continually modified up to the time of Nero. In this theatre the annual Greater Dionysia was held, in honour of the god of wine and patron divinity of the theatre, Dionysos. The dramatic competitions led to the premières of some of the world's greatest tragedies. The stage that remains is from the 4th century BC, while the area before the stage, the **proskenion**, is decorated with 1st century AD scenes based on the life of Dionysos. Beside the theatre stood two temples to Dionysos Eleutherios.

Above the theatre is an **Asklepieion**, a sanctuary to the god of healing. The stoa which remains is from the second rebuilding, while the first and oldest sanctuary to the west first belonged to a water goddess, but very little of it remains. Both the old and new Asklepieions were connected with the parent cult at Epidauros.

The **Theatre of Herodes Atticus** was built and named for the Rockefeller of his day in AD 161 and originally partially covered. Now it hosts the annual mid-May and September **Festival of Athens**, where the cultures of modern Europe and ancient Greece are combined in theatre, ballet, and classical music concerts performed by companies from all over the world.

Other Museums

Benaki Museum: On the corner of Vassilis Sofias and Koumbari St, *open 8.30–3, daily.* This museum holds the collection of Antonios Benaki, who spent 35 years amassing objects from Europe and Asia, Byzantine and Islamic. The Byzantine artworks (6th–14th centuries) are fascinating examples of early Christian art: icons, jewellery, ceramics, silver and embroidery, while the post-Byzantine exhibits (15th–17th century) show the influences of Islamic and Italian art. There are two icons by the Cretan-born El Greco, painted before his departure to Venice and Spain—the *Adoration of the Magi* (1560–65) and the *Evangelist Luke* (1560). The section on folk art, dating from the Ottoman occupation, contains a superb collection of costumes and artefacts from the Ionian islands to Cyprus.

National Archaeology Museum: Patission and Tossitsa Sts, *open 8–5, Sat and Sun 8.30–3, Mon 11–5, free Thurs and Sun.* The National Museum contains some of the most spectacular ancient Greek art anywhere—the Minoan-style frescoes from Santorini, gold from Mycenae (including the famous mask of Agamemnon), statues, reliefs, tomb stelae, and ceramics and vases from every period. The Cycladic collection includes one of the first known musicians of the Greek world, the sculpture of the little harpist that has become the virtual symbol of the Cyclades. The star of the sculpture rooms is a virile bronze of Poseidon (5th-century BC) about to launch his trident, found off the coast of Evia in 1928; around him are some outstanding archaic Kouros statues and the Stele of Hegeso, an Athenian beauty, enveloped by the delicate folds of her robe, seated on a throne. The museum has a shop on the lower level, with reproductions of exhibits by expert craftsmen, so accurate that each piece is issued with a certificate declaring it an authentic fake so you can take it out of the country.

National Gallery: 50 Vass. Konstantinou, across from the Athens Hilton, *open 9–3, Sun 10–2, closed Mon.* Also known as the Alexander Soustou Museum, the National Gallery concentrates on art by modern Greek artists. Works by the leading contemporary painter, Nikos Hadzikyriakos-Ghikas, are permanently displayed on the ground floor, while the lower level is used for rotating exhibitions. The museum shop has posters, cards, catalogues and jewellery, and there's a pleasant outdoor café, for when you've done the rounds.

Historical and Ethnological Museum: At the Palea Vouli (Old Parliament), Stadiou St, *open 9–1, closed Mon.* This imposing neo-Classical edifice is the guardian of Greek history, from the fall of Constantinople to the present day. The bronze warrior on horseback is Theodoros Kolokotronis, hero of the War of Independence, while exhibits within trace the history of modern Greece in paintings, sculptures, armaments (including Byron's sword and helmet), maps, folk costumes, jewellery and more covering every period, from Ottoman rule to resistance against the Nazis in 1940.

Popular Art Museum: 17 Kydathinaion St, *open 10–2, closed Mon.* The museum has a collection of Greek folk art, both religious and secular, along with paintings by naïve artists.

The Pnyx: On the hill west of the Acropolis. The Pnyx once hosted the General Assembly of Athens and the great speeches of Pericles and Demosthenes. On assembly days citizens were literally rounded up to fill the minimum attendance quota of 5000, but they were paid for their services to the state. Later the assembly was transferred to the theatre of Dionysos. On the summit of the nearby Hill of the Muses is the **Philopappos Monument**, the tomb of Caius Julius Antiochos Philopappos, a Syrian Prince and citizen of Athens. The monument was built for him by the Athenians in AD 114 in gratitude for his beneficence to the city.

Roman Agora: Located between the Agora and the Acropolis, *open 8.30–3pm closed Mon. Adm 1000dr.* Dating from the end of the Hellenistic age, the Roman Agora contains the celebrated **Tower of the Winds,** or Clock of Andronikos, built in the 1st century BC. Run by a hydraulic mechanism, it stayed open day and night so that the citizens could know the time. Its name comes from the frieze of the eight winds that decorate its eight sides, although it has lost its ancient bronze Triton weathervane. The Roman Agora also contains the **Gate of Athena Archegetis**, built by money sent over from Julius and Augustus Caesar; there is also a court and the ruins of stoae. Beside the Agora is the Fehiye Camii, the Victory or Corn Market Mosque.

Byzantine Museum: 22 Vassilis Sofias, *open 8.30–3, closed Mon.* This monumental collection of religious treasures and paintings dates from the Early Byzantine period to the 19th century—not only icons but marble sculptures, mosaics, woodcarvings, frescoes, manuscripts and ecclesiastical robes. There are three rooms on the ground floor arranged as chapels, one Early Christian, another Middle Byzantine, and the third post-Byzantine.

Museum of Cycladic Art: 4 Neoforos Douka St (between Byzantine and Benaki museums), *open 10–3.30, Sat 10–2.30, closed Tues and Sun.* This museum houses a vast collection of Cycladic figurines and objects dating back to 3200–2000 BC, illustrating everyday life. The female figurines with folded arms are unique. The newest addition is the 'Treasure of Keros', a small island near Naxos where excavations in the 1950s and 60s unearthed a wealth of figurines.

Keramikos and Museum: 148 Ermou St, *open 8.30–3, closed Mon.* The ancient cemetery or Keramikos was used for burials from the 12th century BC into Roman times, but the most impressive and beautiful finds are in the rich private tombs built by the Athenians in the 4th century BC. Large stone vases mark the graves of the unmarried dead, while others are in the form of miniature temples and stelae; the best are in the National Museum.

Temple of Olympian Zeus: Olgas and Amalias Avenues, *open 8.30–3, closed Mon.* Fifteen columns recall what Livy called 'the only temple on earth of a size adequate to the greatness of the god'. The foundations were laid by the tyrant Pisistratos, but work ground to a halt with the fall of his dynasty, only to be continued in 175 BC by a Roman architect, Cossutius. It was half finished when Cossutius' patron, Antiochos IV of Syria kicked the bucket, leaving the Emperor Hadrian to complete it in AD 131. Nearby are the ruins of ancient houses and a bath and at the far end stands **Hadrian's Arch**, neatly dividing the city of Theseus from the city of Hadrian. The Athenians traditionally come here to celebrate the Easter Resurrection.

Museum of the City of Athens: Plateia Klafthmonos, *open Mon, Wed, Fri, Sat 9–1.30; free Wed.* Located in the re-sited neo-Classical palace of King Otho, this new museum contains photos, memorabilia and a model showing Athens as it was soon after it became the capital of modern Greece.

Byzantine Churches and Monasteries in Athens

Agii Theodori: This 11th-century church in Klafthmonos Square at the end of Dragatsaniou St is most notable for its beautiful door; the bell tower and some of the decorations inside are more recent additions.

Kapnikarea: A few blocks from Agii Theodori, on Ermou St. Tiny Kapnikarea (the chapel of the University of Athens) was built in the late 11th century in the shape of a Greek cross, its central cupola sustained by four columns with Roman capitals.

Panayia Gorgoepikoos (or Ag. Eleftherios): Situated in Mitropoleos Square and known as the little Metropolitan to distinguish it from the nearby cathedral, this is the loveliest church in Athens. Built in the 12th century almost entirely of ancient marbles the builders found lying around; note the ancient calendar of state festivals embedded over the door. Curiously, the **Cathedral** (just to the north) was built in 1840–55 with the same collage technique, using bits and pieces from 72 destroyed churches.

Dafni and its Wine Festival: 10 km from Athens; take bus 282 from Eleftherios Square. The name Dafni derives from the temple of Apollo Dafneios (of the laurel), built near the Sacred Way. The site became a walled monastery in the 6th century and in 1080 a new church was built, decorated with the best Byzantine mosaics in southern Greece. These are dominated in the vault of the dome by the tremendous figure of Christ Pantokrator 'the all powerful', his eyes spellbinding and tragic, 'as though He were in flight from an appalling doom' as Patrick Leigh Fermor has written. From mid-August until September, daily 7.45pm–12.30am, the monastery park holds a festival with over 60 different Greek wines (free once you've paid the 300 dr. admission at the gate) accompanied by (poor and over-priced) food, singing and dancing, an event well-attended by Athenians and visitors alike.

(01–)   ### *Where to Stay in Athens*

Athens is a big noisy city, especially so at night when you want to sleep—unless you do as the Greeks do and take a long afternoon siesta. Piraeus (*see* below) may be a better bet, no less noisy but much more convenient for catching those up-at-the-crack-of-dawn ships to the islands, although women on their own may find too many sailors and working girls about to feel at ease. All accommodation fills up quickly in the summer and if you don't have a reservation, or erratic boat schedules have mangled your booking, it's best to head straight for the EOT office on Syntagma Square (in the National Bank building) and use their hotel finding service.

luxury

New luxury chain hotels are mushrooming up everywhere just outside the city centre—there's the **Ledra Marriott** at 113–115 Syngrou, © 934 7711, fax 935 8603, featuring a Chinese–Japanese restaurant, and a hydrotherapy pool you can soak in with a view of the Parthenon. Another addition to the scene (and one on a human scale) is the 76-room **Astir Palace Athens Hotel** on Syntagma Square, © 364 3112, fax 364 2825 owned by the National Bank of Greece. While it was under construction, ancient foundations and waterpipes were uncovered and these are incorporated into the décor of the hotel's restaurant, the **Apokalypsis**, located below street level (Greek and international cuisine). Despite its location, specially insulated glass windows keep out the hubbub below the rooms. There's a sauna, and each room features a mini bar and colour TV (with an in-house movie channel).

Directly across the square from the Astir is the **Grande Bretagne**, © 323 0251, fax 322 8034 originally built in 1862 to house members of the Greek royal family who couldn't squeeze into the main palace (the current Parliament building) up the square. The Grande Bretagne is the only 'grand' hotel in Greece worthy of the description, with a vast marble lobby, elegant rooms (now air conditioned and appointed with such modern conveniences as direct dial phones and colour TV), a formal dining room, and an appearance of grandeur and style that the newer hotels, with all their plushness, may never achieve. Having said that, on our most recent stay there (Autumn 1993) we found the service to be positively complacent, which is disappointing at the prices they charge. Even if you're not going to stay there, you may want to poke your head in (there's a pleasant bar) to see where the crowned heads of Europe lodge in Athens—and where the Nazis set up their headquarters during the Second World War. Winston Churchill spent Christmas 1944 at the Grande Bretagne and was lucky to escape a bomb meant for him, planted in the hotel's complex sewer system.

On a less exalted level, but with a far more fetching view is the **Royal Olympic Hotel** at 28 Diakou, © 922 6411, fax 923 3317, facing the Temple of Olympian Zeus and Mt Lycavitos. Rooms here are American in spirit, with a number of family-sized suites, and if you have the misfortune to get a room without a view, there's the wonderful panorama from the rooftop bar.

expensive

The **Electra Palace** at 18 Nikodimou St, © 324 1401, fax 324 1875, has views of the Acropolis and a wonderful rooftop swimming pool in a garden setting—something you don't find every day in Athens. Rooms are air conditioned and there's a garage adjacent to the hotel. Half-board is obligatory—unfortunately, because the hotel is quite close to the good tavernas of Plaka. More reasonable, and centrally located just off Syntagma Square, the **Astor**, 16 Karagiorgi Servias, © 325 5555, also has fully air conditioned rooms and a rooftop garden restaurant.

moderate

The best value in this category (and a big favourite with Americans) has long been the **Hotel Alkistis** at 18 Plateia Theatrou, © 321 9811, all rooms with private baths and phones, all very modern and perfectly clean. If the Alkistis is full, a good second bet is the **Hotel Museum** at

16 Bouboulinas St, © 360 5611, right at the back of the Archaeology Museum. The rooms are about the same, but the prices are a bit higher. **Hotel Tempi**, 29 Eolou St, © 321 3175, near Monastiraki, is more downgrade, but is cheaper and has washing facilities. **Art Gallery** at Erekhthiou 5, Veikou, © 923 8376, is a pleasant place at the lower end of this price category, though it is out of the centre; Plaka is a 20-minute walk, more if you're fumbling with a map.

cheap

Most of the inexpensive hotels are around Plaka. For better or worse, the government has shut down many of the old dormitory houses that grew up in the 1960s to contain the vanguard of mass tourism in Greece— every hippy in Europe, or at least so it seemed to the amazed Greeks. Survivors of the government purge have upgraded themselves but are still a bargain—and many still let you sleep on the roof for a thousand drachmas (not an unpleasant option in the thick heat of August). Best bets in the cheaper category include:

Hotel Phaedra, 16 Herefondos St, © 323 8461, just off Filellinon St, with free hot showers; unreconstructed pre-war interior, and pleasant staff (double room 6000dr, more in season).

John's Place, 5 Patroou St, © 322 9719. Around 4000dr.

Hotel Cleo, 3 Patroou St, © 322 9053, small and near Plaka.

Student Inn, 16 Kidathineon, © 324 4808, very conveniently placed in the Plaka, and ideal for the rowdy younger crowd (1.30am curfew though).

Joseph's House, 13 Markou Botsari, © 923 1204, in a quieter area on the south side of the Acropolis; washing facilities available (take advantage of it—if you're travelling in the islands for any length of time, washing clothes will be your biggest headache).

Less savoury, but also less expensive is the city's **IYHF Youth Hostel**, inconveniently located far from the centre at 57 Kypselis St, Kypseli, © (01) 822 5860. A better option, though it is not a member of the YHA, is the **Student's Hostel** at 75 Damareos St, Pangrati, © 751 9530. The nearest **campsites** to Athens are at Dafni Monastery, and down on the coast at Voula. When your make you way through the metro station at Piraeus, you're guaranteed to have fliers thrust in your hand for other rock-bottom options.

Athenians rarely dine out before 10 or 11pm, and they want to be entertained afterwards. If it's warm, chances are they'll drive out to the suburbs or the sea shore. **Glyfada**, near the airport, is a popular destination and on a summer evening the cool sea breeze can be a life saver after the oppressive heat of Athens. The obvious meal to choose is something from the sea, and most of the tavernas specialize in fish (especially red mullet, or *barbounia*), lobster, squid and shrimp, although, as everywhere in Greece, it's the most expensive food you can order. Remember that prices marked for fish usually indicate how much per kilo, not per portion.

Glyfada

Leading off the main square in Glyfada is a street almost entirely devoted to excellent restaurants and friendly, inexpensive bars. At reasonably priced **George's**, the steak will be cooked according to your specifications and the meatballs (*keftedes*) are a speciality. To feed the large foreign community in Glyfada, a plethora of fast food joints has grown up in the area, and now expensive Arab restaurants (complete with imported Middle Eastern singers and belly dancers) have made an appearance on the scene.

central Athens

Costayiannis, 37 Zaimi, near the National Archaeology Museum, with a succulent display of food in the glass cabinets near the entrance preparing you for a memorable culinary evening. Apart from the superb seafood, the 'ready food' is unbeatable—try the quail with roast potatoes, the roast pork in wine and herb sauce or the rabbit *stifado*, accompanied by barrelled retsina, if you've developed a taste for it. Prices here are very reasonable—3500 dr. for a full evening meal (closed lunchtimes and Sundays). As near to a traditional taverna that you'll find, the **Taverna Karavitis** is a few streets up from the old Olympic stadium, on the corner of Arkitinou and Pafsaniou and housed in a long, low white building, with barrels lining the walls. Athenians come here for a good time; the food, served by friendly young lads in jeans, is better than average, wine is served from the barrel, and it's open till late (1500 dr.). Just off Mikalakopoulou St, and not far from the Hilton Hotel is **John's Village (To Chorio tou Yianni)**, a cut above the ordinary taverna and warmly decorated with hand-woven rugs and island pottery. The accompanying music, played by a strolling minstrel, makes this a favourite spot to spend an evening without breaking the bank. There's a good variety of well-prepared dishes and a meal will cost about 3000 dr. Behind the Hilton, on Mikalakopoulou, is the Cypriot restaurant **Othello's**, with delicious, authentic cuisine at around 2500 dr. for a meal.

the Plaka

Plaka is the place to head for for pleasant restaurants and *al fresco* dining in the evening. There are scores of places catering for the passing tourist trade, and they are all very competent, though few serve true, vernacular food that you'll find on the islands (if you make the effort to look for it). Despite this, the Plaka is still the perennial favourite with both Greeks and tourists. The atmosphere at night is exciting with its crowded tavernas perched precariously on uneven steps, Greek dancers whirling and leaping on stages the size of postage stamps, light bulbs flashing and *bouzouki* music filling the air. A typical charming Plaka taverna is the rooftop **Thespes**, 100m along from the Plaka Square, where a selection of starters, such as *tzatziki, taramasalata* and fried aubergine (eggplant) followed by lamb chops and plenty of wine won't cost you much more than 2000 dr. In some of the other tavernas you may not be as lucky and will have to pay well over the odds, particularly if there's live music, for food that rarely rises above the mediocre. One other outstanding exception is **Platanos**, the oldest taverna in the Plaka, near the Tower of the Four Winds. The food here is good and wholesome, but forget about perusing the menu—it's definitely an 'in the kitchen and point' joint, and inexpensive at 1500–2000 dr. for a meal. In the heart of Plaka, in Filomosou Square, where every visitor lands up sooner or later, you can eat well at **O Costas** or **Xynou Taverna**, 4 Geronda St, which serves excellent food in a garden setting, with strolling musicians playing traditional Greek music. It's very popular (closed on Sat and Sun), and reservations are a must (© 322 1065; 2500 dr.). Off touristy Adrianou St, with all its souvenirs, the family-run taverna **Tsegouras**, 2 Epicharmou, is in a walled garden in the shade of an enormous gum tree, with good Greek food for around 2000 dr.

While walking around Plaka, you're likely to pass **Brettos**, a small but colourfully-lit shop selling own-label *mastika* and liqueurs; try some, it beats bringing back a bottle of ouzo with you on the aeroplane.

Just outside the Plaka, two blocks south of Hadrian's arch at 5 Lembessi St, **O Kouvelos** is another typical, reliable Athenian taverna, serving excellent *meze* and barrelled retsina. They'll save you the bother of ordering the meze by planting it on the table in front of you; don't be shy to change it if you want something different (2000 dr.) In the same area (cross Makriyianni St), you could try **Socrates Prison**, 20 Mitseon St, a real favourite with locals and expats. Greek food with a flair in attractive surroundings, though the service can be variable. Bottled or barrelled wine (2000 dr., evenings only, closed Sun). A few blocks west of here, at 7 Garivaldi St, the **Greek House** has dining on a rooftop terrace with a most beautiful view of the Acropolis. Don't be put off by the name; this restaurant serves superb and reasonably priced specialities—try the 'Virginia', slices of *filet mignon* with mushrooms, or the shrimp salad. They also make wonderful spinach and cheese pies (2500 dr.). Near the Monastiraki *elektriko* (underground) station, search out **Taverna Sigalas**, a bustling place where you can soak up the least pretentious side of Athenian life; usual Greek food served at unpredictable temperatures, and Greek folk music to make you feel you never want to go home (1500–2000 dr.).

around Omonia Square

Omonia Square is a great place to try Greek street food. You can buy bags of nuts, coconut sweets, savoury pies (*tyropitta*—cheese, and *spanakopitta*—spinach), late-night souvlaki, and sandwiches, and it's all very cheap. Near Omonia Square are a number of cheap restaurants displaying cuts of roast lamb, pork and the occasional grinning sheep's head. They're really worth a try if you are watching your drachme, but feel like a 'proper' meal—a portion of chicken with rubber fried spuds and a small bottle of retsina will set you back about 1000 dr. Of the half-a-dozen or so places, try **Platanos** on Satombriandou.

ethnic cuisine

Athens is well supplied with ethnic eating places—French, Italian, Spanish, Chinese, Japanese, Mexican, American and restaurants of other nationalities are scattered around the capital. Of particular note for lovers of German food is the **Rittenburg** at 11 Formionos in Pangrati, where the boiled and grilled sausages, and pork with sauerkraut are tops. North German dishes are on the menu in the small, intimate and aptly named

Delicious in Kolonaki at 6 Zalokosta—marinated fish, *bratkartoffeln*, lovely goulash and home-made black bread (2500 dr.). Asian restaurants are all relatively expensive. The Chinese-Malaysian **Rasa Sayang**, in the seaside suburb of Glyfada, on Palea Leoforos Vouliagmenis and 2 Kiou, serves great Peking Duck and beef with mango slices, among many other items (3000 dr.). A little further down the coast at Voula, **Loon Fung Tien** does fixed-price *dim sum* (buffet) lunchtimes on Sunday. Italian restaurants are established in every major European city, and Athens is no exception. **Boschetto**, in the Evangelismos Gardens opposite the Hilton, is one of the city's best. Exquisite spaghetti with *frutti di mare*, inventive main courses (guinea hen with bacon and pomegranate sauce) and fine desserts (4000 dr.). In Kolonaki the trendy **Pane e Vino**, 8 Spefsipou, is popular for its antipasti (aubergine and Gorgonzola rolls) and pasta (tagliolini with smoked salmon), together with main dishes such as sole with mussels or scaloppine with prosciutto (4–5000 dr.) A collection of top class, expensive French restaurants have graced the Athens culinary scene for years. In Kolonaki **Je Reviens**, 49 Xenokratous, is an old favourite, with live music and outdoor seating (5000 dr.). Near the American Embassy **Balthazar**, 27 Tsoha and Vournazou, is a renovated mansion with an attractive bar and a comprehensive selection of international dishes, but it's best to book © 644 1215; 3500 dr.

hotel restaurants

Some of the luxury hotels in Athens have some swish theme restaurants (with swish prices of course). The **Ledra Marriott** (p.81) has the 'Polynesian' **Kona Kai** in an exotic tropical setting, with all the delicacies from that other island paradise; a few blocks down, the **Athenaeum Intercontinental** also has Asian cuisine in its **Kublai Khan** restaurant.

Bars

Watering holes abound in Athens, many of them serving bar food, and most of the English-speaking community do the rounds of the **Red Lion**, the **Underground** and the **Ploughman's**, all within a stone's throw of the Hilton.

Wine bars are a fairly recent addition to Athens' nightlife. If you want to try some finer wines from Greece and Europe, the following places will oblige: **Kelari**, in the Hilton, serving Greek dishes as an accompaniment, in a friendly, warm décor; **Loutro**, 18 Feron, way north near Victoria

Square, decorated in sophisticated Roman bath style, serving imaginative dishes to accompany the French, Italian and lesser known Greek wines; **Le Sommelier d'Athènes**, Leof. Kifissias in Kifissia, in a beautiful old suburban villa, with an emphasis on French and Italian; **Strofilia**, 7 Karitsi (behind the Historical Museum), with mainly Greek labels, and an extensive salad bar.

Piraeus

The port of Athens, Piraeus—pronounced 'Pirefs'—was the greatest port of the ancient world and remains today one of the busiest in the Mediterranean. In Greece, a country that derives most of its livelihood from the sea in one way or another, Piraeus is the true capital, while Athens is a mere sprawling suburb where the bureaucrats live. Still, it takes a special visitor to find much charm in the tall grey buildings and dusty hurly-burly in the streets, although Marina Zea and Mikrolimani with their yachts, brightly-lit tavernas and bars are a handsome sight, as are the neon signs flashing kinetically as you sail to or from Piraeus in the evening. The tall, half-finished building on the waterfront was built and abandoned by the junta when they found that the foundations were mixed with sea water. Somehow its useless silhouette makes a fitting monument to that ignorant and often cruel government.

An Historical Outline

Themistocles founded the port of Piraeus in the 5th century BC when Phaliron, Athens' ancient port, could no longer meet the growing needs of the city. From the beginning Piraeus was cosmopolitan and up-to-date: the Miletian geometrician Hippodamos laid it out in a straight grid of streets that have changed little today. The centre of action was always the huge agora in the middle of the city. Under its stoae the world's first commercial fairs and trade expositions were held, some on an international scale. All religions were tolerated, and women were allowed for the first time to work outside the home.

As Piraeus was so crucial to Athens' power, the conquering Spartan Lysander destroyed the famous Long Walls that linked city and port in 404, at the end of the Peloponnesian War. Piraeus made a brief comeback under Konon and Lykurgos, who rebuilt its arsenals. After the 100-year Macedonian occupation and a period of peace, Sulla decimated the city to prevent any anti-Roman resistance, and for 1900 years Piraeus dwindled away into an insignificant village with a population as low as 20, even losing its name to become Porto Leone (after an ancient lion statue, carved from runes by Harald Hadraada and his Vikings in 1040 and carted off by Morosini as a trophy to embellish Venice's Arsenal). Since the selection of Athens as the capital of independent Greece, Piraeus has regained its former glory as the reigning port of a sea-going nation.

Getting Around

In Piraeus this usually means getting out of town as quickly as possible. **Ships** are grouped according to their destination and almost anyone you ask will be able to tell you the precise location of any vessel. The cluster of ticket agents around the port is very noisy and competitive, but prices to the islands are fixed, so the only reason to shop around is to see if there is an earlier or faster ship to the island of your choice. Beware that ticket agents often don't know or won't tell you information on lines other than the ones they carry. Only the Tourist Police on Akti Miaouli have complete information on boat schedules.

There are three **railway stations.** The half-underground Elektriko serves Athens as far north as the posh suburb of Kifissia, setting off every 10 minutes from 6am to 1.30am from the terminal opposite the quay. Stations for northern Greece and for the Peloponnese are further down the road.

Buses to Athens run day and night, the main 'Green' line (no. 040) taking you directly to Syntagma Square. The express line no. 19 bus service to East and West Airport leaves from Karaiskaki Square.

Tourist Police

Akti Miaouli, ✆ 452 3670.
Irron Politechniou, ✆ 412 0325.

The Sights

If you find yourself in Piraeus with time to kill on a Sunday morning, take a prowl through the flea market parallel to the underground (Elektriko) line, where you may well happen across some oddity brought back by a Greek Sinbad. If culture beckons, there's an **Archaeology Museum** at 31 Har. Trikoupi St, with an above average collection of antiquities (*8.30–3, closed Mon*), or perhaps the **Maritime Museum** on Akti Themistocles by Freatidos St, with intriguing plans of Greece's greatest naval battles, ship models and mementoes from the War of Independence (*8.30–1, closed Sun and Mon*). The **Hellenistic Theatre** at Zea occasionally has performances in the summer.

Beaches are not far away, although the sea isn't exactly sparkling and on most you must pay. Kastella is the closest, followed by New Phaliron which is free. Buses go to Ag. Kosmos by the airport, where you can play tennis or volleyball; at Glyfada, further down the road, there's more wholesome swimming and a golf course for duffers.

Zea, Glyfada and Vouliagmeni are the three **marinas** organized by the National Tourist Organization. Piraeus is also the place to charter yachts or sail boats, from 12-foot dinghies to deluxe twin-screw yachts, if you've missed your island connection (*see* yachting pp. 17–22).

Where to Stay in Piraeus

Hotel accommodation in Piraeus is geared towards businessmen, and unfortunately less so towards people who have arrived on a late-night ship or plan to depart on an early morning one. Brave souls sleep out in the squares, particularly in Karaiskaki, but they have to put up with lights, noise, the neighbouring discotheques and sailors of every nationality who hang around hoping for something to happen.

expensive

If you're with the kids, try the quiet and very clean **Hotel Anemoni**, at Karaoli Demetriou and Evripidou 65–67, © 413 6881; since it's not directly on the port you miss the sailors and some of the racket. All rooms are air conditioned, and there's a free transfer service to the port.

moderate

If you want to be within walking distance of the docks, the **Hotel Triton**, © 417 3457, is one of the best of the many in the area; its B class doubles start at 5500 dr., but go shooting up in high summer. All rooms have private bath and breakfast is available. A mediocre alternative is the **Ideal**, 142 Notara St, © 451 1727, 50 m from the customs house, with air conditioning and private bath.

cheap

On the lower end of the scale there are many D & E class hotels, some of which are not as appetizing as they might be, but their rates range from 3000 dr. to around 5000 dr. Typical of these is **Achillion**, 63 Notara St, © 412 4029.

Around the port the fare is generally fast food and giro spinners, while the tavernas are so greasy it's a wonder they don't slide off the street. For seafood (especially if you're on an expense account), the bijou little harbour of Mikrolimano (or Turkolimano) is the traditional place to go, although too many tourists with too much money have inflated the price to a nasty pitch. A far better idea is to forego fish and eat up at the excellent **Kaliva** in Vass. Pavlou, Kastella, with a splendid view down over the harbour (excellent meat dinners for 2500 dr.) followed by a stroll through Mikrolimano for a coffee and Metaxa on the harbour front. But if it's fish you must have, head over to Frates, around from the Zea Marina yacht harbour, where several moderately-priced places offer fresh fish and sea views. There's really not all that much to distinguish one from another; just stroll around until you find a fish that winks at you. Zea Marina itself is a vast necklace of neon, where the locals haunt the inexpensive **American Pizza**, but there are places with Greek pizza and other fare, both on the harbour and on the streets giving into it.

If you've got time between boats or flights, the stretch of coast between Piraeus and the airport has a few possibilities. Chefs from the eastern Mediterranean are undoubtedly the kings of kebab; try the **Adep Kebab**, 20 Leof. Possidonos in Paleo Phaliron, where the meat is delicately flavoured with the spices of the Levant. Specialities are the *adana* kebab, *domatesli* kebab (cooked with tomatoes on charcoal) and the succulent shish-kebab, marinated in milk, lemon juice, oil and spices. Alternatively, in Nea Smyrni, the **Tria Asteria**, 7 Melitos and 77 Plastira, is run by Armenians from Istanbul. The choice of appetizers is endless, including delicious *cli kofte*, a meatball of veal and lamb, bulgur wheat and pine nuts. This is also the only place in Athens to find *tandir* kebab, lamb which has been smoked and then baked in a red wine sauce. At either of these restaurants, count on around 3000 dr.

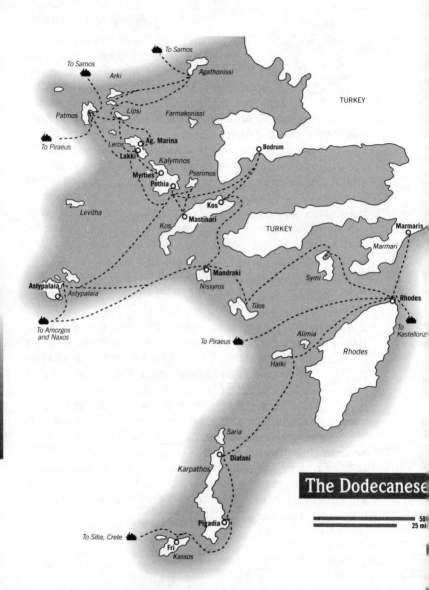

The Dodecanese

50
25 mi

The Dodecanese

Astypalaia

The westernmost island of the Dodecanese, located halfway between Amorgos and Kos, Astypalaia closely resembles the neighbouring Cyclades, particularly in its architecture and austere rocky geography. Unlike many of the Cyclades, however, Astypalaia has a rich fertile valley, Livadia, and equally fertile fishing in the sheltered bays of its wildly indented coastline—in antiquity the island was called *Ichthyoessa*, the fishy island. Besides the lure of seafood, Astypalaia's relative inaccessibility makes it a good place to escape the summer crowds, although there are times when you may find yourself wishing that the locals had more than a couple of streets on which to exercise their scooters in the evening. The women's traditional costumes are famous for their elaborate detail and beauty.

Astypalaia is becoming increasingly trendy as Athenians do up the old houses in the hilly Kastro and Chora. It has also become a package holiday destination for Laskarina Holidays. But as it's difficult to get to, it has kept its charm.

History

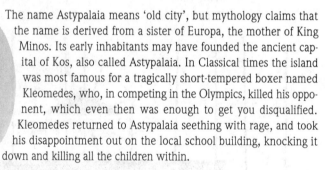

The name Astypalaia means 'old city', but mythology claims that the name is derived from a sister of Europa, the mother of King Minos. Its early inhabitants may have founded the ancient capital of Kos, also called Astypalaia. In Classical times the island was most famous for a tragically short-tempered boxer named Kleomedes, who, in competing in the Olympics, killed his opponent, which even then was enough to get you disqualified. Kleomedes returned to Astypalaia seething with rage, and took his disappointment out on the local school building, knocking it down and killing all the children within.

From 1207 to 1522, the Quirini family of Venice occupied the island, styling themselves the Counts of Astypalaia and building a castle in Chora. During the last Italian occupation of the Dodecanese another fortification called Kastellano was built in the east of the island, south of Vathi.

Astypalaia was the first of the Dodecanese to be annexed by the Italians in 1912.

Connections

Ferries run three times a week Kos, Kalymnos, Mykonos, Tinos and Piraeus; twice a week Rhodes and Syros; once a week in summer Santorini, Andros and Rafina.

A new airport with two flights per week is about to open.

Gournas Travel Agency ✆ (0242) 61334 can give you specific details.

Tourist Police

See regular police, Chora, ✆ (0242) 61 207.

Around Astypalaia

The capital and main port of the island, **Astypalaia** (or Skala) is picturesquely piled beneath the glowering Venetian castle and ruined windmills down to a sandy stretch of beach. Up the narrow stepped streets, lined with pretty, cubist white houses (many fitted with Turkish-style balconies) is **Chora**, the medieval and Venetian capital; the gate of the **fortress** still bears the Quirini coat-of-arms, a display of pride that would have been much-frowned-on back in Venice itself. Within the citadel walls, you can roam through the ruins of stone houses on tiny streets, and two churches, **St George** and the **Madonna of the Castle**, one of the most beautiful in the Dodecanese, topped with a white-tiled dome and decorated inside with intricate lace-like designs. All is being slowly restored.

Green, and comparatively lush **Livadia**, with Astypalaia's best beach, is a little to the west, while a bit further south is an unofficial nudist beach. Other possible excursions from Astypalaia Skala include a walk to the monastery, **Ag. Libies**, or a taxi trip to the more remote village of **Maltezanas** (once a lair of Maltese pirates); or **Vathi**, near Mussolini's **Kastellana** and the stalagmite caves of **Drakou** and **Negri**. It is possible to visit them on foot or by boat, but take a torch with you.

Festivals

21 May, Ag. Konstantinos; 15 August, Panayia.

✆ *(0242–)*

Where to Stay

moderate–cheap

Astypalaia is blessed with several hotels, plus a number of rooms in private houses, all in Skala (also known as Periyialos). The **Hotel Australia** (B), ✆ 61275, is basic and friendly with a restaurant beneath and a flower-filled breakfast terrace; **Hotel Vangelis** © 61281, overlooks the harbour; The **Astynea,** © 61209, is handy for ferries; new **Hotel Carlos** (C) has sea-view rooms; **Vivamare Hotel and Apartments**, © 61328, is smartly done out, inland from the harbour; **Hotel Gallia**, © 61245, is above the bakery, over the road from The Egeon (or Aigaion). Rooms are also availalble in the upper town. Contact the tourist office on © 61217.

Eating Out

Most of the island's eateries are clustered around the wharf and serve local fare at reasonable prices. Good tavernas include **I Moxania**, **Kali Kardia**, and **Astynea** on the wharf, as well as local haunts **Babis** and **To Akroyiali**. Food seems to taste better, however, in the tavernas at Livadia, although the menu is the same; try **Kalamia**. At Maltezanas try **Obelix**, and at **Vathi** the anonymous fish restaurant is excellent.

Halki

Little Halki, basically a big arid rock with its small port overlooked by half-derelict neo-Classical houses—mansions, by Greek island standards—reminds many people of a miniature Symi. Despite its proximity to Rhodes, it is a wonderfully quiet place, with only a few hundred inhabitants and few vehicles; many of those visitors it does get come back year after year. Its name (also spelled Chalki, among other variations) comes from the Greek word for copper which was mined here long ago.

Although puny, Halki is celebrated for its love songs and was designated the 'island of peace and friendship' under a UNESCO scheme which lasted from 1983 to 1988. This was ostensibly to host an annual international youth conference, but in reality this was a project to do up the houses and give work to the locals, a joint project with the mayorality of Rhodes. A Xenia Hotel was built to serve visiting youth groups and bureaucrats under the UNESCO scheme, but in the end the islanders protested because they thought it was a rip-off and an excuse for visitors to abuse the residents' hospitality; one example of this was the (supposedly impoverished) youths using their subsidized meal vouchers from the scheme to order lobsters and other expensive items in the tavernas. This led to a protest with placards, and the end of peace and friendship between UNESCO and Halki.

The building restoration work (conversion to guest houses) has since been taken over by package holiday company Laskarina Holidays, and tourism has taken off in a small way. More and more owners have returned and fixed up houses and rooms, and in 1994 Halki features in several holiday brochures. There are now cars, pick-ups and trucks, mainly for the fishermen and farmers to transport their goods to Rhodes. The only road, Boulevard Tarpon Springs, leads nowhere really, just to the deserted Chorio. A track has been blasted through to the monastery of Agios Ioannis.

Connections

Three times a week with Rhodes, once a week with Karpathos, Kassos, Sitia (Crete), Ag. Nikolaos (Crete), Symi, Santorini, Sikinos, Folegandros, Milos, Sifnos, Piraeus; caique (daily in high season, twice a week at other times) from Kamiros Skala, Rhodes. In summer hydrofoil connection with Rhodes and Tilos.

Emborio and Around

The main claim to fame of **Emborio**, the one town, is that its Ag. Nikolaos has the tallest campanile in the Dodecanese. Other than that, it's an infectiously charming hamlet.

From Emborio a 15-minute walk along 'Boulevard Tarpon Springs' (just wide enough for a single delivery van) will take you to the small sandy beach; the boulevard was paid for by Halkiot immigrants in Florida. Visitors determined to 'see' something else should continue walking along the boulevard's extension another hour for **Chorio**, the ghost-town capital of Halki. Here the Knights of St John built a castle on the earlier acropolis and re-used most of the ancient building stone. Chorio's church has a few Byzantine frescoes and there are good views over rock and sea.

Halki has a few caiques to hire for visiting its quiet swimming coves—Areta, Kania, Yali and Trachia are among the best. The most scenic excursion, however, is to the green isle of **Alimnia**, which has a deep harbour where Italian submarines hid during the war. Now it is a beautifully tranquil place in which to laze about, swim and picnic.

29 August, Ag. Ioannis; 5 August, Ag. Sotiris; 15 August, Panayia; 29 August, Ag. Ioannis Prodomos, John the Baptist; 14 September, Ag. Stavros.

©️ (0286)

Where to Stay
moderate—cheap

Most accommodation is now taken up by the holiday companies. There's the small but very lovely **Captain's House** pension, ©️ 57 201, a turn-of-the-century Halki mansion with three lovely rooms, run with nautical precision by Alex Sakellarides (ex-Greek Royal Navy) and his English wife Christine. It's located near the church. Pay around 5000 dr. for a double room with shared bathroom. Other options are **Hotel Xenontas**, the scheme hotel, to the left of the harbour; **Pension Kleanthe**, ©️ 37648, newly opened near the school on the way to Pondomas beach; **Pension Argyrenia**, self-contained chalet-type rooms past lovely gardens on the way to the beach; and on the beach, **Nick's Pondomas Beach Taverna and Rooms**.

Eating Out

You can get excellent lunches overlooking the sea at **Pondomas Taverna**; at night, **Omonia** is good for fish and grills; **Ouzerie Maria** and Yianni's are fine for real Greek oven dishes; **Taverna Bokolia** is okay, but **O Houvardas**, once arguably one of the best tavernas in the Dodecanese, has never quite been the same under the new management. It's still a good eaterie, popular with yacht people, but the standard depends on who's in the kitchen this year.

Kalymnos

Breathe a sigh of relief when you get to Kalymnos—you're in the real Greece. Although the bustling waterfront has all the usual paraphernalia of tourism, the tavernas, cafés and souvenir shops, and screeching motorbikes everywhere, venture one street back and you'll find yourself in the midst of a fully functioning Greek village, going about its daily life, winter or summer, whether you are there or not. Because of the many Greek visitors, the prices are not sky high, and the food is good and wholesome. Just as it finds an attractive balance between tourism and carrying on its everyday business, Kalymnos also strikes a harmonious geographical equilibrium, with fertile valleys wedged into its dry, rocky face. Even the most fleeting visitor will notice that this island is preoccupied with sponges: Kalymnos has Greece's last active fleet of sponge divers.

History

The first Kalymniotes lived in a Neolithic settlement at Vothini and worshipped Zeus in a cave shrine which still exists. After the destruction of Crete, Argos sent colonists to the island, naming their capital after their mother city. Homer mentions ships from Kalymnos at Troy, and archaeologists have uncovered Homeric tombs on the island. An ally of Persia, the Queen of Halicarnassos, conquered the island at the beginning of the 5th century BC, but after Persia's defeat Kalymnos joined Athens' maritime league at Delos.

Kalymnos next enters history in the 11th century, when Seljik Turks launched a sudden attack on the island and killed almost everyone. The few survivors fled to fortified positions at Kastelli and the virtually impregnable Kastro, which by necessity became the capital of the island. The Vinioli of Genoa occupied Kalymnos, but later sold it to the Knights of St John, who strengthened the fortress of Kastro. In 1522 they abandoned it to succour Rhodes, leaving the Turks quickly to take their place. During the Italian occupation, Kalymnos rioted when the fascists tried to close the Greek schools, and the islanders painted everything in sight Greek blue and white as a sign of solidarity with the motherland.

A Note on Sponges

When fresh from the sea sponges are foul, smelly and black, and have to be stamped, squeezed and soaked until their skeletons (the part you use in the bathtub) are clean. Many sponges are then chemically treated to achieve the familiar yellow colour. Diving for these primitive plant-like porifers is a difficult and dangerous art. In ancient times the divers strapped heavy stones to their chests to bear them down to the sea bed, where they speared the sponges with tridents, then at a signal, were raised to the surface by a lifeline. As modern equipment has permitted divers to plunge to new depths, cases of the 'bends' were frequent; old-timers on Kalymnos remember when, not so long ago, it was common to see sponge divers crippled, paralysed, or made deaf. Nowadays divers wear oxygen tanks and attack the sponges with axes, going down to a depth of 90m. Politics limiting access to Mediterranean sponge beds and the invention of synthetic sponges have undermined Kalymnos' traditional livelihood; in the last century, many divers emmigrated to Florida to exploit the sponge beds off Tarpon Springs.

In the past Kalymnos' sponge fleet left home for seven months of the year to work off the coast of North Africa. Today it makes only one four-month trip a year, sticking mostly to Aegean and Cretan waters. On Kalymnos, the week before the fleet sets out (the week after Orthodox Easter) is sponge week, devoted to giving the sponge divers a rousing send-off, with plenty of food, free drinks, traditional costumes and dances—including the Sponge Dance, where the local schoolmaster mimes the part of the sponge fishermen while his pupils play the sponges. The last night of Sponge Week is tenderly known as *To Ipnos Tis Ayapis*, or the Feast of the Lovers. It ends with the pealing of church bells, calling the divers to their boats for another dangerous four months at sea.

Connections

Daily to Piraeus, Rhodes, Kos, Leros and Patmos; four times a week with Samos, three times a week with Lipsi and Astypalaia, twice a week with Nissyros, Tilos, Symi, and Agathonissi, once a week with Lesbos, Limnos, Ikaria, Mykonos, Santorini, Tinos, Andros, Rafina and Thessaloniki. Summer hydrofoil connection with Kos and Leros. Daily boats to Pserimos, daily caique from Myrties to Xirokambos, on Leros; special boat to connect passengers with Kos airport, arriving on that island at Mastihari.

Tourist Information

NTOG, April–Oct, next to Olympic Hotel, © (0243) 29 310.

Tourist police, *see* regular police on the waterfront, © (0243) 22 100.

Pothia

Pothia, the port, the capital, and one of the largest cities in the Dodecanese, encompasses the harbour and much of Kalymnos' largest valley. More spread out than the typical tightly knotted island town, Pothia has many lovely old mansions along its back streets, walled orchards, and some fine views from the town's upper level. Local sculptors Michail Kokkinos and his daughter Irene have

Kalymnos

5km
3 miles

N

To Leros

Emporios
Skalia
Kalavros Islet
Arginonta
Telendos Islet
Telendos
Stimenia
Kyra Psilas Monastery
Massouri
Myrties
Profitis Ilias (701m / 2300ft)
Dasos
Platanos
Vathi
Platis Yialos
Kamari
Panormos
Cave of Daskaleio
Linaria
Kyriaki Islet
Pigadia
Kantouni
Chorio
KALYMNOS (POTHIA)
Ag. Nikolaos
Argos
Vothini
Kephalas Cave
Thermapiges
Vlyhadia
To Kos and Pserimos
To Astypalaia and Piraeus
Nera Islet
To Leros

adorned Pothia with statues: *Poseidon* by the Olympic Hotel and, near the waterfront, a monument to Liberty with the history of sponge diving in relief. The police occupy one of Kalymnos' most fanciful confections, pink Italianate villa on the sea. On the far side of it is the sponge diving school.

The **archaeological museum**, in an old mansion, contains a typical miscellany of local antiquities and more recent items, including a barrel organ. Pothia also has one of Greece's rarer institutions—an orphanage, and until recently many Orthodox priests came here to choose a dowryless bride before they were ordained. There is a small beach near the yacht club, and beyond that a radioactive spring at **Thermapiges**, reputed to cure rheumatism, arthritis and digestive and kidney disorders. At night Pothia's hilltop landmark is a huge illuminated cement cross.

From Pothia caiques sail to **Nera** islet, south of Kalymnos, with a monastery and a small taverna, or to **Kephalas Cave**, a half-hour trip and a walk of a couple of kilometres. Discovered in 1961, the cave was found to have been a sanctuary of Zeus; it is full of multicoloured stalactites and stalagmites. Another cave never thoroughly explored is the **Cave of the Nymphs** or the **Cave of the Seven Virgins**, after the seven maidens who hid themselves there during a pirate raid and were never seen again. Traces of ancient nymph worship may be seen if you bring a torch. The cave's entrance is at Flakas, by the hospital.

Myli and Chorio

Inland, just behind Pothia, is a suburb called **Myli**, for its three monumental derelict windmills looming over the road. On a hill to the left stands the ruined **Castle of the Knights**, also known as the Chryssocheria (Golden-handed) after the church of the Virgin built within its walls, over an ancient temple of the Dioscuri. A treasure was once supposedly discovered there, and the area has been thoroughly combed on the off-chance of more.

Myli blends imperceptibly into the pretty white town of **Chorio**, the old capital of Kalymnos. It grew up around **Pera Kastro**, the striking though dilapidated citadel that rises over the village and served as a place of refuge during the perilous Middle Ages. The ruined village within the Kastro's walls was inhabited from the 11th to the 18th centuries, and on a gloomy day looks more Transylvanian than Greek. The only undilapidated buildings are nine chapels kept freshly whitewashed by the faithful in Chorio. In Pigadia, just beyond Chorio, only the apse survives of the church of **Christ of Jerusalem**, built by the Byzantine Emperor Arkadios in gratitude for his shelter at Kalymnos during a terrible storm. It replaced a temple of Apollo, and made use of its stone as well; nearby are many rock-cut Mycenaean tombs. A road branching to the west at Chorio leads to **Argos**, named by the settlers from Argos on the mainland of Greece. Although some ruins have been found there, scholars doubt whether the ancient city stood at precisely the same spot as the present village.

North Kalymnos: Beaches, Monasteries and Telendos

North of Chorio the road passes Kalymnos' best beaches, most offering shade if you don't want to bake and sizzle: **Kantouni, Panormos** (known locally as **Elies** because it sits in the olive groves), **Myrties** and **Massouri** (bus every half-hour from Pothia). Although as beaches go they're only just adequate, the deep blue coves offer excellent swimming. These villages are the centre of Kalymnos' tourist industry. Kantouni and Plati Yialos are a bit quieter, but Panormos, Myrties and Massouri have become a bit of a Golden Mile. Myrties runs into Massouri and tourism along the coastal road has unfortunately gone the way of Kos, with neon-sign bars belting out conflicting music. Some tavernas go for the glitzy fast-food photo menus outside. It's all very touristy, with jewellery shops and 'English breakfasts' by the dozen.

From Myrties frequent caiques make the short trip to the islet of **Telendos**, which broke off from Kalymnos in a 6th century AD earthquake. On Telendos, facing the strait are the derelict monastery of **Ag. Vassilos** and a fort, both from the Middle Ages. There are ruins of **Roman houses** on Telendos and up to a mile offshore, and two small beaches. Most of the islanders are fishermen, who have ringside seats for the best sunsets on Kalymnos. See if in the profile of Telendos' mountain you can trace the form of the sleeping or **marble princess**, and the marble prince who faces her on the Kalymnos side of the strait. There are a couple of tavernas on Telendos, and a few rooms for rent.

North of Massouri, **Kastelli** was the refuge of survivors of the terrible 11th century Turkish massacre, and overlooks the sea in a wild region of rocky cave mouths full of fangs. The church **Panayia** is below. **Arginonta**, the next village, lends its name to the entire northern peninsula, a perfect place for strenuous, isolated treks in the quiet hills; **Emborio**, the northernmost village (bus twice a day from Pothia, caiques from Myrties), is within walking distance of some exceptional countryside, and has **Cyclopean walls** and a tower close by. The tower is believed to have been a Neolithic temple; a sacrificial altar was found in the vicinity. Arginonta and Emborio both have quiet beaches; Arginonta has a small taverna, and while Emborio is also very pretty, it does have daily boat trips and is on the island coach tour.

Vathi

The narrow volcanic valley of Vathi ('the deep') is the beauty spot of Kalymnos: it has three charming, lush villages, Rhina, Platanos and Metoki, superbly situated at the mouth of a magnificent fjord. Fragrant groves of mandarins and lemons provide the valley's income, and houses and white-walled roads fill in the gaps between the trees. The middle village, **Platanos** is named for its enormous plane tree and has Cyclopean walls; Rhina has a mysterious 'throne' carved in the rock. North of Vathi you can walk to the Monastery of **Kyra Psilas**, the Tall Lady. Near Vathi, but accessible only by sea, near the mouth of the fjord, is the **Cave of**

Daskaleio, the largest of Kalymnos' grottoes; a trove of Neolithic to Bronze Age items was found in its inner stalactite chamber.

Festivals

15 August, Panayia; 14 September, Stavros on Nera islet; 27 July, Ag. Panteleimonos at Brosta; a week after Easter, the Iprogros (sponge week). Other celebrations are held when the divers return, although each boat arrives at a different time and celebrations are not as general as at the Iprogros.

© (0243–)   ### Where to Stay

moderate

In Pothia, a few strides from the ferry will bring you to the fancy **Olympic Hotel**, © 28 801, with good rates for its C class rooms. The **Thermae Hotel**, © 29 425, is in a pleasant location right on the waterfront, above a restaurant, if you want to be in the thick of it; recently it's become very noisy, and isn't as clean as it used to be. The **Panorama**, © 23 138, provides furnished apartments with a good view of the town and harbour. **Greek House**, © 23 752, near the sponge factory, is pleasant and friendly; **Pension Katerina**, © 22 186, has self-catering facilities; **Patmos Pension**, © 22 750, is okay. In Massouri **Studios Tatsis**, © 47887 is stylish with great views over Telendos; for a peaceful place to stay, try **Galini Studios** or **Hotel Filoxenia**.

In Emborio **Harry's Pension**, **Taverna Paradise** © 47 483, and **Pension Themis**, © 47 277, are good; in Vathi, **Hotel Galini**, © 31 241, is a restful setting for overlooking the fjord-like harbour.

On the island of Telendos for real peace and quiet try **Pension Rita**, © 47 914, over the friendly cafeteria; **Pension Uncle George's**, © 47 502, over the excellent restaurant; and **Dimitrios Harinos** with rooms in a pretty garden, © 47916.

cheap

One of the best in this range, with a certain dilapidated charm, is the **Alma** at 8 Patr. Maximou, © 28 969. Alternatively, try the comfortable, convenient pension by the taxi station, **Aris**. There are also private rooms in Kalymnos town and out at the other popular beaches, although you may have to pound the pavements or mule tracks to find them; best to set forth with a list from the tourist office.

In Pothia most of the restaurants are on the far end of the quay, beyond the Italian villa of the tourist police; the high percentage of Greek clientele ensures that you can't go far wrong. **Uncle Petros** is perhaps the best known. Round by the churches **Vouvaly Fish Restaurant** occupies the original sponge factory and is done out with shells, nets, ship carvings and nautical bric-à-brac; more importantly, it has seawater tanks where you can choose your own lobster or fish—otherwise try their excellent fish casseroles and octopus *keftedes*. On summer nights, there's often Greek music and dancing (3000 dr.). Not far away in the backstreets, search out the friendly, family-run **Xefteris**, near the Metropolis church, where you can sit out in a garden and the fresh fish and roast lamb won't send you running to the bank; try their island versions of *dolmades* and *stifado*. Also in an alley near the church **The Terrace** is family-run and full of locals. On the other side of the harbour, the little **Flaskos** taverna serves delectable roast chicken flavoured with mountain herbs and excellent salads. Order carefully and you'll get change from your 1500 dr. In the village of Argos, you'll find authentic Kalymniot food at the **Argos** taverna; try the *moori*, lamb cooked overnight in a ceramic pot (2000 dr.). In Massouri, enjoy excellent *meze* in the **Mathaios**, and in Kantouni **Ursula's** serves German food (2000 dr.). In Myrties, **Nectar** has a wide menu that makes a change from Greek; in Massouri **To Iliovasilima** (the sunset) is excellent and owned by the butcher; **Matheos** is good value, and on Telendos **Uncle George's** takes some beating.

Karpathos

Nearly halfway in between Crete and Rhodes, Karpathos has for decades been an island-hopper's best kept secret: hard to reach, but well worth the long hours of travelling. For one thing, Karpathos is two islands for the price of one: long and thin, austere and ruggedly mountainous in the north and fertile, prosperous, beach-fringed and 'European' in the south, separated by the two peaks rising over 3000 ft. These two distinct geographical personalities extend to the population; it has even been suggested that the northerners and southerners originally belonged to different races and for long generations had little if any contact with one another. The 'road' connecting the two halves was finished in 1979 and is best-suited to four-wheel drives, though taxis do ply it.

The long isolation of the north has made it a goldmine for students of customs lost a century ago in the rest of Greece. In Olympos, the chief village, women still bake their bread in outdoor ovens; the men, even the young ones, play the traditional three-stringed *lyra*, the goatskin bagpipe *tsabouna*, and the *laouto*. Most striking of all, the women wear their traditional costumes every day—costumes considered the most beautiful in Greece, and the chosen dress of Queen Frederika at the ceremony of 1948 that formally joined the Dodecanese to Greece. So far Olympos has not lost its unique charm, even though Karpathos now boasts a large international airport, bringing in more tourists every year; there are direct flights from the UK. However, Karpathos is by no means overrun, and the north especially has many places offering refuge from the crowds.

History

One of the many ancient names of Karpathos was Porfiris, or 'Red', after a red dye once manufactured on the island and used for the clothes of kings. It was also known as Tetrapolis, describing its four ancient cities of Vrykous, Possidion, Arkessia and Nissyros. Homer referred to the island as Krapathos, although another story claims its name comes from the dark days of piracy, when sheltered Vrontis Bay hid pirate ships that darted out to plunder any passing vessel. Disgruntled captains dubbed the island Arpaktos, or 'robbery', and the name was eventually corrupted to Karpathos. The Venetians knew it as Scarpanto, a name you may occasionally see on maps.

Of the four ancient cities of Karpathos, Nissyros, on the northern islet of Saria, is believed to have been colonized by the island of Nissyros, to exploit the iron and silver mines at Assimovorni. Off the coasts, the prized *scarus* (or parrot fish, which as Aristotle noted, ruminates its food) was so abundant that the Roman Emperors hired special fishing fleets to bring them back for the imperial table. Any signs of prosperity, however, had long ended by the time the pirates made the island their headquarters and one of its towns, Arkessia, their chief slave market. Things were so rough that even the Turks didn't really want Karpathos, and sent only a *cadi*, or judge, to the island a few times a year; he never stayed longer than a few days, and depended entirely on the Greeks to protect him. To this day the bays at Vrontis and Arkessia are said to hold a fortune in sunken pirate treasure.

Connections

By air: daily with Rhodes, several times a week with Kassos and Sitia (Crete); also charters from the UK.

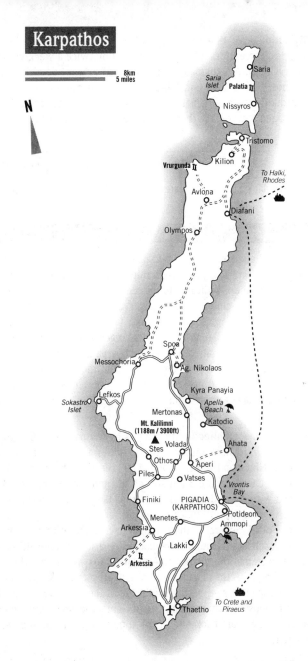

Karpathos

8km
5 miles

N

Saria

Saria Islet

Palatia **II**

Nissyros

Tristomo

Vrurgunda **II**

Kilion

To Halki, Rhodes

Avlona

Diafani

Olympos

Spoa

Messochoria

Ag. Nikolaos

Kyra Panayia

Sokastro Islet

Lefkos

Apella Beach

Mertonas

Katodio

Mt. Kalilimni (1188m / 3900ft)

Ahata

Stes

Volada

Othos

Aperi

Piles

Vatses

Vrontis Bay

PIGADIA (KARPATHOS)

Finiki

Potideon

Menetes

Ammopi

Arkessia

Lakki

II Arkessia

Thaetho

To Crete and Piraeus

By' ship: three times a week with Piraeus, four times a week with Rhodes, three times a week with Santorini, twice a week with Kassos, Sitia (Crete), Ag. Nikolaos (Crete) and Milos, once a week with Paros, Sikinos, Folegandros and Sifnos. Some ships call at both Diafani and Pigadia (Karpathos). Small boats daily in the summer connect the two ports, and at weekends there's a caique from Pigadia to Kassos.

Tourist Police

See regular police on the waterfront, Pigadia, © (0245) 22 218.

Karpathos Town

The island capital and southern port, Karpathos (or Pigadia) is attractively sheltered in that old pirate cove, mountain-ringed Vrontis Bay; Karpathos was the ancient city of Possidion, dedicated to the sea god. Abandoned in the Byzantine era, all that's left are a clutch of Mycenaean tombs and a few stones of the old acropolis on the rocky outcrop to the east. The modern town is just that— modern, with many new buildings, and it's no accident that the local National Bank branch has such an air of prosperity: Karpathos has the distinction of receiving more money from its emigrants abroad (mostly in Baltimore, Maryland) than any other island in Greece. There is now lots of new building in Pigadia, and a package tourist industry developing along the waterfront (loud bars and the like).

The most distinctive architecture in town is by the park and playground: an Italian-built administration building that doubles as a small **museum** containing an early Christian baptismal font, coins, ceramics and inscriptions. From here it is a short walk to the 3-km stretch of sand around Vrontis Bay. The beach is lined with trees, dotted with pleasant tavernas specializing in grilled fish, and on the beach, within an enclosure, are the ruins of a 5th-century basilica, **Ag. Fotini**. Several of the columns have been raised in their original places. The beach area around here has quite a lot of hotel development. Across the bay stands the chapel of **Ag. Nikolaos**, the saint who replaced Poseidon as the protector of sailors; a cave nearby called Kamara has sweet water. Another ancient site, on the south side of the Vrontis bay, **Ag. Kiriaki** (the track is signposted from the road) was a Geometric-era sanctuary dedicated to Demeter; a few years back one of the tombs hewn in the rock yielded a golden statuette.

If you're using public transport, check schedules before setting out; buses are fairly infrequent, and there are villages served only once a day, or even only once or twice a week. South from Karpathos town vegetation is sparse, and the few trees are bent over from the wind. The road passes **Ammopi**, a sandy beach and small resort en route to the airport. This latter occupies the site of the ancient city of Thaetho, although little now remains.

The road west of Karpathos town passes below the picturesque old mountain village of **Menetes**, with a small ethnographic museum. Towards the west coast, **Arkassa** is prettily immersed in orchards. A track leads up to the ruins of its predecessor, ancient **Arkessia** where a Mycenaean acropolis with Cyclopean walls stands on a rocky headland known as Paleokastro. The surrounding cliffs are riddled with caves that have offered shelter to shepherds for centuries. Here you'll find the ruins of an early Byzantine church, **Ag. Sophia,** with brightly coloured floor mosaics just under the fine layer of weeds and dirt; the best sections of these have been moved to the museum at Rhodes. Another ruined basilica, around the chapel **Ag. Anastasia**, dates from the 5th century. The coast below is jagged and wild, but there is a small beach wedged between the cliffs. Further north, **Finiki** is a bijou little fishing harbour with a good, inexpensive restaurant; the sponge divers of Kalymnos call here, and caiques de part for Kassos, if the sea isn't too rough—as is often the case. From Finiki the road approaches the slopes of Karpathos' tallest mountain, Kalilimni, the highest point in the Dodecanese at 1188m, where there's a pretty village, whose name in Roman letters reads **Piles**. From here a rough road continues up the west coast to remote **Lefkos**, with a white sandy beach, a wealth of pine trees and scattering of antiquities, including a large stone that strikingly resembles a Celtic menhir. Lefkos is now being developed, but so far nothing too drastic. A short walk away are the ruins of a small medieval fort; there was another on the offshore islet of **Sokastro**. There are a few small hotels and rooms to rent in Lefkos, which the Karpathiots themselves consider the most beautiful spot on their island.

In the centre of the south, **Othos** is another lovely spot, the highest village of Karpathos, and one of the oldest, its houses decorated with carved wooden balconies. Although you may need a pullover, even in summer, it produces a fine local sweet red wine, *othitiko krasi* and, they say, the island's prettiest girls. A traditional house here has been opened as a small ethnographic museum. Neighbouring **Volada** is a delightful whitewashed village with pretty lanes and well-kept houses, and a ruined castle built by the Cornaros of Venice, who owned the island until 1538.

Circling back towards Karpathos town, **Aperi** with exquisitely tended gardens and houses was the capital of Karpathos up to 1896. It is reputed to be the richest village in Greece per capita; nearly everyone here has lived in New Jersey. One *kafeneíon* still proudly displays a picture of Roosevelt; another, the Eleftheria Café run by a PASOK leprechaun, is full of curios and rubber items from the 1960s. In the new cathedral you can pay your respects to Karpathos' most venerated icon, credited with several miracles, among them that of saving the life of a young boy who was pushed off a cliff. He went on to become a rich American lawyer and contributed the funds for many of the island's new buildings. A track leads down to **Ahata**, a quiet pebbly beach, but it is very steep.

Other beaches along the east coast are easiest reached by caique from Karpathos town, especially **Apella**, the most beautiful, with fine sand, turquoise water and dramatic scenery, and **Kyra Panayia**, a lovely wide beach, varying from fine white sand to large pebbles. An alternative way of getting to Kyra Panayia: a 45-minute walk down through the lush greenery and trees from the mountain village of **Mertonas**. Mertonas is the place to be on 22 August, when it hosts the best *paniyiri* on the Karpathiot calendar with music and folkdancing that goes on well into the following day, and free food to boot. **Messochorio** in the mountains is another pretty village. From here or Spoa the sturdy of foot can begin the long trek to Olympos, or take the somewhat perilous road by taxi-jeep, a long (and rather expensive) proposition. Unfortunately, a massive forest fire in 1983 has left most of the island between Spoa and Diafani denuded and melancholy.

Olympos

The easiest and least expensive way to reach Olympos from Karpathos is by caique to **Diafani**, the village's port, from where a minibus makes the connection to Olympos. The harbour here is being enlarged to enable big ferries to dock, so there's currently a lot of concrete about and a plan to build a big hotel. Diafani has also been discovered by the Italians since the demise of Yugoslavia and Dubrovnik as holiday destinations, so prices have risen; in August it can be more like the back streets of Naples than Greece. There's a beach with flat rocks nearby, and several others within walking distance.

Olympos, one of the most striking villages on the Greek islands, is draped over a stark mountain ridge, with a long line of ruined windmills running like vertebrae down its spine. To the west are magnificent views of mountains plunging head-long into the sea. Decorative painted balconies, many incorporating two-headed Byzantine eagles (one head Rome, one Constantinople), adorn the houses which in many places are literally stacked one on another and opened with wooden locks and keys that Homer himself might have recognized. The village church has smoke-darkened frescoes, perhaps going back to the 18th-century, and an awe-inspiring, sombre ambience, that even the garrulous Greeks speak of in hushed tones.

The origins of Olympos are shrouded in mystery. Some evidence suggests that the original inhabitants of northern Karpathos came from Phrygia in Asia Minor; certainly the village was isolated for so long that linguists were amazed to find people here using ancient Dorian expressions long forgotten elsewhere in the country. Some matrilinear customs have survived, a family's property going to the eldest daughter, the *kanakara*; if you're lucky enough to be in Olympos during a *paniyiri* or wedding, you can recognize a *kanakara* by the weight of gold coins she wears on chains, coins that her forefathers will have earned while working abroad. The women wear their flowing costumes every day, including fine goatskin boots (it is said that snakes hate the smell of goat). The boots, which last for years, are handmade in the village and are perhaps the one souvenir you can buy at Olympos.

Olympos is now firmly on the tourist coach trail, with regular busloads. The best time to visit Olympos is during the weekends, when the women bake bread and vegetable pies in their outdoor ovens, the miller grinds the wheat in the last working windmill, out of 40 that turned a generation ago, and when the two *kafeneíons* are filled with Karpathos' music, uncannily similar to Irish music in one of its wilder moods. But you're not quite as far away as you think; in the *kafeneíon* across from the church the owner displays a certificate from the Governor of Alabama, thanking him for his service in the state militia. Otherwise, there is little to do but stroll the streets and absorb what you can of a vanishing way of life.

From Olympos you can drive most of the way to **Avlona**, a village inhabited only during the harvest season by farmers from Olympos, who work the surrounding valley; some of the tools they use are more commonly seen in museums. From Avlona it is a rough walk down to **Vourgounda** (Vrykus), the ancient Phrygian city, remembered today by a stair, a breakwater, burial chambers and walls. In a cavern in Vourgounda the chapel of **Ag. Ioannis** hosts the largest *paniyiria* in north Karpathos, a two-day event where everyone sleeps out, roasts meat over an open fire and dances to the haunting music.

On Sundays boats from Diafani sail to the islet of **Saria**, which dots the 'i' of long, narrow Karpathos. Here was the ancient kingdom of Nissyros, of which little remains. A chapel now stands on the site of the proto-Christian basilica. More interesting to see are *Ta Palatia* (the palaces), actually a post-Byzantine pirate base, the houses built in the dolmus style, with barrel-vaulted roofs. It is a good walk up from the landing place, so wear sturdy shoes.

Festivals

25 March, Evangelismos at Pigadia; 1 July, Ag. Marinas, near Menetes; 15 August, at Aperi and Menetes; 27–29 August, Ag. Ioannis at Vourgounda; 22–23 August, Kyra Panayia and Mertonas; 6 September, Larniotisa at Pigadia; 8 September, Playias at Messochorio.

© (0245–)

Where to Stay

expensive

The A class **Possirama Bay** at Pigadia is 400m from the town centre, on the sandy beach of Affoti, offering hotel apartments for 2–4 people, with fully equipped kitchen facilities, and large balconies overlooking the sea, © 22 916. In the same area **Miramare Bay Hotel** is another new operation, with swimming pool, sea views and good breakfast included, © 22 802.

moderate

If you've the money the most charming place to stay in the capital is the **Pension Romantica**, © 22 460/1. Located in a grove of citrus trees, and a short walk from the beach, it has 32 rooms and serves a delicious breakfast. Equally pleasant is the modern **Blue Bay Hotel** near the beach at Affoti Pigadia, 1½km from the town, © 22 479. B class **Hotel Apollo** is family owned and comfortable; **Artemis Pension** © 22 724 has self-catering facilities. A good bargain in this category is the D class **Karpathos Hotel** in Pigadia; most of its 16 rooms come with private shower and balcony, © 22 347.

cheap

On the cheap side, in Pigadia, there are quite a few small pensions and rooms for rent. Good value are **Harry's Rooms**, © 22188; **Hotel Annessis**, the oldest in Pigadia, © 22100; and **Hotel Avra**, © 22388. In Diafani, Chryssi Akti, known as **Golden Beach**, has 11 rooms near where the ferry boat lands and is clean and comfortable, © 51 215. Other places include **Diafani Palace**, © 51250, and **Mayflower Hotel**,

© 51228. In Olympos the **Pension Olympos** is highly recommended with great views, © 51252; there's also the **Poseidon Pension**, © 51264.

Eating Out

Karpathos was once a cheap place to eat out, but the recent influx of Italian and German tourists has pushed the prices up. In Pigadia, on the front, is **To Kyma**, which is okay but given over to tourist fare; **Kafeneion Halikas** is still authentic and **Mike's Taverna**, formerly the Restaurant Pizza, is good value. **Le Mirage** is the bar for Greek music. In Diafani **Golden Beach Restaurant** is the main haunt, with **Diafani Palace** the place for fish. In Ammopi, try the **Golden Beach Taverna**.

Kassos

The southernmost Dodecanese island and one of the most remote of all islands, Kassos is a barren rock with steep coasts and sea grottoes, with an odd beach or two wedged in between. The port, Emborio, is small, and if the sea is rough, as it often is, simply landing can be a big headache.

History

Homer mentions Kassos in the *Iliad*, for the ships it sent to Troy to aid the Achaeans. The ancient city stood at the site of the present village of Poli, and at Hellenokamera cave there are Mycenaean walls. During the Turkish occupation, Kassos retained a good deal of its autonomy, especially with regard to its ships, which it quickly put at the disposal of the Greek cause when the War of Independence was declared, in 1821. For the first three years of the war the Greeks generally came out ahead in the struggle, but the Sultan, angered by his setbacks, prepared powerful counter-attacks through Ibrahim Pasha, son of the Ottoman Empire's governor of Egypt. In June 1824 Ibrahim left Egypt with a massive fleet to crush the Greek rebellion. His first stop was Kassos, which he decimated, slaying the men and taking the women and children as slaves. The few who managed to escape went either to Syros or Grambousa, an islet off the northwestern coast of Crete, where they turned to piracy for survival, defiantly flying the Greek flag in

Turkish waters. But Capodistria and his allies put a stop to their activities, and their refuge, Grambousa, was returned to Turkish rule. Thousands of Kassiotes later emigrated to Egypt to work on the Suez Canal.

Connections

By air: daily with Rhodes, two–three times a week with Sitia and Karpathos.

By sea: twice a week with Piraeus, Crete, Milos, Rhodes and Karpathos, once a week with Halki, Symi, Santorini, Sikinos, Folegandros and Sifnos; weekend caique from Finiki, Karpathos.

Around Kassos

Small **Fri** is the capital of the little island, where the main occupation, fishing, is much in evidence. Every year on 7 June a ceremony is held there in memory of the massacre of 1824, and many people from Karpathos also attend, coming on the special boats.

There are hardly any trees on Kassos because, it is claimed, Ibrahim Pasha burnt them all down, but many lighthouses stick out above the rocky terrain. A road and the island's one bus link Fri with Kassos' four other dinky villages. There is a lovely cave with stalactites called Hellenokamara near the beach at **Ammoua**. **Poli** is built on the island's ancient acropolis, and you can still see a few surviving walls at Kastro. Beyond the villages a path leads across the island to **Khelathros Harbour**, with the best beach on the island. Another nice beach is on **Armathia**, the only inhabited islet off Kassos; there are frequent excursions from the port.

Festivals

14 August, at Ag. Marina; 23 April, Ag. Georgios; 7 July, at Fri; late July, Ag. Spyridon.

© (0245–)

Where to Stay

moderate–cheap

The place to stay is the **Hotel Anagennissis**, © 41 323, comfortable and run by an engaging former American. You'll pay more for the rooms facing the sea with bath, less for those in the back. There are also several pensions and rooms, and another small hotel, the class C **Hotel Anessis**,

✆ 41 201, where the doubles tend to be a little less. All of the above are in Fri.

Eating Out

There are a handful of tavernas in Fri; **Restaurant Kassos** and **Taverna Emborio** serve good, cheap island dishes. There are also a couple of tavernas in Ag. Marina and Emborio.

Kastellorizo (Megisti)

The easternmost point of Greece, oddball Kastellorizo is six hours by ship from Rhodes and in spitting distance of Turkey. It is the smallest inhabited island of the Dodecanese, 3km by 6, yet the mother hen of its own small clutch of islets; hence its official name, Megisti, 'the largest'. The Turks know it as Meis Ada, 'eye-land', for one nautical mile away is their town of Kaş ('eyebrow'), while the most commonly heard name is Kastellorizo, in memory of the days when the Neapolitans called it the 'Red Castle'. Dry, depopulated, more than half ruined by numerous vicissitudes, its streets are patrolled by turkeys, and its inhabitants noticeably affected by the isolation. The new airport is slowly bringing the island in closer contact with Greece, and its success as a film set—for the recent Italian film *Mediterraneo*, about a group of Italian soldiers stationed there during the war—has given Kastellorizo a psychological boost. This also explains the swarms of Italian tourists; the *lingua tourista* is Italian, with local Greeks yelling 'stanza' (rooms) as tourists arrive. However, it remains a quirky backwater surrounded by a crystal sea brimming with marine life. And while there aren't any sandy strands, the local people will never fail to tell you that there are plenty of rocks to beach on.

History

According to tradition, Kastellorizo's first settler was King Meges of Echinada who gave his name to the island. Neolithic finds suggest an early arrival for Echinada, and Mycenaean graves coincide with the mention in Homer of the island's ships at Troy. Subsequently, the Dorians built two forts on the island, the Kastro by the present town and on the mountain, called Palaeokastro—the acropolis of the ancient capital, where Apollo and the Dioscuri were the chief gods. The little island had a great fleet of ships based in its sheltered harbour and traded with Lycia on the mainland, transporting its timber to ports in Africa and the Middle East. From 350 to 300 BC Kastellorizo was ruled by Rhodes, and in Roman times the pirates of Cassius used it as their hideout. The island was converted to Christianity from the time of St Paul, who preached along the south coast of Asia Minor at Myra.

During the Byzantine period Kastellorizo's fortifications were repaired, and this work was continued by the Knights of St John after the fall of Jerusalem. They named the island after the red rock of the castle which they used to imprison knights who misbehaved on Rhodes. The Sultan of Egypt captured Kastellorizo in 1440, but ten years later the King of Naples, Alfonso I of Aragon, took it back. Although Kastellorizo belonged to the Ottoman Empire by 1523, the Venetians later occupied it twice in their endless struggles against the Turks, in 1570 and in 1659. Despite all the see-sawing to and fro, Kastellorizo was doing all right for itself; at the beginning of the 19th century it had a population of 15,000, who lived either from the sea or their extensive holdings along the coast of Asia Minor. Things began to go wrong with the outbreak of the Greek War of Independence. The islanders were the first in the Dodecanese to join the cause, and taking matters into their own hands, seized the island's two fortresses from the Turks. The Great Powers forced them to give them back to the Turks in 1833. In 1913 Kastellorizo revolted again only to be put down this time by the Italians, who were trying to get their mitts on Syria. During the First World War the island was bombarded from the Turkish coast. In 1927 an earthquake caused extensive damage but the Italian fascists, then in charge, refused to do any repairs, as Kastellorizo had failed to cooperate with their programme of de-Hellenisation. There was another revolt in 1933, but it was crushed by soldiers from Rhodes. By now Kastellorizo was in sharp decline—in 1941 only 1500 inhabitants remained.

This, however, does not end the tale of misfortunes for the gutsy little island. During the Second World War the Allies shipped the entire population to refugee camps in the Middle East. Although this was done for their safety, the islanders were not allowed to take many of their precious belongings with them, and the occupying Allied troops pillaged the empty houses they left behind. To hide their crime, they burnt the town down, destroying more than 1500 homes. As if this was not enough, the ship carrying the refugees home after the war sank, drowning many. Those who survived to return to Kastellorizo discovered that, although they had finally achieved Greek citizenship they had lost everything else, and that there was nothing to do but emigrate.

Connections

By air: three times a week from Rhodes; **boat** twice a week from Rhodes.

See regular police in the harbour by the post office.

Kastellorizo Town

There is only one town on the island, also called **Kastellorizo,** full of ruined houses and mansions, some burnt, others crumbling from earthquakes or bombardments. One can see how wealthy some of the inhabitants once were from the remaining interiors, with elegant coffered ceilings and lovely carved balustrades. Some are being restored, others are inhabited by cats and chickens. Small tavernas line the waterfront, so close to the edge of the quay that a discreet kick is all it takes to rid yourself of an unwanted guest at your table. A hotel occupies one lip of the harbour mouth, while on the other sits the **fort** (*kastro*), last repaired by the eighth Grand Master of the Knights of St John, Juan Fernando Heredia, whose red coat-of-arms is another possible explanation for the name of the island. If you climb the ladder to the top, you'll have a fine view of the sea and Turkey. An inscription in Doric Greek discovered at the fort suggests the existence of an ancient castle on the same site. A tomb nearby yielded a golden crown, and in the mosque is a small **museum** (*5–7.30*) containing photographs of the days of past prosperity, a few frescoes, folk costumes and items found in the harbour.

Another path leads up to a **Lycian tomb** cut into the living rock and decorated with Doric columns. The whole southwest, or Lycian coast of modern Turkey, is dotted with similar tombs, but this is the only one in modern Greece. The **cathedral of Ag. Konstantinos and Helena** re-uses granite columns from a temple of Apollo in Anatolia. From the town a steep path with steps leads up to four white churches and **Palaeokastro,** the Doric fortress and acropolis. On the gate there is a Doric inscription from the 3rd century BC referring to Megiste; walls, a tower and cisterns also remain.

Kastellorizo's Grotto Azzurro

There are no beaches on Kastellorizo, but the sea is clean, and there are a multitude of tiny islets to swim out to. An excursion not be missed is to the **Blue Cave,** or Parastas, an hour by caique from the town. The effects are best in the morning when some light filters in, for the entrance is so low, you'll have to duck down in the boat to enter. As in the famous Blue Grotto of Capri, the reflections of the water inside bathe the cavern walls with an uncanny blue. There are many stalactites, and if you're very lucky, you may meet the monk seal who lives inside.

The fishing around Kastellorizo is excellent, and serves as the main occupation for the island's 200 souls. Almost everyone, however, is ready to leave, and the only reason they stay is to keep the island Greek. The Turks in Kaş deny it, but many Greeks will tell you that if the population of Kastellorizo drops below 200, it will revert to Turkey. Whatever the case, the Greek government pays people to stay there, has built a desalination plant, and has bent over backwards to bring Greek television, radio and an airport to the island.

Festivals

20 July, Profitis Ilias; 21 May, Ag. Konstantinos; 23 April, Ag. Georgios.

© (0241–)

Where to Stay

expensive

The island's most comfortable digs is the B class **Hotel Megisti**, overlooking the excellent natural harbour, © 29 072; but this will cost you 10000 dr. for a double. For something less expensive, just take up one of the offers you'll receive as you get off the boat. As like as not the room you get will be as quirky as its owner.

Eating Out

Nearly everything's by the harbour; the fish is inexpensive and fresh (and the only thing that doesn't have to be shipped in). Expect to pay around 2000 dr. for a full dinner. **Taverna Mikri Parisi** is the place for fish, **Taerna Lazarakis** is the place for yachtspeople, and **Taverna International** is good for breakfast.

Kos

Dolphin-shaped Kos with its natural beauty, wealth of fascinating antiquities, beaches and comfortable climate is Rhodes' major Dodecanese rival in the tourist industry, so much so that there's a decidedly un-Greek feeling to the place in high season. Nothing remains of the Greece of thirty years ago—the *kafeneío* and *ouzeri*, serving octopus sizzling from the grill, have been replaced with cafés, with brightly coloured plastic chairs, serving international snacks; garlanded donkeys no longer carry their patrons home from the fields, while swarms of rent-a-bikes drone around the island. English, German and Swedish are more commonly heard than Greek. Yet, for all this, the island still holds charm for many people, who find everything they need for a summer vacation. Even the architecture isn't particularly Greek: the Italian occupation provided some attractive buildings, and the pair of minarets rising from the Turkish-built mosques complete its aura of *cosmopolitana*.

History

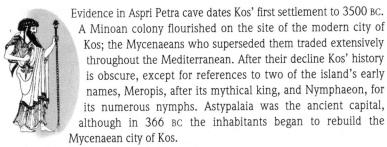

Evidence in Aspri Petra cave dates Kos' first settlement to 3500 BC. A Minoan colony flourished on the site of the modern city of Kos; the Mycenaeans who superseded them traded extensively throughout the Mediterranean. After their decline Kos' history is obscure, except for references to two of the island's early names, Meropis, after its mythical king, and Nymphaeon, for its numerous nymphs. Astypalaia was the ancient capital, although in 366 BC the inhabitants began to rebuild the Mycenaean city of Kos.

Poised between East and West (the ancient city of Halicarnassus, present-day Bodrum in Turkey, is very near), Kos flourished with the trade of precious goods—and revolutionary ideas. Halicarnassus was the birthplace of Herodotus, called the 'father of history' for his attempt to distinguish legend from fact, and in the 5th century BC Kos produced an innovator of its own, Hippocrates, the father of medicine. Hippocrates realized that diseases were not punishments sent from the gods, but had natural causes, and was the first to suggest that healers should discover as much as possible about each patient and their symptoms before making a diagnosis. His school on Kos, where he taught pupils a wholesome medicine based on waters, special diets, herbal remedies and relaxation was renowned throughout the ancient world, and he set a standard of medical ethics incorporated in the Hippocratic oath taken by doctors to this day. When Hippocrates died an Asklepieion (a temple to Asklepios, the god of healing) was founded, and people from all over the Mediterranean world came to be healed in its hospital-sanctuary. Besides physicians, Kos produced a school of Bucolic poetry, led by Theocritus (319–250 BC). The Hellenistic ruler of Egypt, Ptolemy II Philadelphos, was born here, and many of the Ptolemies were sent to Kos for their education. The Romans were later to prize Kos for its silk industry, the only one in the Mediterranean, producing a translucent cloth.

The island's wealth and strategic position excited the envy of others, and from the 6th century BC it was invaded by Persians, Romans and Saracens. The gods themselves, it seems, were jealous, and earthquakes in AD 142, 469, 554 and 1933 levelled most of the island's buildings. In 1315 the Knights of St John took control of Kos, and in 1391, began fortifications using material from the ancient city, incorporating even works of art from the Asklepieion as stone for their walls. In 1457 and 1477 the Turks besieged Kos without success, but they gained the fortress after the fall of Rhodes.

Connections

By air: charters direct from London and several other European cities, three times a day with Athens, three times a week with Rhodes.

By hydrofoil: daily with Rhodes and Samos, several times a week with Patmos and Leros. Also connections with Kalymnos, Nissyros, Tilos and Symi.

By boat: in season, daily boat to Bodrum, Turkey. Ferry every day to Piraeus, Rhodes, Kalymnos, Leros and Patmos; small boats daily in season to Nissyros, Pserimos and Kalymnos, some of these from Mastihari or Kardamena. Three times a week with Tilos, Mykonos, Andros and Rafina, twice a week with Samos, Symi and Astypalaia, once a week with Chios, Lesbos, Limnos, Thessaloniki or Kavala.

Tourist Information

NTOG, waterfront, ℂ (0242) 28 724.

Tourist police, with regular police, by the castle, ℂ (0242) 22 222.

Kos Town

Bustling **Kos**, the capital and main port, looks towards the north, roughly in the region of the dolphin's eye. Its garden setting, the multitude of flowers and stately palm trees make up somewhat for its lack of architectural interest; most of Kos town was built after the 1933 earthquake, this time using anti-seismic construction. From the archaeologist's point of view, the disaster had a good side-effect; when the rubble was cleared away, several ancient sites were revealed, and excavations were carried out throughout the city by the Italians. One block up from the harbour, in Plateia Eleftherias, is the **Museum** (*9–3.30, Sun 10–3, closed Tues*). Fittingly, the prize exhibit is a 4th-century BC statue of Hippocrates; there's

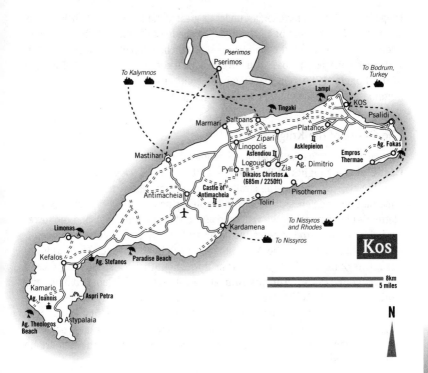

also a good collection of Hellenistic and Roman vases, statues and mosaics from the Casa Romana and the Asklepieion.

Dominated by the 18th-century **Defterdar Mosque** (still used by Kos' 50 or so Moslem families, but not open to the public), Plateia Eleftherias also has the city's fruit market and the **Porta tou Forou**, the gate to Kos' **Agora**. Within its walls the Knights built their town and auberges, and when these collapsed in the earthquake, excavations revealed the Roman Agora, the harbour quarter of the city, a temple of Aphrodite, and a 5th-century Christian basilica.

On the northern end of the Agora, the Plateia Platanou is almost entirely filled by **Hippocrates' plane tree**, its trunk 47ft in diameter, its huge boughs now supported by an intricate metal scaffolding instead of the marble columns that once kept the venerable old tree from disaster. Signs in eight languages warn people not to touch for fear of insecticides. Yet it does still seem quite healthy and, at between 500- and 600-years-old, it may well be the senior plane tree in Europe.

Hippocrates may well have taught under its great grandmother, for he believed, as do modern Greeks, that of all the trees the shade of the plane is the most salubrious. The Turks loved the old plane just as much, and built a fountain under it with a sarcophagus for a basin, and overlooking it constructed the lovely **Mosque of the Loggia** (1786). On 1 September the citizens of Kos come to pluck a leaf from the tree to include in their harvest wreaths as a symbol of abundance.

The Castle of the Knights

A stone bridge off Plateia Platanou takes you over the fosse to the entrance of the **Castle of the Knights of St John** (*9–3.30, Sun 10–3, closed Tues*). Together with their fortress across the strait in Bodrum, this castle served as the most important outer defence of Rhodes. After an earthquake in 1495, Grand Master Pierre d'Aubusson rebuilt the walls and added the outer enceinte, and the tower overlooking the harbour bears his name and coat-of-arms. Since d'Aubusson mostly used stones from the Agora, there's a patchwork of ancient inscriptions and reliefs of the knights' coats-of-arms throughout the castle; some have been removed to the castle's **Antiquarium**, along with stacks of defunct columns and marble. The castle's dishevelled weeds and wildflowers and stillness of the noonday sun attracted director Werner Herzog, who set his first, black-and-white film *Signs of Life* partly within its walls; however, the elaborate cockroach traps and hypnotized chickens that played such a large role in the film are no longer in evidence.

Roman Kos

From Plateia Eleftherias take Vass. Pavlou to Kos' other main archaeological sites. In the quarter called the Seraglio, Minoan and Mycenaean houses were discovered, as well as later structures. Opposite the Olympic Airways office stands a ramped Hellenistic **Altar of Dionysos**, and across Grigoriou St is the **Casa Romana** (*9–3.30, Sun 10–3, closed Tues*), excavated and reconstructed by the Italians in the 1930s. The house and neighbouring baths fell in the earthquake of AD 554; the house has well-preserved mosaics and offers a fair idea of the spacious elegance a wealthy Roman could afford. To the west along Grigoriou St is the **Roman Odeon**, or concert hall, with its rows of marble seats. Opposite, the so-called **western excavations** were also begun by the Italians in the 1930s. On one side are the great Hellenistic walls built around the acropolis, where a minaret stands today; on the other side runs the finely paved *cardo*, the main artery of Roman Kos, lined with houses (many containing fine mosaics, especially the House of Europa), a gymnasium and well-preserved baths used as a basilica by 5th-century Christians. In the baptistry you can see a well-preserved font. Alongside the baths and basilica runs the colonnade of the covered running track, or *xystos*, used in the winter months. The open **stadium** was at the northern end of the *xystos*, down Tsaldari St. Only a few of the seats have yet been excavated, but on the far side near the church is a well-preserved *aphesis*, or starting gate.

The Asklepieion

Many places in Kos hire out bicycles, the ideal transport to the **Asklepieion** (*8–7, Sun 9–6*) a few easy kilometres inland from the town. The German archaeologist Herzog, following the description in Strabo, discovered it in 1902, and it has been partially restored by the Italians. This was one of the ancient world's most important shrines to the healing god Asklepios, worshipped by the Asklepiada, a secret order of priests who found that calm baths in beautiful settings did much to remedy the ills of body and soul. The symbols of the cult were snakes for their supposed aptitude in seeking out healing herbs and their semi-divine status as transmitters of dreams—the Asklepiada made good use of drugs and the power of suggestion in their cures. The sanctuary on Kos was built after the death of Hippocrates, himself a member of the Asklepiada, but most of the buildings you see today are Hellenistic in origin, when it was last reconstructed after an earthquake; many of the structures were dismantled by the Knights, who found it a very convenient quarry. Nowadays, the Greeks have big plans to build a 'City of Hippocrates' near the present Hippocrates Foundation, where every five years they would hold an international medical olympiad. It is amusing to speculate on what that might have encompassed.

Set on a hillside, the Asklepieion is built in a series of terraces. On the lowest level are Roman baths, built in the 3rd century AD; on the next up is the main entrance and another large bath, and near the stair are the remains of a temple dedicated by the Kos-born physician G. Stertinius Xenophon, who went on to become the Emperor Claudius' personal doctor and murdered his patient by sticking a poisoned feather down his throat, before retiring on Kos, hailed as a hero, rather in the face of the Hippocratic Oath. On this level there is a spring, where water has flowed for over 2000 years. On the third terrace is the altar of Asklepios, and Ionic temples of Apollo and Asklepios (a few of the columns have been reconstructed by the Italians); on the fourth level stood a Doric temple of Asklepios from the 2nd century BC, the grandest and most sacred of all, and enjoying a view that in itself might shake away the blues. On the way back to the capital, stop for refreshments in **Platanias**, Kos' main Turkish settlement, with some good tavernas and cafés.

Around Kos

Buses to other points on Kos leave from the terminal behind the Olympic Airways office, but the services are infrequent, and you'll inevitably find yourself at the wrong end of a 100-m line-up, waiting for a taxi. The closest beaches to the east are at **Psalidi** (3km) and **Ag. Fokas**, both along the road to the modern spa, **Empros Thermae**. On the north coast there are beaches at **Lampi** and **Tingaki**; the latter, located near the salt pans, is especially fine and a popular place for a skinny dip.

Just inland, two ruined Byzantine basilicas (Ag. Pavlos and Ag. Ioannis) lie on the outskirts of **Zipario**; from here the road heads up to **Asfendiou**, a pleasant mountain village, although many of its houses have been abandoned as families moved down into town. Up the road, **Zia** has become the official 'traditional village' of package tours on Kos. You can escape them from Zia by following the path up **Mt Oromedon** in an hour, or more ambitiously scale Kos' highest peak, Dikaios Christos. This area is the bucolic Pryioton described by Theocritus, and Mt Dikaios produced much of the marble used by Kos' sculptors.

Another inland road leads to **Pyli**, from where it's a strenuous walk up to **Palaiopili**, a Byzantine ghost town surrounded by concentric walls camouflaged in the rocks. Within its walls is the church of Ypapandi, said to have been built in the 11th century by the Blessed Christodoulos before he went to Patmos. The church and Ag. Nikolaos nearby, have well-preserved 14th-century frescoes. In Pyli itself is the Charmyleion, an ancient hero shrine converted into the church of Stavros.

A sandy beach stretches between the villages of **Toliri** and **Kardamena**, the latter a fishing village famous for its ceramics and now one of Kos' major resorts; it has been commercialized to near Costa Brava proportions. It's very much the Brit and Scandinavian package destination, complete with pubs, chips, and so on. But there is a lovely beach and some superior club-type hotelscomplexes towards the end of it.

A quieter place to stay (although it is being rapidly developed) is **Mastihari** on the north coast. Frequent boats leave Mastihari for Kalymnos and Pserimos, and it is the port for the ungainly village of **Antimacheia**, near the airport. The **Castle of Antimacheia** was built by the Knights as a prison in the mid-14th century. Within its great, battlemented triangular walls are two churches, cisterns and, over the gateway, the arms of Pierre d'Aubusson.

Towards the dolphin's tail, near the beach at **Kamario**, stand the extensive ruins of the twin 5th-century basilicas of **Ag. Stefanos**, with mosaics, Ionian columns and remains of an atrium and baptistries, while out at sea, you can contemplate the dramatic rock of Ag. Nikolaos. A superb beach just to the east called **Paradise** for once deserves its name. Great swimming for children, but you'll have to fight your way through the forest of umbrellas to get to the water.

Kefalos to the west is high up on the headland of the dolphin's tail. When the hotels are full on the rest of Kos, chances are you can find a room here. South of Kefalos are ruins of yet another castle used by the Knights, one that inspired many travellers' tales in the Middle Ages, all involving a dragon; Mandeville claims the serpent was none other than Hippocrates' daughter, enchanted by Artemis and awaiting a knight brave enough to kiss her to transform her back into a maiden. Neolithic remains were found in the **Aspri Petra cave** near Kefalos, which is also near the site of the ancient capital of Kos, **Astypalaia**, the birthplace of Hippocrates; a few bits of the ancient city remain, and on a hill above the town is a fort used by the Knights. Isthmioton, another ancient city on the peninsula, was important enough in the past to send its own delegation to Delos, but not a trace of it remains. The **monastery Ag. Ioannis** is 6km west of Kefalos, along a track through dramatic scenery. Nearby **Ag. Theologos** beach provides some of the island's most secluded swimming.

Festivals

23 April, Ag. Georgios, with horse races at Pyli; 8 September, Panayias at Kardamena; 29 June, Ag. Apostoli at Antimacheia; 29 August, Ag. Ioannis at Kefalos; 25 March, Evangelismos at Asfendiou; 21 November, Isodia tis Panayias at Zia; 6 December, Ag. Nikolaos at Kos. In August the **Hippocrates Cultural Festival** attracts people from all over Greece, and includes art exhibitions, concerts of classical and modern music, and screenings of Greek and foreign films.

© (0242–)   *Where to Stay in Kos Town*

expensive

In the old days those in need of a cure would stay in the Asklepieion at Kos and sacrifice a chicken to the god. If you want to do the same, there's the new **Hippocrates Palace Hotel**, © 24 401, with its Olympic Health Centre, a medical spa supervised by Dr Christian Barnard. However, it will cost you more than a chicken. The nearby **Oceanis Club** (A) is in the same price range, © 23 934. In Kardamena is the new **Club Porto Bello Beach, Hotel and Bungalows**, a luxurious setting with views of Nissyros, © 91217.

moderate

Well located on the harbour is the **Astron Hotel**, © 23 705, a pretty class B with a rooftop garden, and a charming view of the sea and city. With lower prices, the **Helena Hotel**, at 5 Megalou Alexandrou St, © 22 740, is very pleasant, with pretty balconies. **Carda Beach Bungalows** (B), © 91222, is down by the beach.

cheap

There are over a dozen D and E class hotels in the town, but not many have rooms for less than 5000 dr. One good option, however, is **Hara**, 6 Halkonos St, one street back from the waterfront of Vas. Georgiou, © 22 500. For something less expensive, get the list of rooms and pensions at the tourist office, and in the summer have plenty of telephone change handy; these places fill up fast. You could try **Pension Alexis**, 9 Iridotou, © 28 798; or **Pension Andreas**, 2 Argirocastro, © 28740.

130   *The Islands*

expensive

If you don't mind the overwhelming package tourism atmosphere, Kardamena has scores of rooms in its pensions and hotels. Dominant here is the **Norida Beach hotel** complex, ✆ 91 231.

moderate

Smaller and less expensive in Kardamena, **Stelios**, ✆ 91 210, is on the main square and the sea, though do book well in advance. Even more than in Kos town, accommodation fills up quickly in Kardamena, though if you come early in the day you can probably find a room in a private house. Other accommodation is to be found in Mastihari, Kefalos (always the last to fill up) and Tingaki, which is more pricey than the other places, although the pension **Meni Beach**, ✆ 29 217 has rooms for lower rates in this bracket. Enquire at the NTOG office in Kos about renting a house in Asfendiou; currently they are being refurbished as part of the organization's Traditional Settlements scheme.

cheap

Cheapest, but respectable, in Mastihari is **Zevgas**, ✆ 22 577, and all rooms have private bath. Otherwise consult the tourist office handouts for rooms in villages and seaside resorts. The official **campsite** is by the beach at Psalidi about 3km from town, ✆ 23 275.

Eating in Kos Town

...ase all, the typical restaurant food in Kos is notoriously bland and dull, if not downright bad. As on Rhodes, you'd do well to avoid the tacky places that advertise with illuminated photos of meatballs and wurst. In town you can eat reasonably well in the newer quarter, at **Hellas** or **Ageilos** on Psarron Street; in and on the waterfront at Vass. Georgiou the **Miramare** is largely unchanged by tourism and serves good Greek dishes at normal prices. Arguably the most authentic and reasonably priced taverna, hidden way in the backstreets (you'll have to ask half a dozen times to find it, but it's worth it) is **Frangolis**, serving the best *stifado* in town, among many of its other delicious dishes (1800 dr.). The chic **Bristol**, on Vass. Giorgiou, offers some Chinese dishes, and nearby the sparkling **Le Chevalier** has a French menu, with prices to match. The **Kastro**, near the ancient Agora, belongs in the same league, except the setting is much more alluring.

Eating Out of Town

Outside town is Platano, with a handful of tavernas serving Turkish food. The best of the bunch is the **Arap**, offering excellent eggplant with yoghurt, borek, grilled shish kebab and chicken (1500 dr.). Out in Psalidi by the campsite **Nestoras** and **Thessaloniki** both have good Greek fare, and sea views. In Ag. Fokas, on the way to the spa, the beautiful **Villa Café** has an impressive choice of smoked swordfish, barbecue ribs, some Chinese and Japanese dishes, and some delectable homemade pastries, with fine views over to Turkey (2000 dr.).

Kardamena caters very much to the tastes of British package tourists, but it also has an attractive row of tavernas at the water's edge. **Teo's**, by the square where the bus arrives, serves good fish, and standard Greek ready food (2000 dr.). The **Cavo d'Oro**, by the water, also has seafood and pizza. More down to earth is the *ouzeri* **Nikos O Vrahos** in Plateia Konitsis, one block up from the Agora, where a selection of delicious dishes will provide a wholesome, inexpensive meal. The beaches have tavernas as well. One of the best is located above Paradise Beach, serving traditional Greek and Italian dishes for 2000 dr. with Nissyros as a backdrop. If you're from Montréal, you'll get a warm welcome from the owner, who raised his family there.

In Mastihari the long established **Kalia Kardia** (1500–2000 dr.) is the best of several. Up in Zia, **To Vouno** is recommended by locals. It has an outside grill, good food and a beautiful view.

Pserimos

Located between Kos and Kalymnos, Pserimos has a beautiful sandy beach, making it a popular destination for day-trippers from the larger islands. Even in September excursion boats are queueing up to dock, and the sands are covered with trippers lying shoulder-to-shoulder. Fewer than a hundred people live on Pserimos, although the *paniyiri* at its monastery on 15 August attracts many times that number of visitors from Kos and Kalymnos. Regular boats run between Kos town, Mastihari and Kalymnos.

The seaside **Pension Tripolitis** is pleasant, and the **monastery** has simple accommodation for up to 10 people. **Rooms Andreas** and **Kali Kardia** are fine too. There are a few rooms to be had in the village; if they are full, you can sleep out on one of the island's more distant beaches, a kilometre from the village. If you were staying any length of time, you'd probably want to take to the interior by day; the beaches can be murder.

Eating Out

Most of the cafés on the main beach are packed, and the service in them is surly more often than not; but they do regain civility in the evening when the day-trippers go away.

Leros

With one of the most serrated coastlines of any island, Leros defies easy description. Unlike on many of the other Dodecanese, most of the visitors are Greek, and many of those who come to Leros tend to combine their holiday with a visit to a relative in one of the island's three mental hospitals, built during the Italian occupation. For the British, this is still Leros' unfortunate claim to fame, following a scandalous Channel Four television exposé on the appalling conditions the inmates are kept in. However, the people are friendly, and you can walk almost everywhere; there are enough incongruities to make a visit interesting, if not occasionally bizarre. Indeed, here more than on the other islands you are aware of the Italians, to the extent that some older residents have a hard time speaking Greek. Although there are several beaches, none is special, and in the hotels you need all your mosquito defences.

History

When the hero Meleager (of Chalydonian boar hunt fame) died, his sisters mourned him so passionately that Artemis turned them into guinea fowl and put them in her temple at Leros, the wooded island dedicated to her. This worship of the goddess of the chase and the guinea fowl might be traced back to Ionian colonists from Miletus; Robert Graves notes that, perhaps because of their religious conservatism, the Greeks called the Leriots 'evil-livers.' Fittingly for an island dedicated to Artemis, property has been passed down through the female line, to the extent that most of Leros is owned by women.

Homer includes Leros with Kalymnos in his catalogue of ships as the Kalydian isles. The island sided with Sparta in the Peloponnesian War, despite its Ionian ancestry. Under the Romans, pirates preyed among the islets that surround Leros; some nabbed a handsome young lawyer named Julius Caesar on his way home from Bithynia, where according to rumour he had a dissolute affair with the governor; released after a month when his ransom was paid, Julius later got his revenge by capturing and crucifying every brigand around Leros. Under the Byzantines, the island was part of the theme of Samos, but in 1316 it was sold to the Knights of St John and governed by the Duke of Naxos as part of the monastic state of Patmos. The town and harbour of Lakki were badly battered by the combined allied air forces in 1943 during a prolonged bombardment; photographs taken by German paratroopers at the time are on display in the Kastis Travel Agency. During the later Cyprus dispute the Greek government dismantled the military installations to show that it had no warlike intentions against Turkey. When the junta took power in 1967, Communist dissidents were exiled on Leros and kept at a prison camp in Partheni.

Connections

By air: daily from Athens, twice a week from Kos and Rhodes.

By sea: ferry every day from Piraeus, Rhodes, Kos, Kalymnos and Patmos, twice a week with Lipsi and Agathonissi, and from once to three times a week with Samos, Chios, Lesbos, Limnos, Thessaloniki, Nissyros, Tilos, Symi and Ikaria.

By hydrofoil: four times a week from Ag. Marina to Patmos and Lipsi, once a week to Pythagorio (Samos); six times a week excursion boat from Ag. Marina to Lipsi. Daily boat from Myrties (Kalymnos) to Xirokambos.

Tourist Information

Information booth on quay.

Tourist police, *see* regular police, ✆ (0247) 22 222.

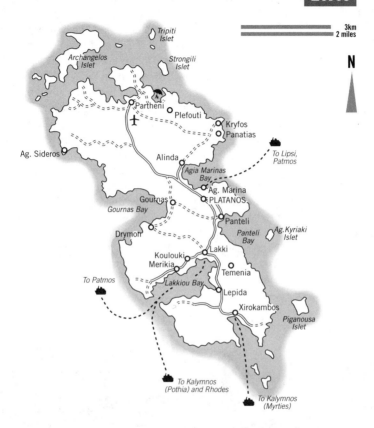

Tripiti
Islet

3km
2 miles

N

Archangelos
Islet

Strongili
Islet

Partheni

Plefouti

Kryfos
Panatias

To Lipsi,
Patmos

Ag. Sideros

Alinda

Agia Marinas
Bay

Gournas

Ag. Marina
PLATANOS

Gournas Bay

Panteli

Ag.Kyriaki
Islet

Drymon

Panteli
Bay

Koulouki
Merikia

Lakki

Temenia

To Patmos

Lakkiou Bay

Lepida

Xirokambos

Piganousa
Islet

To Kalymnos
(Pothia) and Rhodes

To Kalymnos
(Myrties)

Platanos, Alinda and North Leros

Platanos, as near the centre of Leros as possible, is the capital of the island. It is crowned by the **Kastro**, a Byzantine fortress renovated by the Knights of St John and the Venetians, and used even today as a military observation post. Although it seems steep and inaccessible, a fairly easy footpath leads up from the town picturesquely piled below. Once at the top you have a splendid view of Leros' 'four seas': the bays of Panteli, Alindas, Gournas and Lakkiou. Two churches in the fortress walls have been repaired by the Greek Archaeology Service, **Moni Megalochiro** and **Kyras Kastrou**. Of the latter, the following is told: during the Turkish occupation a miraculous icon of the Virgin with a candle set sail from Constantinople and landed at Leros. The inhabitants, led by the bishops, met it and carried it in great procession to the cathedral. The next day, however, the icon had vanished, but before dismay had spread too far the Turkish captain of the Kastro found it with its candle in the powder stores, even though the door had been firmly bolted and locked. The icon was returned to the cathedral, but the next night the very same thing happened. And the next night, and the next. Finally the Turkish captain grew weary of the affair and gave the powder storeroom to the Christians, who turned it into the church Kyras Kastro. Here the wilful icon has decided to remain ever since. In Platanos' main square is a small **museum**, housing local finds, which is usually open in the morning. It is a short walk from Platanos to the beach at **Panteli** in one direction and **Ag. Marina**, Leros' main resort—such as it is—in the other direction. North of Ag. Marina **Alinda**, the old commercial port of Leros, has a long beach, one of the best on the island and recently developed for proper tourist broiling. Near here are the ruins of an Early Christian basilica along with a few vestiges of the ancient city, as well as a British war cemetery from the battle of 1943. Other beaches nearby are at **Gournas**, where the monastery Ag. Sideros was built on a small islet linked to Leros by a long causeway.

Frequent buses run between Platanos and the island's main port, **Lakki**. If Fellini had been Greek, Lakki would have been one of his favourite sets. The streets are perfectly paved and wide enough to accommodate several lanes of traffic, although usually they're perfectly empty, overlooked by stately if forlorn *fascisti* art deco buildings, genteelly dilapidated in empty, litter-strewn lots. Nightlife here centres around the grandiose cinema. Near the waterfront there's a monument to the many who perished when a Greek ship, the *Queen Olga*, was attacked by German planes and sank in Lakki's harbour. A path leading up from the jetty goes to the nearest beach at **Koulouki**, a favourite place for unofficial camping. At **Lepida**, across the harbour, the Moni Panayia is built on the ruins of an old lighthouse, and further south, overlooking Xirokambos, is the fort **Paliokastro**, built near an older fortification dating back to the 3rd century BC. The church inside has mosaics and Xirokambos itself has a pleasant pebble beach with several tavernas and a campsite.

Partheni on the northern shore had an ancient temple to Artemis, near the present church of Ag. Matrona. This former centre of guinea fowl worship on Leros is now the centre of military activity on the island; it was the base used by the colonels to detain political dissidents. There is a better beach with a taverna nearby at **Plefouti**.

Festivals

Carnival at which the children don monks' robes and visit the homes of the newly married, reciting verses made up by their elders: 16–17 July, Ag. Marinas at Ag. Marina; 6 August, Sotiros at Platanos; 15 August, Panayias at the Kastro; 20 August, foreign tourist day at Alinda; 20 October, Ag. Kyras at Partheni; 24–25 September, Ag. Ioannis Theologos at Lakki. Often at the *paniyiria* you can hear the Greek hammer dulcimer, the *santouri.*

Starting on 26 September, three days of memorial services are held for those who lost their lives on the *Queen Olga;* Greek naval vessels always attend this annual commemoration.

© *(0247–)*

Where to Stay

moderate

Miramare has rooms in the heart of Lakki, © 22 043. A new hotel, **Chrissi Palace**, is also worth a look. Other, arguably more comfortable, lodgings may be had at Alinda, in Ag. Marina Bay such as the B class **Xenon Angelou Alinda**, © 22 749, the **Hotel Maleas Beach** class C, © 23 306, and the **Pension Chryssoula**, boasting the best view in town, © 22 460. A useful B pension is **Lakki House**, © 22514. In Panteli there are a number of pensions, including **To Rodon**, © 22 075.

cheap

In Lakki try **Hotel Eleftheria** © 23550; **Venus Pension** © 23389; or **Pension Papa Fotis**, © 22247, behind Maleas beach. At Panteli, **Cavos Pension** (B), © 23247, is smart, and **Monolithos Paradise Pension** (A), 24718, is also a cut above most private rooms. There's a **campsite** at Xirokambos, © 22 236.

Eating Out

In Lakki the fare is generally limited to fast food and pizza, a notable exception being **O Sostos** taverna (behind the Leros Palace Hotel), which enjoys an excellent reputation, especially for its fish dishes (3000 dr.). Ag. Marina has most of the island's tavernas, one of the best being **Ta Kamakia**, where again the fish is excellent; but Ag. Marina is where most of the island's bikers hang out these days. **Finikas** is a dependable favourite in Alinda, while the places to eat in Panteli are **Syrtaki**, **Taverna Maria**, and **Nikola's Taverna**. Generally speaking, wherever you eat on the island, particularly if you choose fish, you cannot go wrong.

Lipsi (Lipsous)

Lipsi is a little gem of an island midway between Leros and Patmos, its lovely beaches a magnet for day excursions from its larger neighbours. However Lipsi is still as quiet a place as one can find with good food and good swimming, near the fine harbour and beach. Other beaches nestling along the jagged coastline are at Katsadia and Lendou; the best, **Plati Yialo**, is a half-hour walk to the south (it is also accessible by taxi). Another pleasant stroll leads to a green cultivated valley beyond the town, where a decent wine is produced. One tradition connects the island with Calypso, and there certainly is a similarity, in the name and the quiet spells the island casts once the trippers have been herded away.

Daily excursion boats from Leros and Patmos. Ferry connections three times a week with Samos, Patmos, Leros and Kalymnos, twice a week with Kos and Agathonissi, once a week with Nissyros, Tilos, Symi, Rhodes and Ikaria.

Where to Stay

moderate–cheap

There's only one hotel on Lipsi, the **Kalypso**, © 41 242, which also has an information service. Plenty of other rooms can be found in the village besides; try **Panorama Pension** or **Pension Flisvos**. On Lendou Beach you'll find **Studios Dream** © 41271. Otherwise you can sleep out at Katsadia or Lendou beach.

Eating Out

The tavernas on the waterfront are good and not very expensive; a fish dinner at **Mr Mungo's**, **Calypso Taverna**, **Barbarossa Restaurant**, or **Taverna O Theologos** will set you back about 2500 dr. Some of the cafés serve breakfast.

Nissyros

In the great war between gods and giants, one of the casualties was the fiery Titan Polyvotis, who so incurred Poseidon's wrath that the sea god yanked off a chunk of Kos and hurled it on top of Polyvotis as he attempted to swim away. This became the island of Nissyros, and the miserable Polyvotis, pinned underneath, eternally sighs and fumes, unable to escape.

Geologically Nissyros was indeed once part of Kos and Polyvotis is the Dodecanese's only volcano. Even in its dormant state it dominates the character of Nissyros, where fertile slopes are green with olives, figs, citrus groves and almond trees. The islanders have traditionally worked the pumice fields, both on Nissyros and its little sister islet **Yiali**. The coasts of both islands are a jumble of black volcanic boulders and black sandy beaches, though Yiali also has a fine golden, sandy beach.

Connections

Ferry once a week from Rafina, Andros, Tinos, Mykonos, three times a week with Kos, Rhodes and Tilos, twice a week with Kalymnos and Symi, once a week with Leros, Patmos, Lipsi, Agathonissi and Samos. In summer, daily excursion boat from Kardamena on Kos; also, less frequently, connections with Rhodes, Symi and Tilos.

Tourist Information

Tourist police, *see* regular police on the quay, ✆ (0242) 31 201.

Tourist office, ✆ (0242) 31 459.

Mandraki and Around

Nissyros, despite the advent of day-trippers, has retained its quiet charm. Even the new houses constructed in bijou **Mandraki**, the capital and port, conform to the old style: tall and narrow with small wooden balconies. Of late it has become fashionable to paint them in deep, almost gaudy colours. One of the houses near the church has opened a small **Historical and Ethnographical Museum**, with household implements and costumes and a tiny library of books about the island.

Fortunately most of the streets of Mandraki are too narrow for traffic, but the town has been kind enough to signpost the way to its major attraction: the stair up to the monastery of **Panayia Spiliani** (1825), in a cave within the walls of the old Venetian **Kastro**. Inside is a finely carved iconostasis and a much-venerated icon of the Virgin, loaded down with a bushel of gold and silver offerings. The Kastro itself isn't much, but the height offers a spectacular view at sunset. Higher up at **Paliokastro** are impressive Cyclopean walls. Nearest swimming to town is at **Hohlaki** beach, covered with small volcanic stones of a light bluish hue. Locals will tell you that the sea is best here, even if the stones can be rather uncomfortable underfoot. A 10-minute walk from Mandraki takes you to **Miramare** beach, just as suitable for swimming and convenient for the nearby fish tavernas.

Just east of Mandraki is the thermal spa of **Loutra** where the hot volcanic springs are used as a cure for arthritis and rheumatism; further east is Nissyros' best sandy beach, **Pali**, where you can top off a swim with a lunch of fresh fish, or try nearby **Yialliskari**, with crystal clear water and a beach of fine, white sand. A modern hotel has been built here.

Into the Volcano

The excursion not to be missed on Nissyros, however, is to **Polyvotis**, ex-Titan and now plugged-up volcano. Buses for the crater leave the port, coinciding with the arrival of the tourist boats, or there is the regular village bus from Mandraki up to Emborios and Nikia, two villages perched on the crater's rim, from where you can walk down (buses wait about 45 minutes before returning to Mandraki).

The winding road manages to take in most of Nissyros' rustic charms before it begins to twist its way down into an other-worldly landscape of pale greys and yellows, the smell of sulphur so pungent that you can almost see cartoonish stink lines curling up out of the great crater (you may have to hang out your clothes to air when you get back to keep from smelling like a rotten egg.) After passing several geothermal pools, the bus stops near the great fuming heart of Polyvotis. A zigzag path descends to the floor of the crater, where you can feel the great heat and turmoil of the volcano underfoot. Stout shoes are essential; rubber soles may melt on the surface hot enough to cook an egg. Beware, too, that your foot can go through the floor, so follow the group heavyweight for safety.

Here and there small fumaroles emit steam and stench, and weird and eerie as it is no one can stand to stick around for long. There is talk of harnessing the volcano's energy to provide electricity for the whole Dodecanese. Even hotter is the natural sauna below **Emborios**, in a cave heated by hot springs. The village with its ruined Byzantine fort and ancient walls offers memorable views of the infernal crater 300m below, as does pretty **Nikia**.

Festivals

29 June, Ag. Apostoli at Pali; 27 July, Ag. Panteleimonos at Nikia; August 15, Panayias at Mandraki.

© (0242–)

Where to Stay

moderate

The B class pension **Haritos**, © 31 322, in Mandraki provides the most comfort; also good is the C-class **Hotel Porfiris**, © 31 376, complete with swimming pool.

cheap

Another comfortable place to stay in Mandraki is the pension/taverna **Romantzo**, near the ferry dock, © 31 340, with a large shady terrace.

Alternatively the small **Tria Adelfia**, © 31 344, has rooms for about the same price, and also has a pleasant taverna. There are also rooms to rent in the village and, if you thread your way through the streets west of town (on the other side from where the ferry docks), you'll find the **Drossia** pension, where the waves crash on the black rocks beneath your balcony.

Eating Out

All of the tavernas in Nissyros are exceptionally friendly and reasonably priced. Not far from the public lavatories are the tavernas **Tsardka** and **Karava**, with excellent ready food and items from the grill, and how good fish tastes when the sea is just a few feet away (2000 dr.). Don't just rely on the waterfront tavernas, though, as there are some pleasant culinary surprises waiting for you in town, where **Sfakianos, Koulakis** and **Magganas** provide good food and Greek music. Just outside the port, **Miramare** has a good name locally. Out at Pali there are some reliable fish tavernas on the beach.

Patmos

Of all the Greek islands, Patmos is the most sacred to Christians, both Orthodox and Western alike, for here St John the Theologian received the vision written in the Apocalypse, or Book of Revelations, and here, in the 11th century, was founded a monastery more wealthy and influential than any in Greece except for Mt Athos. Many find a spirituality in Patmos that the other islands lack, a quiet solemnity, a sacred (though hardly apocalyptic) aura that seems especially strong in the evening, after the cruise ships have sailed away. If a hectic nightlife is what you look forward to, you won't want to stay long on Patmos. It is a quiet place, especially up at Chora, and people tend to retire early.

History

Patmos was inhabited from the 14th century BC, with the capital near present-day Skala, its acropolis and fortifications at Kastelli. It was a subject to Asia Minor and not very important. In AD 95, however, the island's destiny was forever altered when St John the Theologian (or the Divine) was exiled here from Ephesus during the Emperor Domitian's persecution of Christians, and while living here in a cave he received his extraordinary Revelations. Most believe he stayed only a year on Patmos before returning to Ephesus, but in that year John provided not only a

fairly accurate prophecy of the fall of the Roman Empire, but enough to keep fire-eating preachers and literal-minded crank interpreters in material for the next 1900 years.

Patmos was abandoned from the 7th century, its barren, volcanic rock not worth defending against pirates. Destiny remained on hold until the late 11th century, when in faraway Constantinople, things were going badly for Alexis Comnenus 'born to the purple' as the Byzantines put it, but to Alexis, battered by fate and politics, the purple seemed impossible to attain. A saintly hermit named

Christodulos nevertheless predicted his ascent to the throne, and the miserable Alexis promised him that were it to come true, he would grant him any wish in his power. Of course it did, and in 1088, Christodulos made his wish of the Emperor: the island of Patmos, to found a monastery on the site of an ancient temple of Artemis. The Emperor provided not only the island but the building funds.

The entire island of Patmos remained under absolute control of the monastery for centuries, against poverty, pirates, and a thousand other afflictions. The Venetian Dukes of Patmos, its nominal rulers, were content to leave it as an autonomous monastic state. In the 13th century the village of Chora was built in the shadow of the powerful walls of the monastery, offering a safe refuge in case of attack. Patmos flourished particularly during the 16th to 19th centuries, and its school of theology and liberal arts, founded in 1713, cast a healthy glow over the long, dark domination of the Turks. Gradually monastic control lessened as the islanders turned to sea trade, and in 1720 the monks and laymen had divided the land between them. Patmos prospered to the extent that in the 18th century it established colonies abroad; a prosperity nipped in the bud, as in the case of other island shipping centres, with the invention of the steamship.

Connections

Hydrofoils on most days in the summer to Kos, Rhodes, Leros and Pythagorio, Samos; daily excursion boats to Lipsi and Pythagorio (Samos); ferry daily to Piraeus, Kalymnos, Leros, Kos and Rhodes, four times a week with Samos, three times a week with Ikaria, twice a week with Agathonissi, once a week with Nissyros, Tilos, Symi, Chios, Lesbos, Limnos and Thessaloniki.

Tourist Police

See regular police, ✆ (0247) 31 303, in the harbour.

Tourist information office, in Skala, ✆ (0247) 31 666.

Skala

All boats to Patmos drop anchor at **Skala**, the main tourist centre of the island. During the tourist season, this is also where cruise ships disgorge hordes of wealthy tourists. One of the first things you'll see is a statue of Protergatis Xanthos Emmanuel who led an uprising against the Turks in 1821. Skala itself didn't even exist until that year, so fearsome were the pirate raids. Near the beach, marked by a red buoy, is a reminder of another local menace, the evil magician Yenoupas, who at the urging of priests from the temple of Apollo challenged St John to a duel of miracles. Yenoupas' miracle was to dive into the sea and bring back effigies of the dead; John's was to ask God to petrify the submerged magician, which abruptly ended the duel. Behind Skala you can visit what was once one of the world's largest desalination plants, work now performed by a reservoir. The water tastes better without it, but there still isn't enough to meet the island's needs in the summer. You can also hike up to the site of the ancient city, **Kastelli**, in about 20 minutes, a walk rewarded more with stunning views than any archaeological excavations.

Chora

From Skala you can see whitewashed **Chora** clinging to the mighty castle walls of the monastery. Buses make the ascent in a few minutes, but if you have the time it isn't too strenuous to walk up from Skala, to enjoy the ever-widening panorama spread out below. Chora is a lovely, almost Cycladic town, with numerous mansions built during the wealthy days of Patmos' great merchant fleet.

Monastery of St John the Theologian

*(Mon, Wed and Fri 8–2, Tues and Thurs 8–1 and 4–6, Sun 8–12 noon and 4–6); no shorts and women **must** wear skirts)*

If it's your first visit, however, make a beeline for this magnificent monastery. At the entrance, pick up the guide in English by S. A. Papadopoulos, with a good history of the monastery and description of its frescoes and works of art.

Inside the massive walls (restored after the earthquake of 1956) is a charming entrance court of 1698, incorporating the outer narthex of the church. Just before the narthex itself is the chapel and tomb of its founder, the Blessed

Christodulos. The church itself is in the form of a Greek cross set in a square, and still retains its original marble floor; its icon of St John was presented to the monastery by Alexis Comnenus. Beautiful frescoes cover almost all paintable surfaces, although all but those in the 12th-century **Chapel of the Theotokos** are much later than the church. There are more 12th-century frescoes in the Refectory, off the inner courtyard. The **Treasury Museum** contains the priceless 6th-century *Codex Prophyrius*, St Mark's gospel written on purple vellum; the monastery foundation deed—a golden bull, signed and sealed, from the Emperor; remains of the temple of Artemis on which the monastery was built (a temple said to have been founded by Orestes, in gratitude for being rid of the Furies); gold and silver crosses, croziers and stoles; superb icons and ship pendants made of diamonds and emeralds donated by Catherine the Great. The library contains hundreds of rare codices and manuscripts, but may only be visited with permission from the abbot. Lastly, climb up to the roof terrace for a commanding view over the Aegean.

Around Chora

After the monastery, you could spend a day visiting the 40 or so churches wedged in the narrow lanes of Chora: especially good are the **Convent of Zoodochos Pigi** (1607) with fine frescoes and icons (*open mornings and late afternoons*) and 11th-century **Ag. Dimitrios**, contemporary with the monastery, but likely to be locked like many of the others. Nor is hunting out the caretaker particularly easy, as Chora is one of those very old, silent places where the streets always seem to be deserted.

This changes dramatically on Orthodox Maundy Thursday, when Chora is packed with visitors and even TV crews for the Niptiras ceremony, when the abbot of the monastery re-enacts Christ's washing of his disciples' feet—a rite once performed by the proud emperors of Byzantium. It takes place either in Plateia Ag. Levias or Plateia Loza, depending on the weather.

It's a 15-minute walk down from Chora to the **Monastery of the Apocalypse** (*8–12 noon, Thurs 8–12 noon and 2.30–5.30*), where a stair covered with pots of flowers leads down to the cave where St John lived and dreamed and dictated what he saw to his follower. The cave itself has been converted to a church, where you can see the rock where the good saint rested his head and hand (though one can't help thinking he must have been a contortionist to manage it), and the massive overhanging roof, split in three sections by the voice of God.

Caiques from Skala run most days from in front of the Arion Café to the island's many lovely beaches: to the north, **Psiliammos**, with fine white sand is the unofficial nudist beach, an hour away by boat; to the south, **Lampi**, another port of call (or 30-minute walk), has a lovely, multi-coloured pebble beach. Another beach, **Meloi** is close to town and therefore tends to get crowded; enclosed **Grikou** can be reached by bus or boat (or a 45-minute walk) from Skala, and has windsurfs and water skis for hire. Halfway between Skala and Kambos, look for the sign to **Agriolivadi**, pointing the way to a quiet, clean beach. Other beaches in the region are often completely deserted, such as the one at **Sapsila**.

In fertile **Sykamia** is an old Roman bath said to have been used by St John to baptize his converts. In **Stavros**, a tiny village to the south, the **Kalikatsou rock** has carved rooms in rather unlikely places and may have been the 11th-century hermitage mentioned in the writings of Christodulos. Across the island from here, a grotto on **Cape Yenoupas** was the home of the evil magician (*see* above), and even today it's unpleasantly hot and smelly inside.

Heading north, **Kambos** lies in the centre of Patmos' main agricultural valley and has a popular sandy beach, complete with restaurants and the chance to windsurf and waterski. Just over the hill lies the peaceful beach of **Vagia**. Further along are more wild and windswept shores for daring swimmers at **Levkes**. Even more remote is the 19th-century **Hermitage of Apollon**, near a small mineral spring (ask for directions in Kambos).

Boats leave Skala for all these places between 9 and 11am, returning about 4pm. Excursions to Lipsi (one hour away) are especially popular; boats leave at 10 and return at 5.

Festivals

Besides the Maundy Thursday Niptiras ceremony, the monastery holds important services for St John on 8 May and 26 September. More popular (feasting and dancing) *paneyeria* take place 5 August (Sotiris) at Kambos and 15 August, Panayias, also at Kambos; 14 September, Stavros; 27 July, Ag. Panteleimonos, on the islet of Xiliomodi.

moderate

In Skala, **Hotel Chris** © 31403 has a disco downstairs; the new **Hotel Efi**, © 32500 is a good B pension. On the edge of Skala, **Hotel Byzance** is designed in the traditional style featuring a roof garden with a small restaurant and lovely views over the port, © 31 052. Two others that deserve a mention down in the port are the **Patmion**, © 31 313, and the **Skala**, © 31 343, with an attractive pool and just two minutes from the ferry. **Kasteli** commands fine views in the upper part of town, © 31 361; the friendly **Aftsralis**, © 31 576, is beautifully decorated and costs slightly less. In Grikou, the **Panorama** offers furnished apartments by the sea, © 31 209, or try the more economical **Flisvos**, © 31 380. The new **Patmos Paradise**, Kampos, (B) is a club-style development with pool, squash, tennis courts, and fitness centre.

cheap

On the whole the private rooms in Skala are very comfortable and better value than the hotels, and you're sure to be offered one as soon as you get off the boat. **Hotel Rex**, © 31242, is oldish but okay; **Pension Sophia**, © 31501, is also worth a look. There are also rooms up in Chora, and in Kambos, and an excellent campground at Meloi. At Ormos Meloi you'll find **Rooms and Taverna Meloi**, © 31888, almost on the beach; basic facilities, but serving good, reasonably-priced food.

Eating Out

For some reason, everyone hangs out at **Café Arion** on the waterfront. There are other good restaurants in Chora: **Vangelis** and **Olympia** in Plateia Ag. Levias (follow the little signs) both with solid Greek fare at around 2000 dr. and the bonus of sitting in the beautiful old square, where Saturday nights sometimes see some inspired dancing. The third place, **The Patmian House** is an old Patmian mansion that has been converted into a luxury restaurant, a wonderful setting for a romantic dinner (3000 dr., open evenings only). Down in Skala the **Old Harbour** has very elegant service, good seafood, and rather higher prices. **Taverna O Vrachnos** is north of the waterfront, and good for fish; **O Pantelis** a few streets back is good for basic taverna fare. Also down to earth is **Grigoris Grill**, opposite the ferry—good charcoal grilled fish and meat (2000 dr.).

Out at Grikou are two popular tavernas: the small, family-run **Flisvos** up on the hill, with Greek staples and fish (1800–2400 dr.) and, in the middle of the beach, **Stamatis**, serving the same at similar prices. There are tavernas on most other beaches. Meloi has **Stefani's**, where the food is simple but tasty (2000 dr.).

Agathonissi, Arki and Marathi

Agathonissi is a remote island off Patmos, connected only two–three times a week with the outside world, as is its even smaller sister **Arki**. These are poor islets, inhabited only by a few fishing families. Agathonissi has two villages, Megalo Chorio and Mikro Chorio, and a few ancient remains. Occasional caiques run from Patmos to Arki, where there are two cafés and a bit of a beach. You can also visit (but you may have to hire your own caique) the even smaller **Marathi**, which has a better, sandy beach, with excellent swimming, and a taverna.

Rhodes (Rodos)

Rhodes, 'more beautiful than the sun' according to the ancient Greeks, is the largest and most fertile of the Dodecanese, ringed by sandy beaches, bedecked with flowers, blessed with some 300 days of sun a year, dotted with handsome towns and villages full of monuments evoking a long, colourful history—in a nut-shell, all that it takes to sit securely throned as the reigning queen of tourism in Greece. As a year-round resort for cold northerners and major package tour desti-nation, it's not quite fair to compare it with Greece's other islands. Rhodes is rather a Euro-playground, a modern tourist Babylon, where people shed their inhibitions with their woollens and don't feel stupid walking around with 'No Problem!' and 'Relax' emblazoned on their bosoms. If large crowds of tourists bother you, head for the south of the island or try smoking a smelly cigar and pre-tend you only speak Albanian. Or Greek.

Mythology

The first inhabitants of Rhodes were the Children of the Sea, the nine dog-headed enchantresses called Telchines, who had flippers for hands. In spite of this apparent handicap, they made the sickle that Cronus used to castrate Uranus; they carved the first statues of the gods, and founded Kamiros, Ialysos and Lindos before moving to Crete. There Rhea, the goddess of the earth, made them the nurses of Poseidon, and they forged the sea god's trident.

Poseidon fell in love with one of the Telchines and fathered the nymph Rhode, who became the sole heir of the island when Zeus decided to destroy the Telchines for meddling with the weather (they were fond of magical mists); but the real reason he wanted rid of them was because they belonged to a pre-Olympian matriarchal religion. He flooded Rhodes, although the Telchines managed to escape in various forms, most notoriously as the hounds of Artemis, who tore Acteon to bits.

Not long after the patriarchal Olympians were dividing up the world's real estate among themselves, Zeus realized that he had forgotten to set aside a portion for Helios, god of the sun. Dismayed, Zeus asked Helios what he could do to make up for his omission. The sun god replied that he knew of an island just emerging off the coast of Asia Minor which would suit him admirably. Helios married Rhode, and their seven sons, famous astronomers, ruled it. One of the sons, or perhaps Tlepolemos (who led the ships of Rhodes to Troy), refounded the ancient Telchine towns. Kamiros even has another possible founder; one of them is Althaemenes, son of the Cretan King Catreus and grandson of Minos. When an oracle predicted that Catreus would be slain by one of his offspring, Althaemenes went to Rhodes, where he founded Kamiros and built an altar of Zeus, surrounding it with magical metal bulls that would bellow if the island were invaded. Oracles, however, are not often wrong, and in later life Catreus sailed to Rhodes to visit his son, whom he missed dearly. He arrived at night, and what with the darkness and the bellowing of the metal bulls, Althaemenes failed to recognize his father and fellow-Cretans and slew them, thinking that they were invaders. When he realized his error in the morning he begged Mother Earth to swallow him up, which she did.

History

Inhabited since the Stone Age, Rhodes was conquered by the Minoans who built shrines to the moon at Philerimos, Lindos and Kamiros. The Achaeans took the island in the 15th century BC, and according to Homer sent nine ships to Troy, led by Tlepolemos, son of Heracles, who met an unhappy end before the Trojan walls. Before settling on Rhodes for its name, the island was often known as *Telchinia* for its dog-headed Telchines (*see* above), or *Ophioussa*, for its numerous vipers; even today villagers wear snake-repelling goatskin boots when working out in the fields.

The three cities mentioned by Homer—Lindos, Ialysos and Kamiros—long dominated the island's affairs. Rhodes' position along the main Mediterranean trade routes led to its early importance both in trade and naval power. Around 1000 BC, in response to the first Ionian confederacy, the three cities joined the Doric Hexapolis with Kos, Cnidos and Halicarnassus, a prototype EC that united the six city-states politically, religiously and economically. For four centuries the Doric Hexapolis prospered, establishing trade colonies from Naples to the Costa Brava in Spain.

The Founding of Rhodes City, and its Colossus

Rhodes sided with the Persians in both of their major campaigns against Greece, but upon their defeat switched sides and joined the Delian confederacy. In 480 BC, in order to prevent rivalries and increase their wealth and strength, Lindos, Ialysos, and Kamiros united to found one central capital, Rhodes, in Greek *Rodos*, the rose. Hippodamos of Miletus, the geometrician, designed the new town on a grid plan as he had with Piraeus, and the result was considered one of the most beautiful cities of ancient times, surrounded by walls encompassing a much greater area than that enclosed by the existing medieval walls. Celebrated schools of Philosophy, Philology and Oratory were founded, and the port had facilities far in advance of its time. Although Lindos, Kamiros and Ialysos continued to exist, they lost all their importance and most of their populations to the mighty new city they had created.

During the Peloponnesian War, Rhodes sided with whichever power was on top at any given time, and later supported the rising star of Alexander the Great. He in turn lent his support to Rhodes and its commerce, enabling the island to surpass politically-hostile Athens; thanks to Alexander, Rhodes dominated Mediterranean trade, its navy ruled the waves and policed the seas, and it founded colonies all over the known world. Rhodes' trade and navigation laws were later adopted by the Romans and remain the basis of maritime trade today.

Egypt was one of Rhodes' most lucrative trading partners, and in the struggles between the Macedonian generals after Alexander's death, Rhodes allied itself with Ptolemy, who had taken Egypt as his spoils. When another of Alexander's generals, the powerful Antigonas, ordered Rhodes to join him against Ptolemy, the Rhodians refused. Furious, Antigonas sent his son Dimitrios Poliorketes (the Besieger), the army of Syria and the Phoenician fleet to besiege the uppity islanders.

The ensuing year-long siege by one of the greatest generals of all time against the greatest city of the day has gone down in history, not only as a contest of great strength and endurance, but as a battle of wits. Over and over again Dimitrios would invent some new ingenious machine, such as the ten-storey Helepolis siege tower only to have it ingeniously foiled by the Rhodian defenders (who tripped up the Helepolis with a hidden, shallow ditch). After a year both sides grew weary of fighting and made a truce, Rhodes agreeing to assist Dimitrios' father Antigonas except in battles against Ptolemy.

So Dimitrios departed, leaving the Rhodians all of his vast siege machinery. This they either sold or melted down to construct a great bronze statue of Helios, their patron god of the sun. The famous sculptor from Lindos, Chares, was put in charge of the project, and in 290 BC, after twelve years of work and a cost of 20,000 pounds of silver, Chares completed the Colossus. Standing somewhere between 30 to 40m tall (at her crown the Statue of Liberty is 34m), the Colossus did not straddle the entrance of Rhodes harbour, as popularly believed, but probably stood near the present Castle of the Knights, gleaming bright in the sun, one of the Seven Wonders of the Ancient World. But of all the Wonders, the Colossus had the shortest lifespan; in 225 BC, an earthquake brought it crashing to the ground. It lay forlorn until AD 653 when the Saracens, who had captured Rhodes, sold it as scrap metal to a merchant from Edessa. According to legend, it took 900 camels to transport it to the ships.

In 164 BC, when they had repaired their city and walls, the Rhodians signed a peace treaty with Rome. Alexandria was their only rival in wealth, and tiny Delos, with all its trade concessions, their only rival in Mediterranean trade. A famous school of rhetoric on Rhodes attracted Roman students such as Cicero, Cassius, Julius Caesar and Mark Anthony. However, entanglement in Roman politics brought Rhodes trouble as well as privileges. When Rhodes supported Augustus after the death of Caesar, Cassius sacked the island city, destroyed or captured its fleet, and sent many of its treasures to Rome. It was a blow from which Rhodes never recovered; she lost control of her colonies and islands, and other Roman allies muscled in on her booming trade. In the first century St Paul preached on the island and converted many of the inhabitants; by the end of the Roman empire, Rhodes was a sleepy backwater.

Two Hundred Years of Knights

Byzantium brought many invaders and adventurers to Rhodes: Saracens, Genoese, Venetians and the Crusaders all passed through; in 1191 Richard the Lionheart and Philip Augustus of France came to Rhodes in search of mercenaries to fight in the Holy Land. After the fall of Jerusalem in 1291, the Knights

Hospitallers of St John took refuge on Cyprus, but by 1306 they had become interested in the wealthier and better positioned Rhodes. They asked the Emperor Andronicus Palaeologus to cede them the island in return for their loyalty, but after 1204 the rulers of Byzantium had learned better than to trust the Franks. The Knights, under Grand Master Foulques de Villaret, then took the matter into their own hands. Although they purchased the Dodecanese from the Genoese pirates who controlled them, it was a prize the Knights had to fight for; they had to spend their first three years subduing the Rhodians themselves.

By 1309, with the help of the Pope, the Knights were secure in their possession and began to build their hospital and inns in Rhodes town. They built eight inns or auberges in all, one for each of the 'tongues', or nationalities, in the Order (England, France, Germany, Italy, Castile, Aragon, Auvergne and Provence). Each tongue had a bailiff, and the eight bailiffs elected the Grand Master, who lived in a special palace. There were never more than 600 men in the Order, sworn to care for and protect pilgrims to the Holy Land. As time went on, they became more and more warlike, and although they built a hospital on Rhodes, defence and raiding were their primary concerns. Already wealthy to begin with, they were given a tremendous boost in 1312, when Pope Clement and Philip the Fair gave them the property of the recently-dissolved Knights Templars.

With their new fortune, the Knights of St John replaced the outdated Byzantine fortifications—and continued to replace them up until the 16th century, hiring the best Italian fortification engineers of the time, who perfected one of the most splendid defences of the day. The knights were besieged without success by the Sultan of Egypt in 1444 and by Mohammed II the Conqueror in 1480. Then in 1522 Suleiman the Magnificent moved in with 100,000 troops. The siege lasted for six months, and Suleiman was on the point of abandoning it when a traitor informed him that of the original 650 Knights, supplemented by 250 Genoese and Venetians and a thousand Greeks, only 180 survived, and they were on their last legs. The Sultan redoubled his efforts and the Knights at last were forced to surrender. They were permitted to leave in safety, with their Christian retainers and possessions, and set up a new headquarters in Malta. In 1831 they ended up in Rome.

The Turks were very fond of Rhodes, but for the Greeks their rule brought 400 years of darkness. When the inhabitants revolted during the War of Independence, the Turks reacted by slaughtering a quarter of the population. The Italian rulers in 1912 brought material prosperity but spiritual tyranny. They claimed that the island was their inheritance from the Knights of St John, although of course only an eighth of the knights had been Italian. Mussolini even had the Palace of the Grand Masters reconstructed (it and many other of the medieval buildings of the old town had been destroyed in the Great Gunpowder Explosion of 1856, when lightning struck a minaret and exploded a Turkish powder magazine). During the Second World War Rhodes remained in the hands of a German garrison until May 1945. By then most of the island's Jewish community, originally 2000 strong, had been sent off to the concentration camps. Rhodes, with the rest of the Dodecanese, officially joined Greece in 1945, whereupon the government declared it a free port, boosting its already great tourist potential.

Connections

By air: In summer at least five daily flights from Athens, and frequent connections with Thessaloniki, Herakleon (Crete), Karpathos, Kos, Kastellorizo and Kassos. Numerous charter flights.

By sea: daily ferry to Piraeus, Patmos, Leros, Kalymnos, Kos and Symi, 4–5 times a week with Crete, Santorini and Paros, less frequently with the other Cyclades and Rafina, and Samos, Chios, Lesbos, Limnos, Thessaloniki, Nissyros, Tilos, Halki, Karpathos, Kassos and Astypalaia. Daily excursion boats to Lindos, Symi, Marmaris (Turkey) and twice a week to Limassol (Cyprus) and Haifa (Israel).

By hydrofoil: daily with Kos, Patmos and Symi, three times a week with Leros, once a week with Samos, also connections with Kalymnos, Halki, Nissyros, Karpathos and Kastellorizo.

Tourist Information

NTOG, Papagon and Makariou St, ✆ (0241) 23 255.

City of Rhodes Tourist Information Centre, Sound and Light Sq, ✆ (0241) 35 945. Both have town maps and copies of the English events paper, *The Rhodes Tourist*.

Tourist Police, Papagon and Makariou St, ✆ (0241) 27 423.

British Consulate 17, 25th Martiou, ✆ (0241) 27 306.

Lindos Information, Lindos, ✆ (0244) 39 227

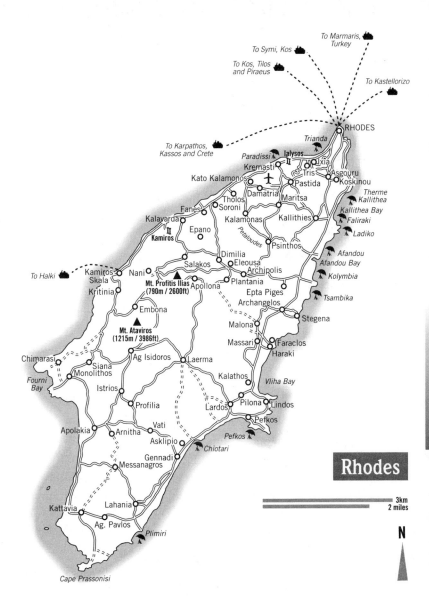

To Marmaris, Turkey
To Symi, Kos
To Kos, Tilos and Piraeus
To Kastellorizo
RHODES
Trianda
Paradissi
Ialysos
Kremasti
Ixia
Tris
Asgourou
Koskinou
To Karpathos, Kassos and Crete
Kato Kalamonas
Pastida
Therme Kallithea
Damatria
Maritsa
Kallithea Bay
Tholos
Soroni
Kalamonas
Kallithies
Faliraki
Fanes
Ladiko
Kalavarda
Epano
Petaloudes
Psinthos
Afandou
Kamiros
Afandou Bay
Dimilia
Salakos
Eleousa
Archipolis
Kolymbia
To Halki
Kamiros Skala
Nani
Plantania
Tsambika
Kritinia
Mt. Profitis Ilias (790m / 2600ft)
Apollona
Epta Piges
Archangelos
Embona
Stegena
Mt. Ataviros (1215m / 3986ft)
Malona
Massari
Faraclos
Chimarasi
Ag Isidoros
Laerma
Haraki
Siana
Monolithos
Kalathos
Vliha Bay
Fourni Bay
Istrios
Profilia
Lardos
Pilona
Lindos
Apolakia
Vati
Pefkos
Arnitha
Asklipio
Pefkos
Gennadi
Chiotari
Messanagros
Kattavia
Lahania
Ag. Pavlos
Plimiri
Cape Prassonisi

Rhodes

3km
2 miles

N

Spread across the northern tip of the island, **Rhodes** (pop. 39,000) is the largest town and capital of the Dodecanese. It presents an opulent face to the sea: the massive walls of the old town and the Castle of the Knights rise out of a lush sub-tropical garden; graceful minarets and the arcaded waterfront market, bright with strings of lightbulbs at night, add an exotic, Eastern touch. Monumental Italian public buildings loom to one side, trying to look serious, while opposite three windmills turn lazily. If your vessel is small, you'll disembark at the smallest of three harbours, **Mandraki**, guarded by a bronze doe and buck and the old fort of **Ag. Nikolaos**, with its small church. On larger ferry and cruise ships you'll enter the **commercial harbour**, nearer the Old Town walls.

These **walls** are a masterpiece of late medieval fortifications, and although you'll often be tempted to climb up for a walk or view, *access is by guided tour only, Tues and Sat at 2.45pm*. Constructed on the foundation of the old Byzantine walls under four of the most ambitious Grand Masters, d'Aubusson, d'Amboise, del Carretto and Villiers de l'Isle Adam, they stretch 4km and average 12m thick. They are curved to better deflect missiles, and the landward sides were safe-guarded by a 30m wide moat. Each national group of Knights was assigned its own bastion and towers to defend. Of the many gates that linked the walled Old Town with the village outside, the most magnificent is the **Gate of Emery d'Amboise** near the Palace of the Grand Masters, built in 1512. The Turks blocked up the two harbour gates; they also made a law that all Greeks had to be outside the inner walls by sundown or forfeit their heads.

Within the Inner Walls

The town within these walls was called the **Collachium**, where the Knights could retreat if the outer wall were taken. Most of their buildings are here, begin-ning with the **Palace of the Grand Masters** (*8.30–3, closed Mon*), or Kastelli, as the Greeks call it. Construction of this citadel, on the site of a sanctuary of Helios, was completed in the 14th century and it survived intact under the Turks, who used it as a prison until it accidentally blew up in the Great Gunpowder Explosion of 1856. Mussolini, fancying himself a Grand Master, ordered it be reconstructed as his summer villa. The Italians filled it with lovely Roman mosaics and Hellenistic sculptures from Kos, a hodgepodge of Renaissance furniture and installed an elevator and modern plumbing, but the war broke out and ended before Il Duce could ever make use of it. In the garden below the palace a Sound and Light show is held most evenings (*in English on Mon and Tues at 8.15pm, Wed, Fri and Sat at 9.15pm, Thurs 10.15pm*).

Quiet, cobblestoned Ippoton Street ('of the Knights') has been carefully spared souvenir claptrap, the better to evoke the medieval city. It leads down from the palace into the centre of the Collachium, passing first the arcaded **Loggia** where the Knights would muster, then several of their inns: the **Inn of Provence** on the left and the two buildings of the **Inn of Spain** on the right, then the French chapel and elaborate **Inn of France** (1509), adorned with escutcheons and crocodile gargoyles; as there were always more French knights than any other 'tongue', their inn was the most spacious. Opposite is the handsome Catalan **House of Villaragut**; further down, the **Inn of Italy** (1519), and at the end of the street, the 13th-century **St Mary**, a Byzantine church used by the Knights as their cathedral until they built their own—destroyed in the Gunpowder debacle. St Mary's is now used as a little **Byzantine Museum**. To the right, at the end of Ippoton Street, **Inn of England** (1483) was abandoned by the English Knights in 1534, when the Pope excommunicated Henry VIII. It was hard hit by an earthquake in 1851, then rebuilt by the British, bombed and rebuilt again in 1947. The British consul of Rhodes (*see* above for the address) has the key to it.

Across the street stands the Flamboyant Gothic Hospital of the Knights, built between 1440 and 1481 and restored by the Italians in 1918, which now houses the **Archaeology Museum** (*daily except Mon 8–3*). The long ward, where the Knight's surgeons cared for patients in elaborate canopy beds, still has coats-of-arms and other heraldic devices. In the sculpture gallery the star attraction is the kneeling *Aphrodite of Rhodes* (90 BC), combing out her hair after emerging from the sea; it was she who provided the title for Lawrence Durrell's *Reflections on a Marine Venus*. Other rooms contain funerary stelae, Mycenaean jewellery, and a mosaic from Karpathos.

Through the arch just to the north, charming Argyrokastro Square has the most beautiful auberge of all, the 15th-century **Inn of Auvergne** (now a cultural centre) with a **fountain** reconstructed from bits found in the Byzantine fort at Arnitha. Here, too, is the 14th-century **Palace of the Armeria**, constructed by Grand Master Roger de Pins as the Knight's first hospital on Rhodes. The

Museum of Decorative Arts (*8.30–3, closed Mon*), has folk arts and handicrafts from all over the Dodecanese, including costumes, embroideries and a reconstruction of a traditional room. In Plateia Symis, the next square north, are the ruins of a 3rd-century BC **temple of Aphrodite**, discovered by the Italians in 1922. Fragments of another temple of the same epoch, dedicated to **Dionysos**, are in a corner behind the Ionian and Popular Bank.

The Turkish Quarter

South of the Collachium of the Knights is the former Turkish bazaar and Old Town's shopping district, centred around bustling **Sokratous Street**, thick with tourist and duty-free luxury shops (many on the isle of eternal sun sell nothing but umbrellas and fur coats). On the top of Sokratous St stands the slender minaret of the lovely **Mosque of Suleiman**, built in 1523 by Suleiman to celebrate his conquest of Rhodes (now closed). The **Turkish library** (1793) opposite contains rare Persian and Arabian manuscripts and illuminated Korans.

Off Sokratous Street, the Turkish Quarter dissolves into a zigzag of narrow streets, where charming Turkish balconies of latticed wood project beside crumbling stone arches and houses built directly over the street. On the square off Archelaos Street is the hammam, or **Turkish baths**, built in 1765 (*Wed–Sat 7am–7pm, Tues 1–7, closed Sun and Mon, reduced adm on Thurs and Fri*). Although heavily bombed, they have been restored to full working order. Another old mosque, **Ibrahim Pasha** (1531) is off Sophocles St; its minaret was restored by the Italians.

On Hippocrates Square, where Sokratous St turns into Aristotelous St, stands the **Kastellania Palace**, built by d'Amboise in 1507, perhaps as a tribunal or commercial exchange for the Knights. It stands at the head of Pithagora St, the main street of **Evriaki**, the Jewish quarter. Continuing east along Aristotelous St, the **Plateia Evrion Martyron** (the Square of Hebrew Martyrs), recalls the inhabitants of Rhodes sent off to die in the concentration camps. The so-called **Admiral's Palace** is here, with a bronze seahorse fountain; it was more likely the seat of Rhodes' bishop. From here, Pindarou St continues to the ruins of **Our Lady of Victory**, built by the Knights in thanksgiving for their defeat of the Turks in 1480. The Turkish and Jewish Quarters offer many other little cobbled lanes to explore, dotted with old frescoed churches converted into mosques and converted back again.

New Town

Outside the walls, facing the little port of Mandraki, is a seafront row of sweet shops, a good bet for a quick snack; behind them is the **Market** and bus depot for Rhodes' west coast. Beyond them is a fairly austere ensemble of public buildings built by the fascists in the 1920s—post office, theatre, city hall. The Italians also left Rhodes some attractive buildings: the fine Venetian-Gothic **Governor's Palace** and the cathedral **Evangelismos**, designed after the church of St John, the Knights' cathedral (demolished in 1856); the fountain is a copy of Viterbo's Gothic Fontana Grande.

For the Turks, Rhodes was an island paradise, and many Moslem notables in exile (including a Shah of Persia) chose to spend the rest of their lives here. Many lie buried in the cemetery north of the theatre, next to the **Mosque of Murad Reis**, named for the admiral of the Egyptian Sultan, killed during the siege of Rhodes, and buried in a turban-shaped tomb, or *turbeh*. The mosque has a lovely, though crumbling, minaret. Next to it looms the grand, forlorn art Deco Hotel des Roses, awaiting resurrection of some kind, and a long, crowded stretch of public beach. At the northernmost tip of the island is the **Aquarium** (*daily 9am –9pm*), said to be the only one in the Balkans, with tanks of Mediterranean fish and sea turtles, and a startling horror show collection of stuffed denizens of the deep, their twisted grimaces the result not of any prolonged agony but amateur taxidermy. Another beach stretches from the aquarium down the west coast, but it's often battered by strong winds and frequently deserted.

Many places hire out bicycles, scooters and cars, but any reasonably active visitor can walk south of the New Town to the ancient acropolis of Rhodes, **Monte Smith**, named after Admiral Sydney Smith who kept track of Napoleon's Egyptian escapades from here. On the way (North Epirous St) are the ruins of an **Asklepieion**, dedicated to the god of healing, and a **Cave of the Nymphs**. On the top of Mt Smith, the Italians have partly reconstructed a 2nd-century BC Doric **temple of Pythian Apollo** who was later associated with Rhodian Helios. A few columns also remain of temples of Zeus and Athena, and you can trace the outline of a 3rd-century BC **stadium**. The **ancient theatre**, the only square one on the islands, has been reconstructed, and hosts Classical dramas in July (*see* the Tourist Office for programme details).

Other Rhodian distractions include the **Casino** at the Grand Hotel on Akti Miaoulis where the guests may win or lose their fortunes at roulette and baccarat. **Folkdances** by the Nelly Dimoglou company are performed in the Old City Theatre (*nightly except Sat, June–Oct; for information © (0241) 20 157 or*

27 524). Two km from the centre, lovely **Rodini Park** is where Aeschines built his School of Rhetoric in 330 BC—there's a rock-cut tomb from the same period, a later tomb of the Ptolemies, and ruins of a Roman aqueduct. The Knights grew their medicinal herbs here, and now in July and August merry drinkers join Rodini's peacocks for a **Wine Festival**; *open from 7pm to 1am,* buses transport revellers to and from Mandraki harbour. Try Rhodes' own wines: *Chevaliers de Rhodes*, *Lindos* and *Embonas* as well as other Greek vintages, celebrated with music, dance and food.

Bus connections for points east on the island depart from Papagou St in Rhodes town; for the west they leave from the market. **Excursion boats** to Lindos and Symi and the diving school boat dock near here, in Mandraki, while other caiques leave in the mornings for the beaches at Lardos, Tsambika, Faliraki, Kallithea, Ladiko, Kolymbia and Lindos.

Around Rhodes: Down the East Coast

The sandy shore just southeast of Rhodes town is lined with luxury hotels, from the coves of **Kallithea**, an old, disused thermal spa in a magnificent kitsch Italianate-Moorish building; to **Faliraki**, a major resort near a long beach, popular with the 18–30s crowd. The fast food, wet T-shirt competitions, throbbing nightlife, and masses of watersports conspire to make Faliraki over-commercialized.

Afandou has the ultimate rarity in this part of the world—a golf course with 18 holes as well as tennis courts. There are fine beaches in the bay below and next to **Ladiko**, and a beautiful pebbly beach named Anthony Queen (sic) after Anthony Quinn, so named because *The Guns of Navarone* was filmed here. There are boat trips to Anthony Queen Beach from Rhodes town. At **Kolymbia** down the coast, farms are irrigated thanks to the nymph-haunted pool set in the pines in the hamlet of **Epta Piges**, the 'Seven Springs'. Epta Piges is a wooded beauty spot, very tranquil with peacocks, lush vegetation and a small streamside taverna. You can paddle through the pitch black subterranean channel; this then opens out into a lake. The Greeks wade back up again, going against the flow of human traffic.

Long sandy **Tsambika** beach is very popular, set in a cliff-edged bay. The road then goes down to the charming village of **Stegena**, set by a shingle beach in a pretty bay.

Continuing down the main highway, **Archangelos** (pop. 3500), the largest village on Rhodes, has a North African feel, its little white houses spread under a ruined castle of the Knights. Its churches, **Archangelos Gabriel** and

Archangelos Michael are considered two of the prettiest on the island; another nearby, **Ag. Theodoroi**, has 14th-century frescoes. The villagers have a reputation for their musicianship, their carpets, pottery and bootmaking; local cobblers can make footwear to order.

One of the strongest citadels on Rhodes towers on a promontory below Malona called **Faraclos**. Faraclos was occupied by pirates, until the Knights gave them the boot, repaired the walls and used the fort as a prison. Even after the rest of the island fell to Suleiman, Faraclos held, only surrendering after a long determined siege. The nearby fishing hamlet of **Haraki** has a lovely shaded esplanade running along the enclosed bay; there's excellent swimming and postcard views of Lindos.

Lindos

Dramatically situated on a promontory high over the sea, beautiful Lindos is Rhodes' second town and a National Historic Landmark. Of the island's three ancient cities it was the most important, first inhabited around 2000 BC; the first temple on its magnificent acropolis was erected in 1510 BC. It grew rich from its many colonies, especially Parthenope (modern Naples). Lindos owed its precocious importance to its twin natural harbours, the only ones on Rhodes, and to its 6th-century BC ruler Cleoboulos, one of the Seven Sages of Greece: his maxim 'Measure is in all the best' (Moderation in all things) was engraved on the oracle at Delphi and his reservoir supplies water to Lindos to this day. The town was important enough to merit a visit from St Paul; the Knights fortified it, and during the Turkish occupation, merchants from Lindos handled most of the island's trade. Their elegant flat-roofed 'Captain's mansions', built between the 15th and 17th centuries, line the serpentine pebbled lanes and stairs. Below town are two fine beaches, while high overhead is Lindos' **Acropolis**, one of the most stunningly sited in all of Greece—accessible by foot or hired donkey (*daily except Mon 8.30–3*). The route up is lined with billowing blouses, tablecloths and other items put out for sale by the good women of Lindos, who sit by the wares, needles clicking away as if they'd made it all themselves (most of it is mass-produced and imported).

Near the top, before the Knights' stairway, note the prow of a trireme carved into the living rock. This once served as a podium for a statue of Agesander, priest of Poseidon, sculpted by Pythocretes, best known for his *Victory of Samothrace*. At the top of the stair are two vaulted rooms and to the right, a crumbling 13th-century **church of St John**. Continue straight on for the raised Dorian arcade, or stoa of Lindian Athenas, the patron goddess of the city. From here the 'stairway to Heaven' leads up to the mighty foundations of the **Propylaea** and on the edge of the precipice, the **temple of Athena** itself, of which only seven columns are standing. Both were built in the 4th century BC and reconstructed by the Italians. In ancient times, the temple was celebrated for its golden inscription of Pindar's Seventh Ode, now gone without a trace. The views from the acropolis are extraordinary, especially towards the round azure pool of the small harbour, or **St Paul's Bay** where St Paul landed in AD 58; its small white chapel has a huge *paniyiri* on 28 June. The larger harbour was the home port of Lindos' navy, 500 ships strong.

Many of the houses in the village have collections of Lindian ware, faience painted with highly stylized Oriental motifs first manufactured in Asia Minor; the oldest ones date back to Byzantium. Potters who took refuge in Lindos taught their craft to the islanders. Some of their finest works are displayed in the town's most lavish house, the Papakonstandis mansion (or **Lindos museum**). Lindos' reputation for embroideries dates back to the time of Alexander the Great. A *sperveri*, the fine bridal dress that all Lindian girls once wore, can be seen at **Kashines house**. Among the shady plane trees and restaurants in the Plateia where the bus stops, the **church of the Panayia** (1479) has good 18th-century frescoes. To the northeast of the larger harbour, the cylindrical **tomb of Cleoboulos** actually pre-dates Cleoboulos, and in the Middle Ages was converted into a church.

In more recent times, Lindos has become heavily touristed. During the high season, the cobbled streets are heaving with tourists and day-trippers.The beautiful, sandy Pallas Beach is packed by day, then the crowds migrate to the bars at night. The locals have adjusted to this since its hey-day in the swinging sixties, but they've become rather jaded with the annual circus and aren't very friendly. With a preservation order to prevent high-rise development, Lindos is still visually stunning. If you want to avoid the hordes, it's best to go in spring or autumn; during the summer it's one of the hottest spots on Rhodes.

Around South Rhodes: Lindos to Monolithos

Lardos, west of Lindos, is a pretty little valley village. The beach below Lardos has sand dunes; indeed the whole southeast coast of Rhodes is a series of beaches, many deserted, although good fish tavernas and rooms to rent may be found at **Pefkos**, just south of Lindos, which is being extensively developed with holiday apartments and now has fish and chips on sale. Other progressively quieter beaches with tavernas are at **Chiotari** (where you can detour inland to the medieval hill village **Asklipio**, with a frescoed church of 1060), **Gennadi** and **Plimiri**. As you approach the southernmost tip of Rhodes, **Cape Prassonisi**, the desolate landscape may as well be the end of the world. You can spend the night at Skiadi Monastery nearby.

Heading up the west coast from Katavia are yet more beaches and scenic views (often battered by strong winds) on the way to **Mesanagros**, an old fashioned mountain village. In the Kourkourtahi valley below, **Apolakia** is a charming village that produces the best watermelons and marriage feasts on Rhodes. It has a few eating spots and rooms for rent. Further up the west coast, **Monolithos** is the most important village of the region, the monolith in its name a 200m high rocky spur rising above the sea, capped by a castle built by the Grand Master d'Aubusson. A fairly difficult footpath winds to the top, where you can see the frescoed chapel of **Ag. Panteleimon** (15th century), and at sunset a view across to little Halki. Below, the shady bay of **Fourni** has a beach, and ancient cave dwellings, and not far away is the monastery Ag. Anastasia. The road continues through **Siana**, an attractive old stone village built on a hillside, offering a superb view of the coast and islets; it's famous for its superb wild honey.

In the face of all of Rhodes' cosmopolitan urges, **Embona** in the mountains keeps to its traditional ways. The dances of the women are exceptionally beautiful, as are the homespun costumes that a few older people wear every day. Increasingly though, Embona's purity is polluted by tour buses from Rhodes town. The island's highest peak, **Mt Ataviros** (1215m) is a tough 2-hour climb from Embona. Here Althaemenes is said to have built the temple of Zeus Atavros, although little remains of it now. But there are views of the whole island from the summit, and on a clear day they say you can see Crete from the peak; perhaps poor Althaemenes used to come up here when he longed, like all Cretans, for his mother island. Althaemenes supposedly founded the village below Embona, **Kritinia**, which he named in honour of Crete.

Kamiros and the West Coast

But Althaemenes' most celebrated foundation was **Kamiros**, one of the three Dorian cities of Rhodes, destroyed by an earthquake in the 2nd century BC, abandoned in the Dark Ages and covered with the dust of centuries and forgotten until 1859, when two archaeologists, Biliotti and Salzmann, began excavating where some villagers had uncovered a few graves. The city they eventually brought to light is well preserved; the **cemetery**, in particular, rendered many beautiful items and in archaeological terms was one of the richest ever discovered in Greece. An excellent water and drainage system, supplied by a large reservoir, served the many excavated Hellenistic-era houses. Also to see are the baths, the agora with its rostrum for public speeches, the agora's Great Stoa with its Doric portico, and two temples, one 5th-century BC dedicated to Athena and the other, from the 3rd century, possibly to Apollo Kamiros (*daily except Mon 8.30–3*).

Kamiros Skala, a small fishing harbour about 16km south of Kamiros, was ancient Kamiros' port, although these days it more modestly sends out local ferries for Halki. There are two good fish tavernas here, both popular for lunch. **Fanes**, further north, has a long, narrow stony beach with a few tavernas.

Inland, on a high hill over the village of **Salakos** are the ruins of another medieval fort; Salakos itself is beloved for its shade and fresh water from the Spring of the Nymphs. This region, with its cedar and pine forests and views of the sea, is one of the prettiest in Rhodes for walks. Further up the road leads to **Mt Profitis Ilias** (790m). The trees here belong to the Prophet Elijah, who according to legend strikes down any sinner who dares to cut one down. The chief settlements on its slopes are **Apollona** with a museum of popular art and **Eleousa** with a pretty Byzantine church.

Another enchanting spot, if you manage to get there before or after the tour buses, is **Petaloudes**, the '**Valley of the Butterflies**'. Sliced by a tiny stream and laughing waterfalls, the long, narrow valley has a roof of fairytale trees, crossed by a winding path and little wooden bridges. From June to September tiger moths (*Callimorpha quadripuntaria*) flock here, attracted by the sweet resin of the storax tree, which is used in the making of frankincense (*daily 9–6*). Just up the road the monastery, **Panayia Kalopetra**, claimed to have been built in 1782 by Alexander Ypsilantis, grandfather of the the leader of the Greek uprising in 1821.

Below Kalamonas is the tiny village of **Paradissi**, a useful waiting spot next to the airport; it even has a small beach.

Kremasti is a village busy with Greek soldiers (there are large barracks here) and foreign tourists, and is best known for its wonder-working icon, Panayias Kremasti, occasioning one of biggest *paniyiri* in the Dodecanese, lasting from 15–23 August. At the climax on the 23rd the villagers don traditional costumes and dance a very fast *sousta*. On nearby **Mt Philerimos** stood Orychoime, the acropolis of the ancient city of **Ialysos**. Ialysos, the least important of the three Dorian cities, was situated near present-day Trianda village, but its acropolis presents the greatest interest. Built over the foundations of a Phoenician temple are the remains of a 3rd-century BC **temple of Athena** and a way down below, a reconstructed 4th-century **Doric fountain**. An early Christian basilica from around the 5th century still has its cruciform font and frescoes from the 1300s. The **cemetery** yielded finds from Mycenaean to Hellenistic times. At the Byzantine fortress at Orychoime, **Our Lady of Philerimos**, the Genoese fought John Cantacuzene in 1248. There are a few Byzantine churches nearby; the one used by the Knights had both Catholic and Orthodox altars.

Nearby **Trianda**, the modern name for Ialysos, is the west coast's main resort with wall-to-wall hotels, blending into **Ixia**. Ialysos was settled by Minoans in 1600 BC, and may have been damaged in the explosions and subsequent tidal wave from Santorini; more recently it has been devastated by masses of grotty bars and 'English breakfast' caffs. The still functioning mosque at **Asgouru** was originally a church of St John.

Festivals

In August, dance festivals at Kallithies, Maritsa and Embona; 29–30 July, Ag. Soula at Soroni, an occasion for donkey races; 28 June at Lindos; 14 June, Profitis Ammos at Faliraki; 26 July, Ag. Panteleimonos at Siana; 7 September, at Monastery Tsambikas, when barren women go to pray for fertility; 14–22 August at Kremasti; 26 August, Ag. Fanourious in the Old Town; 5 September, Ag. Trias near Rhodes; 13 September, Stavros at Apollona and Kallithies; 26 September, Ag. Ioannis Theologos at Artamiti; 18 October, Ag. Lukos at Afandou; 7 November at Archangelos; Lenten carnival just before Easter; Scandinavian midsummer festivities in Rhodes town (yes, really).

© (0241–)   ### Where to Stay

Rhodes has a plethora of accommodation in every class and price range. Many places are booked solid by package tours 12 months of the year, but there are so many rooms available on the island that you're bound to find something without booking, although it may be inconvenient.

luxury

Most of the luxury hotels are in Ixia. **Rodos Palace Hotel**, © 25222, fax 25350 also has apartments and bungalows, indoor and outdoor pools, a sauna, gym, tennis courts and all the trimmings. In Rhodes town, at the top of the list, is the deluxe **Grand Hotel Astir Palace** on Akti Miaouli,

✆ 26 284, fax 35589 with the island's casino, a nightclub, tennis courts and what's reputed to be the largest swimming pool in the country.

expensive

With similar facilities at a lower price, the **Miramare Beach** is directly on the beach in Ixia, just south of Rhodes town, ✆ 24 251/4, and offers bungalows as well as hotel rooms. Also in Ixia the **Rodos Bay**, ✆ 23 661/5, has a pool and bungalows by its private beach, while the rooftop restaurant has one of Rhodes' finest views. One of the nicer places in Faliraki is the **Rodos Beach Hotel**, which also has bungalows, ✆ 85 471. In Lindos, where it's illegal to build hotels, nearly every other house has been converted into a holiday villa, and if you want to stay at one you're best to book through a holiday company before you arrive. If you do want to take pot luck, try the **Pension Electra**, ✆ 31 2266, or seek help from **Pallas Travel**, ✆ 31 275, who have rooms and villas in Lindos. Outside Lindos is the **Lindos Bay Hotel**, ✆ (0244) 42 212, fax 42210, on the beach and within walking distance of town. Three km from Lindos, in the bay of Vlyha, the **Steps of Lindos** has luxury rooms and facilities, and offers a variety of watersports, ✆ (0244) 42 262. To get away from the sun-and-fun crowds, there are two Swiss chalets that lost their way and ended up in the eastern Mediterranean, near the top of pine-forested Mt Profitis Ilias, to be specific. These are the **Elafos** (the stag) and the **Elafina** (doe), both class A, quiet and comfortable and not as silly as they sound. The telephone number is (0244) 21 221 for both.

moderate

There are scores of class B, C and D hotels in and around Rhodes town, especially in the new quarter. One of the best value here is the **Ambassadeur**, a class C hotel at 53 Othonos & Amalias, ✆ 24 679. **Marie Rodos**, by Elli Beach, 2 minutes walk from the town centre, at 7 Kos St, ✆ 30 577, has a swimming pool and English-style pub. Other, less expensive (on the whole) beach hotels run down the west coast of the island solidly to Paradissi. If you want to be in Mandraki harbour to catch ferries to Symi and other islands, then the **Hotel Spartalis** (B), ✆ 24 371, is basic but handy and just over the road from the quay. It has a nice breakfast terrace and harbour views. The **Hotel Hermes** (C), ✆ 27 677, opposite is also useful if you're just passing through and allows you to store luggage.

Most of the inexpensive (and to be honest, the most interesting) places to stay are in the old town. Look around Omirou Street, where a clean and friendly spot is **Steve's Pension** at no. 60, ℂ 24 357. Another very informal pension is the **Apollon** at no. 28, with laundry facilities and hot showers. **Athinea**, 45 Pythagora, also has decent rooms and shared facilities. A must for budget travellers, **Pithagora**, 56 Fanouriou, is a friendly little place for the young, or young at heart. It's one of the cheapest places in town; even if it's full, drop into their miniscule bar to swap travelling yarns. At **Iliana Hotel**, 1 Gavala Street, ℂ 30 251, childen under 10 are free; **Minos Pension**, 5 Omirou, ℂ 31 813 is okay; **Cavo d'Oro Hotel**, 14 Kisthiniou, ℂ 36 980, is a 13th Century house restored by the owner and his German wife (he'll even meet you from the ferry); **Pension Andreas** 28D Omirou, ℂ 34 156, has French/Greek management; and **Hotel St Nikolas**, 61 Ippodhamou, ℂ 34 561, does excellent bed and breakfast (the Greek/Danish proprietors also have a cheaper pension, booking essential). Cheap accommodation can be difficult to find in the purpose-built resorts. In the southern half of the island the pickings are sparse—little rooms over tavernas and the like. There are **campsites** at Lardos, 2km from Lindos, ℂ (0244) 44 203, and at Faliraki, ℂ 85 358.

Eating Out

in Rhodes Town

Getting lost in the old city and finding your own little taverna is the best way to enjoy eating out in Rhodes town. After an aperitif in Ippocratous Square, possibly at **Café Brazil**, take the plunge into the maze of backstreets—in some of the industrious little shops you'll see tailors and cobblers still hard at work—and come across several decent tavernas, the most reasonable and authentic places to eat in town. **Alexis**, on Socratous St, is expensive but good, and specializes in fish. Nearby, **Argo** is a local favourite, with all the Greek standards. If you're down to your last 1000 dr. before your ferry or flight, eat at the **Astra**, underneath the Sydney Hotel in Apellou St, where you'll get change from 600 dr. for chicken and chips, plus a drink. Also in the old town, try **Taverna Kostas**, 62 Pythagora, friendly and good value; **Nireas**, 22 Plateia Sofokleous, for Greek home cooking, and the nearby **Taverna Sea Star** for good fish; **Restaurant Pandesia**, Plateia Aristostofanous, has authentic and unusual dishes; don't be put off by the photos outside. One of the cheapest places to eat in Rhodes is the market, where numerous greasy spoons offer several varieties of grilled meats and souvlaki. If you have a taste for Scandinavian food there are many possibilities. **The Danish House** on Akti Miaouli is the real thing, serving *smorgasbord* and other specialities; 3500 dr. for dinner, with healthy belts of Danish beer and schnapps. The **Mascot**, on Sofokleous St, is worth a visit for its ultra-kitsch décor alone—artificial tree, plastic waterfall, model of the Colossus—and the food is tops: souvlaki stuffed with garlic and cheese, oven-baked tomatoes with cheese and garlic, and decent local Rhodian wines (2000 dr.). Incidentally, the local sparkling white wine from CAIR makes a superb Buck's Fizz, so start squeezing those oranges now.

outside Rhodes

Outside Rhodes, try not to miss **Ta Koupia**, on the road to Trianda (best to take a short taxi ride); wonderfully decorated with antique Greek furniture, the food matches the décor in quality—excellent *meze* and upmarket Greek dishes with an Eastern influence (4000 dr.). Also in Ixia, the **Restaurant Tzaki** is known for its *mezedes*, and has bouzouki music. **Alatopipero** (Salt and Pepper) at 76 M. Petridi St in the new town is a taverna/ouzerie specialising in Greek nouvelle cuisine, and has a good wine list. On the road to Lindos, near the seven palms, more refined Greek cuisine can be sampled at **The Old Story**, with a zany ex-actor owner and particularly good vegetarian dishes (2500 dr.). Most tavernas in Koskinou are like the village itself, small and typically Greek. **Yiannis** here serves meze, ouzo and a meal for under 2000 dr. Don't be put off by the elegant air of **Le Chef**, also in Koskinou. It looks like a luxury restaurant, and serves international fare (good steaks and schnitzel), but at everyday prices (2–3000 dr.). For good fish tavernas head for Kamiros Skala, where the tavernas on the beach are popular. In Lindos international cuisine rules and prices are high. **Mavriko's** just off the square is outstanding, and **Xenomania** also has a great menu is you want to splash out. On a more modest budget, **Dionysos Taverna** has all the usual Greek favourites in a rooftop setting while **Maria's** and **Agostino's** tavernas are good, cheap and cheerful.

Dhiakou St in the new town is heaving with bars and packed at night with British and Scandinavian tourists. You can hang out for coffee and people-watch at **Dolce Italia**, take in a movie at the **Rodon Cinema**, sample the cocktails from the **Underground** to **Tramps**, or the **Symposium Garden** in the old town. **La Scala** is the best disco in town. Lindos has scores of bars, try **Lindos By Night**.

Symi

Few other islands have the crisp brightness of Symi, with its amphitheatre of half-restored, half-derelict neo-Classical mansions, stacked one on top of the other like a Cubist lemon meringue. There are few trees to block the sun, for unlike its neighbour Rhodes, Symi is an arid island, unable to support many visitors. Most who do come arrive and depart on the excursion boat from Rhodes, and when they're gone, Symi regains much of its serenity. Although it can get as hot as a cat on a tin roof from July to September because it's in a basin and the heat beats off the surrounding rock, its climate is particularly pleasant in spring and late autumn.

History

According to legend, Symi was a princess of Ialysos on Rhodes, who was abducted by Glaukos, the builder of the *Argo*, before she ended up on the little island that bears her name. If such was the case, Princess Symi's descendants inherited Glaukos' shipbuilding skills; throughout history Symi was famous for its ships.

Pelasgian walls in Chorio attest to the prehistoric settlement of Symi. In the *Iliad* Homer tells how the island mustered three ships for the Achaeans at Troy, led by King Nireus. After Achilles, Nireus was the most beautiful of all the Greeks, but as in Achilles' case, beauty was no defence against the Trojans. In historic times Symi was part of the Dorian Hexapolis, dominated by Rhodes. The Romans fortified the acropolis at Chorio; the Byzantines converted it into a fort, which was renovated by the first Grand Master of the Knights of Rhodes, Foulques de Villaret. From Symi's Kastro the Knights could signal to Rhodes, and they favoured swift Symiot skiffs for their raiding activities.

Thanks to the Knights, Symi began to know a certain measure of prosperity through shipbuilding and trade. When Suleiman the Magnificent came to the Dodecanese in 1522, the Symiotes, known as the most daring divers in the Aegean, avoided the inevitable invasion by offering him the most beautiful sponges he had ever seen. A consignment of sponges became Symi's yearly tribute to the Sultan in return for a relative degree of independence. Like the Knights, the Turks made use of the swift Symiot ships, this time for relaying messages. In order to keep Symi thriving, the Sultan declared it a free port and gave the inhabitants the rights to dive freely for sponges in Turkish waters.

Little Symi thus became the third richest island of the Dodecanese, a position it held from the 17th to the 19th centuries. Large mansions were constructed befitting the islanders' new status; many bought forests in Asia Minor. Schools thrived. Even after certain privileges were withdrawn because of its participation in the 1821 revolution, Symi continued to flourish. The Italian occupation and the steamship, however, spelt the end of the little island's fortunes: the Italians closed the lands of Asia Minor and the steamship killed the demand for wooden sailing vessels altogether; during the Italian tenure the population of Symi dropped from 23,000 to 6000 at the outbreak of World War II. At its end the treaty giving the Dodecanese to Greece was signed on Symi on 8 May 1945, but this handover wasn't officially enacted until 7 March 1948 .

Connections

At least three tourist boats a day from Rhodes; plus the island's own ferries, Symi I and Symi II, daily. Hydrofoils from Rhodes and Kos; two ferries a week with the other Dodecanese. Excursion boats daily around the island.

Tourist Information

Clock Tower, Yialos, ✆ (0241) 71 215.

Yialos and Chorio

Symi's capital is divided into two quarters: Yialos around the harbour and Chorio, the older settlement on the hill. In **Yialos** you'll find most of Symi's tourist facilities and what is left of its shipyards. In honour of its shipbuilding tradition, a copy of the stone trireme in Lindos has been carved into the rock on the waterfront. Nearby, the restaurant **Les Katerinettes** has a plaque commemorating the signing of the 1945 treaty of the Dodecanese. At the end of the harbour behind the ungainly concrete clock tower and the statue of the fishing boy is small

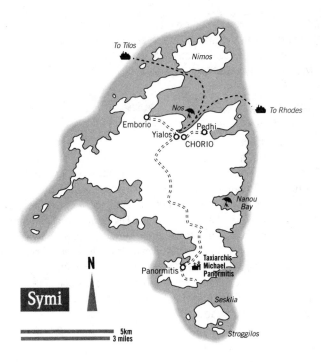

Charani bay where ships wait to be finished or repaired. Here one can see traces of the bombing during World War II, but many of the houses are now being renovated. There are no beaches near Yialos, but **Nos**, at the end of Charani, is where the local people swim; it's also the first place that day-trippers descend on. It's better to walk on to **Emborio**, a pretty harbour with a good taverna.

Most of the neo-Classical houses in Yialos date from the 19th century, while older architecture dominates at **Chorio**, connected to the port by road or mansion-lined stairway, called the Kali Strata, with nearly 400 steps from Plateia tis Skala. By the derelict windmills, a **stone monument** was erected by the Spartans for their victory over the Athenians off the coast of Symi. Houses in Chorio are similar to Cycladic houses, small and asymmetrical, often with neo-Classical elements incorporated into their doorways and windows. Many houses have very lovely interiors with carved woodwork.

Among the most interesting buildings at Chorio are the **19th-century pharmacy;** the fortress-mansion **Chatziagapitos;** and the churches with their pebble mosaics of evil mermaids sinking hapless ships. The island's **museum** up at Chorio houses objects dating from Hellenistic times to the present. Up at the top, the **Kastro's** Byzantine and medieval walls were built from an ancient temple of Athena; the coat-of-arms belongs to d'Aubusson; the church near the walls, **Megali Panayia**, has good frescoes and post-Byzantine icons.

Around Symi

From Chorio it's a half-hour walk to **Pedhi**, the only fertile area on Symi. On a small bay, it has a beach and is the best place on the island to camp out. A new road from Chorio travels to the extreme southern tip of the island and Symi's main attraction, the 18th-century **monastery of Taxiarchis Michael Panormitis** (in the summer there are also caiques, and the tourist boat from Rhodes often stops there). Archangel Michael of Panormitis bay is Symi's patron saint and a big favourite of all Greek sailors. The carved wooden **iconostasis** in the monastery church is remarkable, while the walls are liberally adorned with frescoes. Gold and silver ship ex-votos dangle from the ceiling, and the **sacristy** contains more rich gifts from faithful sailors, and little bottles which drifted to shore with money for the monastery. Panormitis also has one of the best beaches on Symi, and there are restaurants and cafés and rooms to rent, more in the spirit of a resort than a religious sanctuary.

Sesklia, an islet near Panormitis, also belongs to the monastery. Its ancient name was Teutlousa, and Thucydides writes that it was here that the Athenians took refuge after their defeat by the Spartan navy during the Peloponnesian War. A few Pelasgian walls remain, and there are also a few ruins on the nearby islet **Stroggilos**.

The other sites of Symi are also religious in nature. Of its 77 churches, the most interesting is **Michael Roukouniotis**, an hour's walk from Yialos. Built in the 18th century, it is a curious combination of Gothic and folk architecture, and holds its feast day beneath an old umbrella-shaped cypress. **Ag. Emilianos** is on an islet in the bay of the same name, connected to the shore by a causeway with a pleasant pebbly beach nearby. Another 18th-century church, **Ag. Noulias** is a half-hour walk from Chorio, and nearby **Ag. Marina** had a famous school before the War of Independence broke out. On the east coast, best reached by caique, **Nanou Bay** has an excellent shingly beach.

Festivals

5 May, Ag. Athanasios; 21 May, Ag. Konstantinos; 4 June, Analypsis; 24 June, Ag. Ioannis; 17 July, Ag. Marinas; 6 August, Nymborio and Panormitis; 15 August, Panayias; 8 November, Taxiarchis at the monastery.

Most of the island's accommodation is in town, but there are also rooms to let at Pedhi.

expensive

The new **Hotel Chorio** (A) near the windmills has lovely views and has been built in the traditional style © 71 800; also in Chorio, **Taxiarchis Hotel and Apartments**, © 72012, is well appointed and in the island style. The two prettiest places to stay are both in old sea captains' mansions, each lovingly restored with fine wood interiors. These are the **Aliki**, © 71 665, where you can almost dive straight out of the front door into the sea, and the **Dorian**, © 71 181. Outside town, the **Pedhi Beach Hotel** has a pool.

moderate

The **Hotel Grace**, © 71 415, is in another traditional house, with lower rates than the above, and has recently added new studios. Older **Hotel Glafkos**, © 71 358, is still good value; new **Hotel Kokona** © 71 549, is another option; **Pension Les Katerinettes** overlooks the harbour, © 71 676; or there's **Hotel Albatross** © 71 707, a B class pension. Otherwise, Symi Tours by the harbour, © 71 307, has a large listing of houses for rent in town.

cheap

Prices on Symi are expensive in the high season. Try **Pension Egli** © 71 392. On the less expensive side there are rooms to let here and there, usually on the condition that you stay three nights (to economize on sheet washing—water is scarce).

Eating Out

The eateries in Symi fall into two clear categories: really good and genuine, and rip-off tourist traps. The portside tavernas of Symi can be expensive, especially during the day when they're full of day-trippers. **O Meraklis**, in Yialos beyond Symi Tours, offers excellent Greek home cooking and is good value; **The Trawler** in the square is legendary for its fish; **Taverna Vrachos**, opposite Vapori Bar and **The Nereida** near the OTE, both serve good untouristy Greek dishes. In the Chorio have a drink at **Jean and Tonic** then eat at **George's** for atmosphere and for the accordion, **The Panorama** or **Dallaras**.

Tilos

Tilos now has package holidays and a few day trips, but is still very peaceful. It's famous for its miniature elephant fossils and petrified bodies of sailors, known as beach rocks, on the beach at Agios Antonis. Tilos was also the home of the poetess Irinna, a rival (though not a contemporary) of Sappho. It's also known for its Byzantine monastery of Agios Panteleimon, and a huge three-day knees-up in July. Knees-up apart, it's as fine a place as any to do nothing; a dreaminess surrounds all practical activities and the visitor who neglects to wind his watch is in danger of losing all track of time. While parts of Tilos are arable and there's water, much of Tilos is desolate; pockets of sandy beach may be found along the island's indented shoreline.

Connections

Two to three times a week by ferry to the other Dodecanese islands; once a week with Samos, Mykonos, Tinos, Andros and Rafina; in the summer occasional tourist boat and hydrofoil arrivals from Rhodes, Symi and Kos; twice a week from Halki.

Tourist Police

See regular police in Megalo Chorio, © (0241) 53 222.

Livadia and Megalo Chorio

The islanders live in two settlements: the port **Livadia**, with a rocky beach, and in the capital **Megalo Chorio**, 8km up the road. Megalo Chorio stands on the site of ancient Tilos, and near the castle you can see Pelasgian walls built by the earliest known residents (if you discount the mastodons) dating back to 1000 BC. The castle, or Kastro, was built by the Venetians, who incorporated a Classical gateway and stone from the ancient acropolis. There is a pleasant beach and taverna near Megalo Chorio at **Nausica**, and paths lead down to other small beaches. In Megalo Chorio a one-room museum awaits a brilliant discovery. Further north is the deserted village of Mikro Chorio and the cave where the mastodon bones were discovered. The best beaches are at **Erestos** and **Plaka**.

There is now a minibus service with an erratic timetable running between Livadia and Megalo Chorio; there are no taxis, but you can hire elderly mopeds and motorbikes if you dare. Fresh food is still hard to get here, but at least there's a bakery now. The people are very kind and help as much they can.

Festivals

25–27 July, Ag. Panteleimonos; 28 June, Ag. Pavlos; 17 January, Ag. Antonio at Megalo Chorio.

© (0241–)

Where to Stay

moderate–cheap

In Livadia you'll find the **Irini**, a class C with 18 rooms, © 53 293, which is very ritzy with lovely gardens. The same management also lets cheaper rooms in Livadia. **George's Apartments** are new and sparkling, © 53 243; there are plenty of small pensions with adequate rooms including **Pension Kastello**, © 53 292, **Stamatia**, © 53 255, and **Galini**, © 53 280. **Hotel Livadia** is a down-at-heel class E establishment, © 52 202, but it's cheap. Of the many village rooms; **Alex** and **Stamata** are among the best. There are also municipal bungalows in Livadia, © 53 258. In Megalo Chorio, Sevasti Ikonomou runs the restaurant and has rooms; © 53 236. At Agios Antonis, the **Hotel Australia**, © 53 296, is okay. The fancy apartments in Livadia are always booked by a holiday company. You can also camp out on any beach without protest, and at the other end of the scale, plans are afoot to build the Tilos Oasis Hotel in Livadia during 1994.

Eating Out

The old favourite Blue Sky Taverna on the jetty has now become **La Luna** bar, and is where the locals hang out. The current in-place is **Taverna Sophia**; other good eateries include **Taverna Kostas**, beneath Stefanakis Travel; the **Trata Fish Restaurant**, pricey but good; and **Taverna Irini**.

7000–2800	Neolithic Era
4000	Precocious civilization at Palaeochoe, Limnos
3000	Milos exports obsidian
3000–2000	Early Cycladic civilization
2800–1000	Bronze Age
2600–2000	Early Minoan civilization in Crete
2000–1700	Middle Minoan: Cretan thalassocracy rules the Aegean
1700–1450	Late Minoan
1600–1150	Mycenaean civilization begins with invasion of the Peloponnese
c.1450	Eruption of Santorini's volcano decimates the Minoans; Mycenaeans occupy ruined Crete and Rhodes
1180	Traditional date of the fall of Troy (4 July)
c.1150	Beginning of the dark ages: Dorian invasion disrupts Mycenaean culture; Ionians settle Asia Minor and islands.
1000	Kos and the three cities of Rhodes join Doric Hexapolis
1100–100	Iron Age
1100–700	Geometric Period
700–500	Archaic Period
650	Aegina is first in Greece to mint coins
Late 600s	Sappho born on Lesbos
570–480	Pythagoras of Samos
500–323	Classical Age
490–479	Persian Wars end with defeat of Persian army and fleet
478	Delos becomes HQ of the Athenian-dominated Maritime League
460–377	Hippocrates of Kos
431–404	Peloponnesian War cripples Athens
378	Second Delian League
338	Philip of Macedon conquers Athens and the rest of Greece
334–323	Conquests of Alexander the Great
323–146	Hellenistic Age
146–AD 410	Roman Age

Chronology

88	Mithridates of Pontus, enemy of Rome, devastates many islands
86	Romans under Sulla destroy Athens and other Greek rebels who supported Mithridates

AD

58	St Paul visits Lindos, Rhodes
95	St John the Divine writes the Apocalypse on Patmos
391	Paganism outlawed in Roman Empire

410–1453	Byzantine Era
727–843	Iconoclasm in the Eastern Church
824–861	Saracen/Arab Occupation
961	Emperor Nikephoros Phokas reconquers Crete from the Saracens
1054	Pope ex-communicates Patriarch of Constantinople over differences in the creed
1088	Foundation of the Monastery on Patmos
1204	Venetians lead Fourth Crusade conquest of Contantinople and take the islands as their share of the booty
1261	Greeks retake Constantinople from Latins
1309	Knights of St John, chased out of Jerusalem, establish on Rhodes
1453	Turks begin conquest of Greece
1522	Ottomans defeat Knights of St John
1541	El Greco born on Crete
1669	Venetians lose Herakleon, Crete to the Turks after a 20-year siege
1771–74	Catherine the Great sends Russian fleet into the Aegean to harry the Sultan
1796	Napoleon captures Venice and her Ionian islands
1815–64	British rule Ionian islands
1821–27	Greek War of Independence begins
1823	Aegina made the capital of free Greece
1827	Annihilation of Turkish fleet by the British, French and Russian allies at the Battle of Navarino
1833	Otho of Bavaria becomes the first king of the Greeks
1883–1957	Cretan writer Nikos Kazantzakis
1912–13	Balkan Wars give Greece Macedonia, Crete and the Northeast Aegean Islands; the Italians pick up the Dodecanese
1922–23	Greece invades Turkey with catastrophic results
1924	Greece becomes a republic
1935	Restoration of the monarchy
1941	Nazi paratroopers complete first ever invasion by air on Crete
1945	Treaty signed returning Dodecanese islands to Greece
1948	Dodecanese islands reunite with Greece
1949	End of civil war between communists and US-backed government
1953	Earthquake shatters the Ionian islands
1967	Colonels' coup establishes a dictatorship
1974	Failure of the Junta's Cyprus adventure leads to the regime's collapse and restoration of democracy
1981	First-ever nominally socialist government (PASOK) elected
1983	Greece joins the EEC
1990	PASOK lose election to conservative New Democracy (ND)
1993	PASOK re-elected

Language

Although modern Greek, or Romaíka is a minor language spoken by few non-Greeks, it has the distinction of having caused riots and the fall of a government (in 1901). In Greece today there are basically two languages, the purist or katharevoúsa and the popular or demotikí. Both are developments of ancient Greek, but although the purist is consciously Classical, the popular is as close to its ancient origins as French is to Latin. While many purist words are common in the speech of the people, the popular dominates, especially in the countryside.

Until the turn of the century all literature appeared in the purist language. What shook Athens with riots in 1901 was the appearance of the Iliad and the New Testament in the demotic. When the fury had died down a bit, more and more writers were found to be turning their pens to the demotic. Cavafy, the first great modern Greek poet, wrote in both the popular and purist. In its 'moral cleansing' of Greece the Papadopoulos government tried to revive the purist, but with little success.

Knowing the language of any country makes the stay twice as enjoyable; in Greece, especially, people spend much of the day talking. But modern Greek isn't a particularly easy language to pick by ear, and it is often spoken at great velocity (if you speak slowly someone is sure to interrupt). If you buy a modern Greek grammar, check to see if it has the demotic and not just the purist. Even if you have no desire to learn Greek, it is helpful to know at least the alphabet—so that you can find your way around—and a few basic words and phrases.

The Greek Alphabet

			Pronunciation/English Equivalent
A	α	*álfa*	short 'a' as in 'father'
B	β	*víta*	v
Γ	γ	*gámma*	gutteral *g* or *y* sound
Δ	δ	*thélta*	hard *th* as in 'though'
E	ε	*épsilon*	short 'e' as in 'bet'
Z	ζ	*zíta*	z
H	η	*íta*	long 'e' as in 'bee'
Θ	θ	*thíta*	soft *th* as in 'thin'

I ι	*yóta*	long 'e' as in 'bee';	
		sometimes like the 'y' in 'yet'	
K κ	*káppa*	k	
Λ λ	*lámtha*	I	
M μ	*mi*	m	
N ν	*ni*	n	
Ξ ξ	*ksi*	'x' as in 'ox'	
O o	*ómicron*	'o' as in 'cot'	
Π π	*pi*	p	
P ρ	*ro*	r	
Σ σ	*sígma*	s	
T τ	*taf*	t	
Υ υ	*ípsilon*	long 'e' as in 'bee'	
Φ φ	*fi*	f	
X χ	*chi*	German *ch* as in 'doch'	
Ψ ψ	*psi*	*ps* as in 'stops'	
Ω ω	*oméga*	'o' as in 'cot'	

Dipthongs and Consonant Combinations

AI αι		short 'e' as in 'bet'
EI ει, OI οι		'i' as in 'machine'
OY ου		*oo* as in 'too'
AY αυ		*av* or *af*
EY ευ		*ev* or *ef*
HY ηυ		*iv* or *if*
ΓΓ γγ		*ng* as in 'angry'
ΓK γκ		hard 'g'; *ng* within word
NT ντ		'd'; *nd* within word
MΠ μπ		'b'; *mp* within word

Vocabulary

Yes	*né*	Ναί
	(with a short nod or tilt of the head)	
	málista (formal)	Μάλιστα
No	*óchi*	Οχι
	(with a backwards jerk of the head,	
	with a click of the tongue, smack of	
	the lips or raise of the eyebrows)	

English	Transliteration	Greek
I don't know	*then xéro* (An even greater throwing back of the head, or a display of empty hands)	Δέν ξέρω
I don't understand ... (Greek)	*then katalavéno ...* (*elliniká*)	Δέν καταλαβαίνω ... (Ελληνικά)
Does someone speak English?	*milái kanis angliká?*	Μιλάει κανείς αγγλικά;
Go away	*fíyete*	Φύγετε
Help!	*voíthia!*	Βοήθεια!
My friend	*o fílos moo* (*m*) *ee fíli moo* (*f*)	Ο φίλος μου Η φίλη μου
Please	*parakaló*	Παρακαλώ
Thank you (very much)	*evcharistó* (*pára polí*)	Ευχαριστώ (πάρα πολύ)
You're welcome	*parakaló*	Παρακαλώ
It doesn't matter	*then pirázi*	Δέν πιράζει
Alright	*en daxi*	Εν τάξι
Of course	*vevéos*	Βεβαίος
Excuse me	*signómi*	Συγνώμη
Pardon?	*oríste?*	Ορίστε;
Be careful!	*proséchete!*	Προσέχεται!
Nothing	*típota*	Τίποτα
What is your name?	*pos sas léne?* (*formal*) *pos se léne?*	Πώς σάς λένε; Πώς σέ λένε;
How are you?	*ti kánete?* (*formal/pl*) *ti kanis?*	Τί κάνεται; Τί κάνεις;
Hello	*yásas, hérete* (*formal/pl*) *yásou*	Γειάσας, Χέρεται Γειάσου
Goodbye	*yásas, hérete* (*formal/pl*) *yásou, adío*	Γειάσας, Χέρεται Γειάσου, Αντίο
Good morning	*kaliméra*	Καλημέρα
Good evening	*kalispéra*	Καλησπέρα
Good night	*kaliníchta*	Καληνύχτα
What is that?	*ti íne aftó?*	Τί είναι αυτό;
What?	*ti?*	Τί;
Who?	*piós?* (*m*), *piá?* (*f*)	Ποιός; Ποιά;

Where?	*poo?*	Ποιός;
When?	*póte?*	Πότε;
why?	*yiatí?*	Γιατί;
how?	*pos?*	Πώς;
I am	*íme*	Είμαι
You are (*sing*)	*ísse*	Είσε
He, she, it is	*íne*	Είναι
We are	*ímaste*	Είμαστε
You are (*pl*)	*íssaste*	Είσαστε
They are	*íne*	Είναι
I have	*écho*	Εχω
You have (*sing*)	*échis*	Εχεις
He, she, it has	*échi*	Εχει
We have	*échome*	Εχομαι
You have (*pl*)	*échete*	Εχεται
They have	*échoon*	Εχουν
I am lost	*échasa to thrómo*	Εχασα το δρόμο
I am hungry	*pinó*	Πεινώ
I am thirsty	*thipsó*	Διψώ
I am tired	*íme kourasménos*	Είμαι κουρασμένος
I am sleepy	*nistázo*	Νυστάζω
I am ill	*íme árostos*	Είμαι άρρωστος
I am poor	*íme ftochós*	Είμαι φτωχός
I love you	*s'agapó*	Σ'αγαπώ
good	*kaló*	καλό
bad	*kakó*	κακό
so-so	*étsi kétsi*	έτσι κ'έτσι
slowly	*sigá sigá*	σιγά σιγά
fast	*grígora*	γρήγορα
big	*megálo*	μεγάλο
small	*mikró*	μικρό
hot	*zestó*	ζεστό
cold	*crío*	κρίο

Shops, Services, Sightseeing

I would like ...	*tha íthela ...*	Θά ήθελα ...
where is ...?	*poo íne ...?*	Πού είναι ...;
how much is it?	*póso káni?*	Πόσο κάνει;

bakery	*fournos*	φούρνος
	artopiíon (antiquated, above entrance)	Αρτοποιείον
bank	*trápeza*	τράπεζα
beach	*paralía*	παραλία
bed	*kreváti*	κρεβάτι
book	*vivlío*	βιβλίο
bookshop	*vivliopolío*	βιβλιοπολείο
butcher	*kreopolío*	κρεοπωλείο
church	*eklisía*	εκκλησία
cinema	*kinimatográfos*	κινηματογράφος
food	*fayitó*	φαγητό
hospital	*nosokomío*	νοσοκομείο
hotel	*xenodochío*	ξενοδοχείο
hot water	*zestó neró*	ζεστό νερό
house	*spíti*	σπίτι
kiosk	*períptero*	περίπτερο
money	*leftá*	λεφτά
museum	*moosío*	μουσείο
music	*musikí*	μουσική
newspaper (foreign)	*efimerítha (xéni)*	εφημερίδα (ξένη)
pharmacy	*farmakío*	φαρμακείο
police station	*astinomía*	αστυνομία
policeman	*astifílakas*	αστιφύλακας
post office	*tachithromío*	ταχυδρομείο
restaurant	*estiatório*	εστιατόριο
ruins	*archéa*	αρχαία
sea	*thálassa*	θάλασσα
shoe store	*papootsís*	παπουτσής
shower	*doush*	ντούς
student	*fititís*	φοιτητής
telephone office	*OTE*	OTE
theatre	*théatro*	θέατρο

toilet	*tooaléta*	τουαλέττα
tourist policeman	*astifílakas tooristikís*	αστιφύλακας
		τουριστικής
a walk	*vólta*	βόλτα

Time

What time is it?	*ti óra íne?*	Τί ώρα είναι;
month	*mína*	μήνα
week	*evthomáda*	εβδομάδα
day	*méra*	μέρα
morning	*proí*	πρωί
afternoon	*apóyevma*	απόγευμα
evening	*vráthi*	βράδυ
yesterday	*chthés*	χθές
today	*símera*	σήμερα
tomorrow	*ávrio*	αύριο
now	*tóra*	τώρα
later	*metá*	μετά
it is early	*íne norís*	είναι νωρίς
it is late	*íne argá*	είναι αργά

Travel Directions

I want to go to ...	*thélo na páo sto (m), sti (f) ...*	Θέλω νά πάω στό, στη ...;
How can I get to ...?	*pós boró na páo sto (m), sti (f) ...?*	Πώς μπορώ νά πάω στό, στη ...;
Can you give me a ride to ...?	*boréte na me páte sto (m), sti (f) ...?*	Μπορείτε νά μέ πάτε στό, στή ...;
Where is ...?	*poo íne ...?*	Πού είναι ...;
How far is it?	*póso makriá íne?*	Πόσο μακριά είναι;
When will the ... come?	*póte tha érthi to (n), ee (f), o (m) ...?*	Πότε θά έρθη τό, ή, ό ...;
When will the ... leave?	*póte tha fíyí to (n), ee (f), o (m) ...?*	Πότε θά φύγη τό, ή, ό ...;
From where do I catch ...?	*apó poo pérno ...?*	Από πού πέρνω ...;
How long does the trip take?	*póso keró pérni to taxíthi?*	Πόσο καιρό πέρνει τό ταξίδι;

Please show me	parakaló thíkstemoo	Παρακαλώ δείξτε μου
How much is it?	póso káni?	Πόσο κάνει;
the (nearest) town	to horió (to pió kondinó)	Το χωριό (το πιό κοντινό)
Have a good trip	kaló taxíthi	Καλό ταξίδι
here	ethó	εδώ
there	ekí	εκεί
near	kondá	κοντά
far	makriá	μακριά
full	yemáto	γεμάτο
left	aristerá	αριστερά
right	thexiá	δεξιά
forward	brostá	μροστά
back	píso	πίσω
north	vória	βόρεια
south	nótia	νότια
east	anatoliká	ανατολικά
west	thitiká	δυτικά
corner	goniá	γωνιά
square	platía	πλατεία

Driving

where can I rent ...?	poo boró na nikiáso ...?	Πού μποπώ νά νοικιάσω ...;
a car	éna aftokínito	ένα αυτοκινητο
a motorbike	éna michanáki	ένα μηχανάκι
a bicycle	éna pothílato	ένα ποδήλατο
where can I buy petrol?	poo boró nagorásso venzíni?	Πού μπορώ ν'αγοράσω βενζίνη;
where is a garage?	poo íne éna garáz?	Πού είναι ένα γκαράζ;
a mechanic	énan mikanikó	έναν μηχανικό
a map	enan chárti	έναν χάρτη
where is the road to ...?	poo íne o thrómos yiá ...?	Πού είναι ο δρόμος γιά ...;
where does this road lead?	poo pái aftós o thrómos?	Πού πάει αυτός ο δρόμος;
is the road good?	íne kalós o thrómos?	Είναι καλός ο δρόμος;

EXIT	*éxothos*	ΕΞΟΔΟΣ
ENTRANCE	*ísothos*	ΕΙΣΟΔΟΣ
DANGER	*kínthinos*	ΚΙΝΔΥΝΟΣ
SLOW	*argá*	ΑΡΓΑ
NO PARKING	*apagorévete ee státhmevsis*	ΑΠΑΓΟΡΕΥΕΤΑΙ Η ΣΤΑΘΜΕΥΣΙΣ
KEEP OUT	*apagorévete ee ísothos*	ΑΠΑΓΟΡΕΥΕΤΑΙ Η ΕΙΣΟΔΟΣ

Numbers

one	*énas* (*m*), *mía* (*f*), *éna* (*n*)	ένας, μία, ένα
two	*thío*	δύο
three	*tris* (*m, f*), *tría* (*n*)	τρείς, τρία
four	*téseris* (*m, f*), *téssera* (*n*)	τέσσερεις, τέσσερα
five	*pénde*	πέντε
six	*éxi*	έξι
seven	*eptá*	επτά
eight	*októ*	οκτώ
nine	*ennéa*	εννέα
ten	*théka*	δέκα
eleven	*éntheka*	έντεκα
twelve	*thótheka*	δώδεκα
thirteen	*thekatría*	δεκατρία
fourteen	*thekatéssera*	δεκατέσσερα
twenty	*íkosi*	είκοσι
twenty-one	*íkosi éna* (*m, n*) *mía* (*f*)	είκοσι ένα, μία
thirty	*triánda*	τριάντα
forty	*saránda*	σαράντα
fifty	*penínda*	πενήντα
sixty	*exínda*	εξήντα
seventy	*evthomínda*	ευδομήντα
eighty	*ogthónda*	ογδόντα
ninety	*enenínda*	ενενήντα
one hundred	*ekató*	εκατό
one thousand	*chília*	χίλια

Months/Days

January	*Ianooários*	Ιανουάριος
February	*Fevrooários*	Φεβουάριος
March	*Mártios*	Μάρτιος
April	*Aprílios*	Απρίλιος
May	*Máios*	Μάιος
June	*Ioónios*	Ιούνιος
July	*Ioólios*	Ιούλιος
August	*Avgoostos*	Αύγουστος
September	*Septémvrios*	Σεπτέμβριος
October	*Októvrios*	Οκτώβριος
November	*Noémvrios*	Νοέμβριος
December	*Thekémvrios*	Δεκέμβριος
Sunday	*Kiriakí*	Κυριακή
Monday	*Theftéra*	Δευτέρα
Tuesday	*Tríti*	Τρίτη
Wednesday	*Tetárti*	Τετάρτη
Thursday	*Pémpti*	Πέμπτη
Friday	*Paraskeví*	Παρασκευή
Saturday	*Sávato*	Σάββατο

Transport

the airport	*to arothrómio*	τό αεροδρόμιο
the aeroplane	*to aropláno*	τό αεροπλάνο
the bus station	*ee stási leoforíou*	ή στάση λεωφορείου
the bus	*to leoforío*	τό λεωφορείο
the railway station	*o stathmós too trénou*	ό σταθμός τού τραίνου
the train	*to tréno*	τό τραίνο
the port	*to limáni*	τό λιμάνι
the port authority	*to limenarchío*	τό λιμεναρχείο
the ship	*to plío, to karávi*	τό πλοίο, τό καράβι
the steamship	*to vapóri*	τό βαπόρι
the car	*to aftokínito*	τό αυτοκίνητο
a ticket	*éna isitírio*	ένα εισιτήριο

The Menu

Hors d'oeuvres	Orektiká (Mezéthes)	Ορεκτικά (Μεζέδες)
yoghurt and cucumbers	*tzatziki*	τζατζίκι
olives	*eliés*	ελιές
stuffed vine leaves	*dolmáthes*	ντολμάδες
cod's roe dip	*taramosalata*	ταραμοσαλάτα
mixed hors d'oeuvres	*thiáfora orektiká*	διάφορα ορεκτικά

Soups | Soópes | Σούπες

egg and lemon soup	*avgolémono*	αυγολέμονο
vegetable soup	*chortósoupa*	χορτόσουπα
fish soup	*psarósoupa*	ψαρόσουπα
giblets in egg and lemon soup	*magirítsa*	μαγειρίτσα

Pasta and Rice | Zimariká | Ζυμαρικά

pilaf	*piláfi*	πιλάφι
spaghetti	*spagéti*	σπαγκέτι
macaroni	*makarónia*	μακαρόνια

Vegetables (in oil) | Latherá | Λαδερά

potatoes	*patátes*	πατάτες
stuffed tomatoes	*tomátes yemistés*	ντομάτες γεμιστές
stuffed aubergines/ eggplants	*melitzánes yemistés*	μελιτζάνες γεμιστές
stuffed peppers	*piperíes yemistés*	πιπεριές γεμιστές
beans	*fasólia*	φασόλια
lentils	*fakí*	φακή
greens	*chórta*	χόρτα

Fish | Psária | Ψάρια

lobster	*astakós*	αστακός
little squid	*kalamarákia*	καλαμαράκια
octopus	*achtapóthi*	αχταπόδι
red mullet	*barboúni*	μπαρμπούνι
prawns (shrimps)	*garíthes*	γαρίδες
whitebait	*maríthes*	μαρίδες
sea bream	*sinagrítha*	συναγρίδα

fried cod (with garlic and vinegar sauce)	*bakaliáros (skorthaliá)*	μπακαλιάρος (σκορδαλιά)
oysters	*stríthia*	στρείδια
bass	*lithrínia*	λιθρίνια

Eggs	**Avgá**	**Αυγά**
ham omelette	*omeléta me zambón*	ομελέττα μέ ζαμπόν
cheese omelette	*omeléta me tirí*	ομελέττα μέ τυρί
fried (scrambled) eggs	*avgá tiganitá (brouyé)*	αυγά τηγανιτά (μπρουγέ)

Main Courses	**Kíria Piáta**	**Κύρια Πιάτα**
chicken	*kotópoulo*	κοτόπουλο
beefsteak	*biftéki*	μπιφτέκι
rabbit	*kounéli*	κουνέλι
meat and macaroni	*pastítsio*	παστίτσιο
meat and aubergine/ eggplant with white sauce	*mousaká*	μουσακά
liver	*seekóti*	συκώτι
veal	*moschári*	μοσχάρι
lamb	*arnáki*	αρνάκι
pork chops	*brizólas chirinés*	μπριζόλες χοιρινές
meat balls in tomato sauce	*soutsoukákia*	σουτζουκάκια
sausage	*lukániko*	λουκάνικο

Grills	**Skáras**	**Σχάρας**
meat on a skewer	*souvláki*	σουβλάκι
veal chops	*kotelétes*	κοτελέτες
roast chicken	*kotópoulo psistó*	κοτόπουλο ψηστό
meat balls	*keftéthes*	κεφτέδες

Salads	**Salátes**	**Σαλάτες**
tomatoes	*domátes*	ντομάτες
cucumber	*angoúri*	αγγούρι
Russian salad	*róssiki saláta*	ρώσσικη σαλάτα

English	Transliteration	Greek
village salad with cheese and olives	*choriatiki*	χοριάτικη
courgettes/zucchini	*kolokithákia*	κολοκυθάκια

Cheeses / **Tiriá** / **Τυριά**

cheese pie	*tirópitta*	τυρόπιττα
goat's cheese	*féta*	φέτα
hard buttery cheese	*kasséri*	κασέρι
blue cheese (roquefort)	*rokfór*	ροκφόρ
Greek 'Gruyère'	*graviéra*	γραβιέρα

Sweets / **Glyká** / **Γλυκά**

ice cream	*pagotó*	παγωτό
sugared biscuits	*kourabiéthes*	κουραμπιέδες
hot honey fritters	*loukoumáthes*	λουκουμάδες
sesame seed sweet	*halvá*	χαλβά
nuts and honey in fillo pastry	*baklavá*	μπακλαβά
custard in fillo pastry	*galaktoboúreko*	γαλακτομπούρεκο
yoghurt	*yiaoúrti*	γιαούρτι
rice pudding	*rizógalo*	ρυζόγαλο
shredded wheat with nuts and honey	*kataifi*	καταΐφι
custard tart	*bougátsa*	μπουγάτσα
soft almond biscuits	*amigthalotá*	αμιγδαλωτά

Fruit / **Froóta** / **Φρούτα**

pear	*achláthi*	αχλάδι
orange	*portokáli*	πορτοκάλι
apple	*mílo*	μήλο
peach	*rothákino*	ροδάκινο
melon	*pepóni*	πεπόνι
watermelon	*karpoúzi*	καρπούζι
plum	*thamáskino*	δαμάσκινο
figs	*síka*	σύκα
grapes	*stafília*	σταφύλια
banana	*banána*	μπανάνα
apricot	*veríkoko*	βερύκοκο

Miscellaneous

water (boiled)	*neró (vrastó)*	νερό (βραστό)
bread	*psomí*	ψωμί
butter	*voútiro*	βούτυρο
honey	*méli*	μέλι
jam	*marmelátha*	μαρμελάδα
salt	*aláti*	αλάτι
pepper	*pipéri*	πιπερι
sugar	*záchari*	ζάχαρη
oil	*láthi*	λάδι
vinegar	*xíthi*	ξύδι
mustard	*mustárda*	μουστάρδα
lemon	*lemóni*	λεμόνι
milk	*gála*	γάλα
tea	*tsái*	τσάι
chocolate	*sokoláta*	σοκολάτα
the bill/check	*logariasmó*	λογαριασμό
to your health!	*stín iyásas (formal, pl)*	στήν ηγειά σας!
	stín iyásou (sing)	στήν ηγειά σου!

Note: Page references in **bold** indicate main sections and those in *italics* indicate maps.

Index